THE POLITICS OF PLANNING

*A Review and Critique
of Centralized Economic Planning*

THE POLITICS OF PLANNING

A Review and Critique of Centralized Economic Planning

B. Bruce Briggs

James Buchanan

A. Lawrence Chickering, *Editor*

Ralph Harris

Robert B. Hawkins, Jr.

George Hilton

Richard Mancke

Richard Muth

Vincent Ostrom

Svetozar Pejovich

Myron Sharpe

John Sheahan

Herbert Stein

Gordon Tullock

Ernest van den Haag

Paul H. Weaver

Murray L. Weidenbaum

Hans Willgerodt

Peter P. Witonski

Institute for Contemporary Studies
San Francisco, California

CONTENTS

CONTRIBUTORS

B. Bruce Briggs, Resident Consultant, Hudson Institute

James Buchanan, Professor of Economics, Center for Public Choice, Virginia Polytechnic Institute

A. Lawrence Chickering, Institute for Contemporary Studies

Ralph Harris, Director, The Institute of Economic Affairs, London

Robert B. Hawkins, Fellow, Woodrow Wilson International Center for Scholars

George Hilton, Professor of Economics, University of California, Los Angeles

Richard Mancke, Professor of Economics, Fletcher School of Law and Diplomacy, Tufts University

Richard Muth, Professor of Economics, Stanford University

Vincent Ostrom, Professor of Political Science, University of Indiana

Svetozar Pejovich, Professor of Economics, University of Dallas

Myron Sharpe, Editor, *Challenge* magazine

John Sheahan, Professor of Economics, Williams College

Herbert Stein, Professor of Economics, University of Virginia

Gordon Tullock, Professor of Economics, Center for Public Choice, Virginia Polytechnic Institute

Ernest van den Haag, Lecturer in Sociology and Psychology, New School for Social Research

Paul H. Weaver, Associate Editor, *Fortune* magazine

Murray L. Weidenbaum, Center for the Study of American Business, Washington University, St. Louis

Hans Willgerodt, Professor of Economics, University of Cologne, West Germany

Peter P. Witonski, Historian

PREFACE

In the two years that have elapsed since the Arab oil boycott in the fall of 1973, mounting economic problems in the United States and abroad have increased public pressures for government intervention in the American economy. Several years of "stagflation," with rising rates of both inflation and unemployment, have encouraged many people to conclude that new conditions have anachronized the laws of economics and that nagging problems can only be brought under control by centralized economic planning.

In the wake of these increasing problems, in June 1975, the Initiative Committee for National Economic Planning, co-chaired by United Auto Worker President Leonard Woodcock and Harvard economist Wassily Leontief, and bearing the names of many prominent academic, professional and business leaders, released a statement calling for the establishment of a national planning agency for the American economy. In the spring the principal recommendations of the Initiative Committee were drafted into The Balanced Growth and Economic Planning Act of 1975, introduced into the Senate under the co-sponsorship of Senator Jacob Javits (R, N.Y.) and Hubert Humphrey (D, Minn.).

The Javits-Humphrey Bill is important of and for itself. If it passes, it will have fundamental implications for our entire economic and social life as a nation. But beyond the particular legislation, the Balanced Growth and Economic Planning Act of 1975 represents the culmination of a growing body of economic planning legislation which now touches most areas of our economic life.

It is in the nature of the legislative process that individual pieces of legislation are proposed, debated and either passed or not. But rarely do legislatures have opportunities to step back from their daily routines and consider the substance of their work as a totality. Each of twenty individual pieces of legislation might be worthwhile if considered separately; but taken together they may raise serious questions that tend not to be asked when the bills are considered one at a time.

Because of the importance of the planning proposals, the Institute decided to assemble a series of essays examining the following issues: First, what is the record of central economic planning? Has it worked? If so, where and how? And if not, why not? And secondly, if planning has not worked, what are the factors underlying its continued popularity? The most cursory survey of economic planning suggests it has not been notable for its successes. But if planning has not been successful, why does it continue to be presented throughout educated circles in both industrialized and non-industrialized countries as the answer to growing economic problems? And finally, is there some connection between the enduring (even increasing) popularity and the problems themselves?

We trust that this volume will offer a useful and important contribution to the public debate on the planning issue.

H. Monroe Browne
President
Institute for Contemporary Studies

San Francisco, Calif.
February, 1976

EDITOR'S NOTE

All of the essays in this book were originally commissioned except three. We included two essays from *Challenge* magazine, whose editor Myron Sharpe is also the Coordinator and primary organizer of the Initiative Committee for National Economic Planning. Sharpe's endorsement of the Planning Bill, which is reprinted here as the lead essay, describes his own part in drafting the Javits-Humphrey bill. We included John Sheahan's essay on France as representative of the kinds of arguments that proponents of central planning make in support of their case.

We are also reprinting excerpts of Herbert Stein's analysis of the planning bill, which he wrote for the American Enterprise Institute in August 1975.

The overall organization is obvious enough. The general movement from analysis of specific planning efforts to a consideration of broader issues reveals certain underlying forces that go far beyond planning to most other economic and social issues. Understanding these underlying forces will almost certainly increase our understanding of the limits of reason in public discussions of social policy.

A. L. C.

PART I
INTRODUCTION

THE PLANNING BILL*

MYRON SHARPE
Editor, Challenge *Magazine*

Senators Humphrey and Javits, joined by other members of the
Congress, will shortly announce their sponsorship of "The
Balanced Growth and Economic Planning Act of 1975," a proposed piece of legislation that clearly has far-reaching implications.[1] The bill was originally drafted by members of The Initiative Committee for National Economic Planning, of which
Wassily Leontief and Leonard Woodcock are Co-chairmen. The
final draft is the joint product of the Initiative Committee and the
original Senate sponsors. A great deal of thinking went into the
bill, and I should like to share it with the reader. It is always the
case that each person who takes part in a project has a different
emphasis when called upon to interpret it. I do not pretend that
what follows is any but my own.

An attractive feature of the bill is that it is exceptionally neat
and simple. It sets up an Office of Balanced Growth and Eco-
nomic Planning in the Executive Office of the President. This
Office consists of a Council, a Director, and Deputy Director,
and staff. The Council has sixteen members: the Director of
the Office, who acts as Chairman; members of the Cabinet; the
Chairman of the Federal Reserve Board; the Chairman of the
Council of Economic Advisers; the Director of the Office of
Management and Budget; and the Chairman of the Advisory
Committee. The Advisory Committee, reasonably balanced to

*Reprinted with permission of *Challenge,* 1975.

1

represent various interests, will be formed to consult with the Director on the work of the Office. Four of its twelve members will be chosen by the Director; four by the Speaker of the House; and four by the President of the Senate.

The Director and Deputy Director of the Office are appointed by the President with the advice and consent of the Senate. The Director has Cabinet rank and supervises the activities of the Office. He or she is directly responsible to the President and acts as chief officer for economic planning in the Executive Branch of government.

The functions of the Office of Balanced Growth and Economic Planning are:

1. to prepare a proposed Balanced Economic Growth Plan, to be approved by the Council and then to be submitted to the President;
2. to monitor and report on the implementation and results of the plan;
3. to review the budgets of the departments and agencies of the federal government, legislation proposed by the Executive Branch to Congress, legislation reported to the Senate or House by their Committees, and major new programs or actions of the Executive Branch if they have an important bearing on the plan;
4. to make reports on the consistency of budgets, legislation, and new programs with the plan;
5. to conduct other activities pertaining to national economic planning as the President directs.

The bill provides that the Office contain a Bureau of Economic Information to supervise and coordinate the activities of the departments and agencies of the Executive Branch with respect to the collection and analysis of economic data and information. In order to ensure that the necessary detailed economic information is available to the Office as a foundation for its planning activities, the Bureau is authorized to establish standards and methods for the acquisition, collation, analysis, and reporting of economic data by any department or agency of the Executive Branch and to initiate new programs for gathering and processing economic information essential to support the planning functions of the Office.

The Director of the Office is empowered to employ a staff with the necessary qualifications to carry out the functions of the Office.

The Council of Economic Advisers will continue to advise the President directly on short-run economic problems and its staff will remain separate from the staff of the Office. The CEA will be required to include an analysis of the consistency of the Economic Report of the President with the Balanced Economic Growth Plan.

For the purpose of carrying out the act, the Director of the Office is empowered to hold such hearings as he or she considers necessary.

The Office is given the authority to appoint advisory committees composed of representatives of labor, management, and the public to advise it on subjects in which committee members have specialized knowledge.

The bill requires the President to submit a proposed Balanced Economic Growth Plan to Congress biennially, prepared by the Office and approved by the Council. The proposed plan will include:

1. an examination of long-run economic and social trends and objectives;
2. a recommended six-year economic and social plan, embodying coherent and realizable economic and social goals, including specific goals for each major sector of the economy;
3. identification of the resources required for achieving the stated goals and objectives and a statement of the governmental policies and programs needed;
4. a review of economic and social goals contained in existing legislation, with analysis of the progress toward meeting such goals that can reasonably be expected in the six-year period;
5. identification of the resources, policies, and programs necessary to achieve such progress, and the extent to which the achievement of such progress will compete with other goals and objectives that the President considers of equal or greater importance;

6. pertinent data, estimates, and recommendations which the Office considers useful to the President, Congress, or the public.

After the proposed plan is submitted to Congress, the Joint Economic Committee will hold hearings to ensure comment, criticism, analysis, and reaction from interested groups, government agencies, officials, and the public. Chairmen of Congressional Committees will be asked to report on aspects of the plan that come within the competence of their Committees. Within 90 days of receipt of the proposed plan, the Joint Economic Committee will make a report to Congress accompanied by concurrent resolutions (one for each House) recommending approval, disapproval or modifications of the plan as submitted by the President.

The staff of the Joint Economic Committee is authorized to conduct a continuing, nonpartisan analysis of national economic goals and the policies necessary to achieve them, and to provide the Joint Economic Committee with the information and analyses necessary for enlightened decisions concerning proposed and existing plans.

The Congress will also be assisted by a Division of Balanced Growth and Economic Planning, to be set up in the Congressional Budget Office. This Division, headed by a Deputy Director, will be responsible for the long-term budget planning that must be an integral part of the six-year plan.

After receiving the report of the Joint Economic Committee accompanied by concurrent resolutions, the Congress will debate the resolutions and vote on them, going on record as a body with respect to the plan. If approved, the proposed plan becomes the national economic plan. If not approved, it will be necessary for the President to submit a revised plan to Congress within 30 days.

The Office of Balanced Growth and Economic Planning is instructed to make a biennial report to the President and Congress evaluating the progress made toward fulfillment of the plan.

The President is authorized to ensure that departments and

agencies subject to his direction conform as nearly as possible with the plan. The Congress, for its part, directs that United States laws, policies, and regulations be interpreted and administered as nearly as possible in accordance with the policies set forth in this act and with the plan then in effect.

The Director of the Office of Balanced Growth and Economic Planning may ask any federal department or agency to submit a statement assessing the consistency of proposals or actions that have a significant impact on the fulfillment of the plan. The Director will review the statements, and if he or she finds any serious inconsistency with the plan, he will inform the Council, which then will report its views and recommendations to the President.

Finally, the bill requires that the national economic plan take account of regional, state, and local plans to the maximum extent feasible. It calls on the Director to establish procedures for regular consultation with regional, state, and local planning agencies; if they request it, to review the consistency of their plans with the national economic plan and to recommend changes to bring such plans into conformity with the national plan; and to make grants to regional, state, and local planning agencies to improve their capability for long-range planning. In addition, the governor of each state may hold hearings on the proposed plan, and submit a report of findings and recommendations to the Joint Economic Committee. This report will include the views of state and local officials and private citizens.

So much by way of summary. Now to explain the considerations that shaped the bill.

The members of the Initiative Committee proceeded from two premises: to write a bill that would result in effective planning; and to do it in an American context, taking into account the realities of the U.S. political system and economy. The planning institutions proposed in the bill are built squarely on the Presidency and the Congress. The Office of Balanced Growth and Economic Planning, the Joint Economic Committee, and the Division of Balanced Growth and Economic Planning in the Congressional Budget Office are the principal planning instruments of these branches of government. The President, through the Office, develops a planning program, including legislative recommendations, which he presents to Congress. The Joint Economic Committee examines the program in consultation with Committee Chairmen and the Budget Office, proposes alternatives where it sees fit, and recommends legislation to the appropriate Congressional Committees to carry out the plan. Congress passes the laws. The President executes them. If the President and Congress are of like mind, the concurrent resolutions and the legislation needed to implement the national economic plan will be passed. If they differ, they will have to seek a compromise.

Some who have given thought to this question and who fear an imperial presidency, would put the planning agency entirely in Congress. But this is impossible, since the President must carry out the laws that pertain to planning and must have the institutional means to do so. Moreover, the President, as the leader of the party in power, must have the staff to develop a planning program.

Others who fear that planning will fall into the hands of an elite, remote from the pressure of public opinion, would establish an independent Planning Commission somewhere between the Executive Branch and Congress, and select its directors—proportionally—from among representatives of labor, business, consumers, and other sectors of the public. The Initiative Committee rejected this idea. It is an illusion to think that the plans of any such commission can survive if they are contrary to the wishes of the President and Congress. The only way to get better plans is to elect better representatives. There is no shortcut.

The institutional arrangement proposed in the planning bill strengthens neither the President nor the Congress at the expense of the other, but allows them both to deal with economic problems more efficiently.

The Office of Balanced Growth and Economic Planning is located in the Executive Office of the President precisely so that it can be effective. The members of the Cabinet, the Chairman of the Federal Reserve Board, the Chairman of the Council of Economic Advisers, and the Director of the Office of Management and Budget are included in the leadership Council so that they will be parties to the making of planning policy. Without their participation, planning cannot succeed and a plan will remain a scrap of paper, as we know by examining the experience of anemic planning councils that exist abroad. The Director of the planning office is given the power to examine all proposed actions of the Cabinet, of federal agencies, and of Congress, for their consistency with the national economic plan. This is an indispensable means to ensure the coherence of all economic and social programs of the federal government.

The bill provides that the President shall submit a proposed national economic plan to Congress. The Initiative Committee deliberately did not specify in this bill what the goals of the plan should be. We have received letters that say: start with the goals, then set up the planning mechanism. We profoundly disagree with this view. In a society as diverse as ours, we shall never reach permanent agreement on goals. Majority opinion changes over the years. But planning provides the intellectual and institutional framework within which to consider goals, to consider their feasibility, the cost of reaching them, and the alternatives we have to forego if we adopt them. The establishment of a framework for the rational consideration of goals is an immense step forward. The present method of government decision-making can best be described as a series of reactions to one emergency after another. Neither officials nor the public have a chance to consider goals in a systematic way. The process of planning will force us to think about the long run. It will also force us into a debate in which we will have to make our goals explicit. Anyone who recognizes the value of such a debate should welcome the prospect of setting up a planning system.

What will a plan be like?

The planning bill specifies that the proposed national economic plan include an examination of trends and general objectives covering a protracted period beyond six years. This provision implies scanning the distant horizon for possible dangers as well as opportunities that might be discerned; and devoting attention to undertakings that have a long gestation period—research on alternative sources of energy, for instance. But most of the planning staff will devote its time to working out a six-year plan embodying coherent and realizable economic and social goals, including specific goals for each major sector of the economy. It will identify the resources needed to achieve the goals. It will prepare a statement of the government policies and programs needed. And it will review progress toward achieving previously adopted goals.

This means that a plan will analyze the economy industry by industry and sector by sector. Of necessity it will have to deal with interindustry relations, using analytical techniques designed for this purpose. A great deal of detailed data will be required. The background material for the plan will undoubtedly fill several thick volumes, but its main features can and should be summarized in a small booklet. It will take a staff of perhaps 500 people to do the work and will cost possibly $50,000,000 a year. The plan will analyze and set general objectives for the allocation of resources, labor, and capital to specific sectors of the economy; and will set general objectives for the goods and services produced by those sectors. It will also analyze and set strategic objectives for the future structure of production and consumption. It will incorporate special projects for the development of energy, transportation, housing, health, research, and numerous other requirements of pressing importance. It will take into account "the quality of life" and the environment. And—what monetary and fiscal policy is supposed to do now—it will deal with such familiar matters as employment, GNP, and the price level.

No disparagement of monetary and fiscal policy is intended. The Council of Economic Advisers is preserved intact to advise the President on measures needed to influence the general level of economic activity. But the manipulation of monetary and fiscal aggregates is necessarily a short-run proposition, and deals with—it is perfectly clear—aggregates, not component parts of the economy. Restrictive measures cannot, for example, stop inflation caused by shortages or by administered prices that occur in specific parts of the economy without destroying jobs and wasting billions in potential output. The planning bill will probably return monetary and fiscal policy to its proper function, since it requires that recommendations of the Council of Economic Advisers be consistent with the national economic plan. It is not likely that the plan will call for mass unemployment.

By contrast, a plan not only allows us to look at the general picture, but at its details. Plans are guides to the relationships between different parts of the economy and allow us to adopt coherent policies for the separate parts as required. The means to implement these policies are not specified in the bill. Just as in the case of goals, the bill provides a framework. A wide range of instruments can be used to accomplish specific, interrelated aims. These instruments are already familiar in nonplanning contexts or where the planning has been applied *ad hoc:* they are tax incentives and penalties; capital and credit allocation; laws requiring or prohibiting definite actions, such as those specifying how air, water, and land may be used; and projects within the public sector itself—the space program, for example. Incomes policy, now under a cloud, is also a possible planning instrument. Whether or not it is used depends, like everything else, on the circumstances. Some who like neat definitions have asked what kind of model we have in mind. Is it indicative planning, like the French version? The fact is that the Initiative Committee didn't start with any foreign model at all, but tried to analyze American conditions and needs. Anyone who reads John Sheahan's article in the March/April issue of *Challenge* will see that French planning leaves much to be desired. The same may be said about Japanese planning, as one can learn by reading Ryutaro Komiya's article in the current issue. A planning commission that makes forecasts to which nobody pays attention is not what we have in mind. Nor do we have in mind a tug-of-war between planning technocrats, the Finance Ministry, and the Prime Minister. Nor yet a summary of the investment intentions of all the businesses in the country. Nor a planning system that is boycotted by unions because they are aligned with opposition parties. Least of all do we have in mind a *pro forma* planning procedure that is rubber-stamped by parliament and actually negotiated by chairmen of the boards of the largest corporations.

What we envisage is an effective planning agency, the Office of Balanced Growth and Economic Planning, that is the direct instrument of the President and that actually has the authority to plan. On the Congressional side, we envisage a complementary and equally effective planning agency, the Joint Economic Committee, supported by an expanded staff, working with the Budget Office, able to recommend planning legislation to Congress. The bill also encourages and supports planning agencies at the regional, state, and local levels. It is therefore inevitable that a continuous public discussion will take place about what planning should be and how it is working.

We expect that the normal American political process, through which the President, Congress, and state and local officials are elected, through which issues are discussed, and through which labor, business, farmers, minorities, and other parts of the public are heard, will determine how we plan.

This kind of planning consists neither in making elaborate forecasts spiced with wishful thinking, nor in issuing detailed orders to businesses about how to run their affairs. The detailed decisions about purchases, sales, production, employment, prices, and investment remain private. All the virtues of decentralized decision-making are kept intact. Undoubtedly many sectors of the economy which are in a state of good health, where projections look favorable, will not call for any planning action at all. But in a modern industrial economy, a collection of private decisions does not necessarily guarantee that private and social needs are met automatically. The purpose of planning is to provide, where it is lacking, the mechanism to relate needs to available labor, plant, and materials. The plan is a guide to the market.

One last consideration. The President is required by this act to transmit to Congress biennially a six-year economic and social plan. What is the point of issuing six-year plans every two years? The answer is that as circumstances change, plans must change. The six-year plan is a rolling plan, subject to change as unforeseen difficulties or opportunities arise. Those skeptical of planning say that it is impossible to see a year ahead, much less six. That is true. Nevertheless, these same skeptics plan their businesses, their vacations, and their children's educations. If something unforeseen happens, the plan is changed. Still it provides a sense of direction. When you plan to drive from Boston to Washington, you cannot tell in advance which lights will be red and which green. You find that out when you come to them. If a bridge is washed out, you do not try to drive over it. You detour. The same kind of common sense that is useful in driving from Boston to Washington is also useful in planning a national economy.

ECONOMIC PLANNING AND THE IMPROVEMENT OF ECONOMIC POLICY*

HERBERT STEIN
Professor of Economics, University of Virginia

Senator Jacob Javits, cosponsor with Senator Hubert Humphrey and others of the Balanced Growth and Economic Planning Act of 1975, has expressed the opinion that the bill has ''opened a great national debate on the American economy and its future.''[1] The idea of a great debate on the economy is appealing. It seems especially appropriate as we approach the bicentennial of the Declaration of Independence and of *The Wealth of Nations,* in an economy that is operating beyond the dreams of the Founding Fathers and beneath the contempt of many of our contemporaries.

However, the notion of a great debate, like the notion of economic planning itself, reflects a romantic, overrationalized view of how things get done in our economic and political system. It conjures up the picture of statesmen in knee breeches and powdered wigs, amateurs in economics, political science and philosophy, debating in classical rhetoric the proposition: Resolved, That Congress shall pass no law abridging freedom of contact among consenting adults. An electorate, all of whom

*Excerpted from the author's ''Economic Planning and the Improvement of Economic Policy'' (American Enterprise Institute for Public Policy Research, 1975); reprinted with permission of the American Enterprise Institute.

have read The Great Books, then makes a decision which fixes the Constitution of the American economy for the next 200 years.

History does not work like that. A great debate requires great debaters, a great audience, and a great issue. This conjuncture may sometimes arise; it can hardly be summoned on order. Our economic system evolves gradually in response to emerging problems, which are usually felt most keenly by those with special interests, but the responses are made within the range of public understanding of the proper nature of the system. This understanding changes through time as a result of experience and discussion. The changes made are incremental, often described as only codifications, improvements, or minimum necessary extensions of what already has come into existence. They are not debated or accepted as radical transformations of the system.

Surely any prudent person would want change in the system to come about in this way. The system works so well, by comparison with anything else we have ever seen, that to make a great leap to something we have only imagined would be foolhardy. This is an especially necessary attitude for those who value freedom highly. Since change decided upon by the government process is almost certain to be change towards more government power, one must hope it will not come so rapidly as to outpace the efforts of private individuals to escape government control—efforts which are also going on.

The current proponents of national economic planning seem to recognize that there is little appetite in the country for what is seen as radical economic change. They describe today's economic situation in desperate language and describe the planning bill as being of historic importance. Yet, when pressed about the implications of the proposed planning system, they tend to belittle them, saying that it only would give more information, or ensure more coordination, or do better what is being done anyhow.

Discussion of the planning proposal is not going to bring

about a fundamental change in thinking about the constitution of the American economic system, and adoption or rejection of the bill will not by itself fundamentally change the system. But this discussion and this action will *contribute,* along with hundreds of other steps, to a direction and degree of change that may be very significant in the next decade or two. In this context the planning issue deserves the most careful consideration we can give it.

WHY THE CURRENT INTEREST?

The idea that the economy should be planned has had continuing appeal in the United States and elsewhere. In fact, nothing is more natural than to believe that the best way, or indeed the only way, to ensure that an economy will serve the national interest is to have the government identify the national interest, make a plan for achieving it, and enforce the plan. The notion that the spontaneous interaction of individuals is a way to organize an economic system that serves well the interests of its members is a sophisticated idea that has never been accepted by many people. That the American economy has been basically organized in the spontaneous, free-market way is less a reflection of deliberate choice by the majority of Americans than of failure to pay attention.

So there has always been an undercurrent of support for something called economic planning. Even Herbert Hoover, great individualist that he was, was also the Great Engineer, and something of a planner.

But planning, though it has great latent appeal, only surfaces from time to time as a serious issue. It arose during the Great Depression, and during the period of national concern about the shape of the postwar economy, and again in the early 1960s when the rest of the world seemed to be outstripping the United States economically.

The present wave of interest in planning is stimulated chiefly by the fact that the economy is not performing well. We have been going through the most severe recession of the postwar period along with a serious inflation. This inevitably sets off a search for different ways of doing things. For the advocates of planning, the fact that the economy is not doing well is a large part of the argument for planning. For some of them, it is the sole and sufficient argument, despite the lack of any demonstration that planning is relevant to the current economic problem.

Beyond Keynesianism

Although, as we shall discuss further, the content of "economic planning" is exceedingly vague, most of its advocates would recognize that they are proposing something other than a better or different execution of fiscal and monetary policy to manage aggregate demand—which has been the staple of economic policy for the past generation. They are seeking to go "beyond" Keynesianism, and perhaps especially beyond the current brand of Keynesianism which is completely synthesized with monetarism. In this they are reopening an issue which was important in the 1930s but resolved or submerged subsequently.

During the 1930s there were two competing strands of thought among those who had positive programs for dealing with the acute economic problem. There were some who thought that what was needed, and essentially all that was needed, was a fiscal-monetary policy that would first expand and then stabilize aggregate demand. Others thought the difficulties were "structural," having to do with the real relations in the system and requiring more change in its internal organization. Supporters of the National Recovery Act, Agricultural Adjustment Administration, minimum wage, National Labor Relations Board, undistributed profits tax, and other New Deal measures fell in this latter camp. This issue was resolved in favor of the fiscal-monetary approach as Keynes swept the intellectuals, as World War II demonstrated what miracles demand expansion could deliver, and as the conservatives came to see that the threat to their values was not in fiscal-monetary policy but in radical structural "reform." Debate continued between Keynesians and anti-Keynesians, between fiscalists and monetarists, but this was a family quarrel among people who were generally on the same side of the larger issue.

There seem to be two reasons for the current push to get beyond demand-management policy. One is the perceived nature of the present economic problem, which makes that problem seem different from the problem with which Keynesian policy dealt. The combination of heavy unemployment with rapid inflation is an aspect of that but, oddly, the discussion of planning places little emphasis on this dilemma, and the proposal as usually described does not seem to aim at it. The aspect of the present situation which is most relevant to the planning proposal is ''shortages.'' Whereas general fiscal and monetary policy were designed to deal with the failure of spontaneous forces to generate total demand equal to potential supply, a prime concern of present planners is the claimed failure of either private forces or public policies to bring forth supplies of particular products equal to the need or demand for them. Thus we have shortages, which make for inefficiency, slow growth, and possibly also inflation. The term ''Balanced Growth'' in the title of the Humphrey-Javits bill reveals the weight the bill's sponsors give to this consideration.

The worry about shortages is largely derived from the energy problem. Indeed, there is no other example of nearly comparable magnitude. Yet to cite the energy shortage as an example of a problem for which government planning is the solution is ironic, in two respects.

First, in the process of reconsidering its oil import policy the government conducted a study of the energy problem in 1970, on a large scale and involving competent, responsible people. The study did not identify the difficulties that were then three years off. It weighed the possibility of an effective oil cartel emerging and concluded that it was unlikely. This is not a criticism of the study. It does, however, indicate that the problem of foresight is not solved by telling a government agency to have foresight.

Second, almost two years have passed since the energy problem ceased to be a forecast and became an actuality. In that period the Administration has put forward many proposals for dealing with the problem. But we still do not have an energy policy, let alone a solution. The reason we have neither a policy nor a solution is not lack of planning. It is the belief that the shortage can be corrected while energy is kept cheap.

Aside from the shortage problem, the other reason for the drive to go beyond Keynesianism, of which the planning movement is a part, is that Keynesianism no longer serves the intellectual's needs. It no longer serves, as it once did, to mark him as free thinking, avant-garde anti-establishment, and all those other qualities that intellectuals esteem. Keynesianism began losing its cachet when it was embraced by the business community. Probably the last straw was President Nixon's saying in 1971 that he was a Keynesian. After that, what assistant professor or editorial writer for an eastern newspaper would want to say that he was a Keynesian? They even began to discover that Keynes himself was a narrow, arrogant fellow, snobbish and elitist. Planning is not the farthest out of the post-Keynesian causes. It is just far enough out for a coalition of respectable professors and fashionable senators.

Foreign Experience as Precedent

On earlier occasions the planning movement in the United States has been inspired by examples of planning elsewhere. For a while, in the 1920s and 1930s, there were some who pointed to the Soviet model. However, the thoroughgoing compulsion involved in the Soviet plan has turned away most Americans. And if that were not enough, the continued Soviet food crises after almost sixty years of trying to increase farm output are a poor advertisement for Soviet-style planning.

In the 1960s many in the United States, including President John Kennedy, were fascinated by economic planning in democratic countries, especially France. The French seemed to have found the secret of planning without tears—or how to get everyone to do what the government wants them to do voluntarily, only by pointing the way. The spectacular growth of the

Japanese economy also stimulated interest in Japan's planning system. But in the last ten years the glamour has gone from these foreign systems, too. The plans were discovered to be the frosting on cakes whose size and composition they did little to influence. They were not the important determinants or instruments of government economic policy and they neither guided private behavior nor even forecast it very well. Neither has there been evidence that planning enabled the French or Japanese to avoid the common problems of recession, inflation, shortages, pollution, urban congestion, or other evils to which planners direct their attention. Their long-range plans did not, for example, foresee the world energy problem.

The present U.S. planning movement does not draw its inspiration from foreign experience. Although the procedures envisaged are certainly influenced by foreign examples, the U.S. planners seek to disassociate themselves from the foreign models. This can be seen in the comments of Myron E. Sharpe, a leading member of the Initiative Committee for National Economic Planning. This committee, whose cochairmen are Wassily Leontief and Leonard Woodcock, is a private organization that includes businessmen, academicians, and others. It did much to generate interest in the subject of planning in 1975 and it assisted in the drafting of the Senate bill. Mr. Sharpe wrote:

> Some who like neat definitions have asked what kind of model we have in mind. [Apparently this is a finicky and unimportant question to the planners.] Is it indicative planning, like the French version? The fact is that the Initiative Committee didn't start with any foreign model at all, but tried to analyze American conditions and needs. Anyone who reads John Sheahan's article in the March/April (1975) issue of *Challenge* will see that French planning leaves much to be desired. The same can be said about Japanese planning, as one can learn by reading Ryutaro Komiya's article in the current issue. A planning commission that makes forecasts to which nobody pays attention is not what we have in mind. Nor do we have in mind a tug-of-war between planning technocrats, the Finance Minister, and the Prime Minister. Nor yet a summary of the investment intentions of all the businesses in the country. Nor a planning system that is boycotted by unions because they are aligned with opposition

parties. Least of all do we have in mind a *pro forma* planning
procedure that is rubber-stamped by parliament and actually
negotiated by chairmen of the boards of the largest corporations.[2]

So the present surge of enthusiasm for planning in the United
States arises not because of the success of foreign planning but
despite its failure. American planning is to be unlike any planning known anywhere up to now. This leaves open, of course,
the question what it is to be like.

WHAT IS PLANNING?

Careful consideration of the proposals for more economic planning is made almost impossibly difficult by the lack of any
precise and agreed meaning for the term ''economic planning.''
Its opponents sometimes talk as if it means converting the
United States into the Gulag Archipelago. Its supporters sometimes seem to mean that the American economy should be run
like a progressive kindergarten, in which the pupils reach a
consensus each morning on what they will do that day—who
will pour the lemonade and who will serve the cookies. But
the first interpretation is not inevitable and the second is not
possible.

At hearings before the Joint Economic Committee of the
Congress on June 12, 1975, George Hagedorn pointed out this
uncertainty and difference of opinion about what ''planning''
meant. In reply, Senator Humphrey said: ''That is exactly the
purpose of these hearings. . . . This is advisory and consulta-
tive and hopefully out of this dialogue and discussion . . . we
will come down to a much more clear and precise understanding
of exactly what we are talking about and what we mean.''[3] It
may seem odd that the advocates of rationality and foresight
should be unable to give a clear picture of ''exactly what we are
talking about and what we mean.'' But it is really not. They do
not have to. The label on their package, ''planning,'' has great

appeal and any specification of the contents would only make the whole less attractive.

There is another aspect of Senator Humphrey's answer to Mr. Hagedorn which reveals one of the two basic themes of the modern philosophy of planning. That aspect is confidence in talking as a way to solve problems. If we do not know what we mean by "planning" we will have a dialogue until we agree on what it is, at which point we will all like it. Similarly, if we do not know how many automobiles should be produced, for example, we will have talk among the persons "involved" until we agree on an answer.

The other basic theme is confidence in the ability to answer questions by scientific, objective methods. The relation between these themes raises some of the main questions about planning. How far is it possible to answer economic and social questions by talk, and how far by science? How likely is it that the two methods will give the same or consistent answers, and what happens to planning if they do not? But for the time being the proponents of planning are still in the stage of willingness to talk about what we mean by it.

Possible Meanings

Critics of planning have paid more attention to the definition of planning. They have had to, for the same reason that the planners have not had to. Since they are in the position of not accepting something as intuitively appealing as "planning," they are forced to spell out the characteristics of that process so that they can then specify what they find to be objectionable.

A good classification of what might be meant by "planning" is given by Vera Lutz in her study *Central Planning for the Market Economy,* which is one of the best works on the subject:

> Any discussion of comparative economic systems must keep in mind that the terms "central economic planning" and "planned economy" have both in recent times been applied to differing concepts which still need to be kept apart. The first term, some-

times replaced by the second, is used to refer to three distinct things:

    a. a system of *integral* planning from the centre, implying that all economic operations are centrally "guided," "coordinated," or "directed" by a "National Plan";

    b. a system of *partial* planning from the centre, entailing measures of government intervention for purposes of modifying specific aspects of the pattern of production, consumption, or distribution;

    c. the government's programme for the public sector of the economy, or what M. Massé calls the "Plan of the State" as distinct from the "National Plan" of which it would constitute only a part.

The second term is used in still a further sense:

    d. to denote that every economy is "planned" in the sense that the various economic agents (government departments, local authorities, public enterprises, private firms, households, etc.) almost all engage individually in some sort of forward planning or "programming" of their activities.[4]

Planning as Ad Hoc Intervention

Insofar as the leaders of the present move for economic planning in the United States have given hints about what they have in mind, different ones seem to have different ideas. Senator Javits emphasizes his desire to see certain important but specific and limited policies of government changed. Replying to the charge that "planning" would interfere with consumers' freedom of choice, he says: "What is lost in the obfuscation on this issue is that the Swedes can make the same choices, but also get a national health care scheme and a safe environment." To the argument that "planning" would reduce efficiency, he says: "It just may be that one source of our current economic difficulty is too great a concern with 'efficiency' in government. In the name of efficiency millions of Americans would be consigned to the scrap heap of endemic unemployment in order to try to shave some mathematical fractions from the rate of inflation."[5]

Achievement of the objectives that Senator Javits seeks—a national health care scheme, more rigorous environmental regulations, a different choice in balancing inflation against un-employment—does not require "planning" in the sense of any different decision-making process or any qualitatively different relation between the government and the private sector. All that is required is that the President and a majority of the Congress should agree with Senator Javits on matters about which they have up to now disagreed. Something called "planning" is neither necessary nor sufficient for that.

Senator Javits's main interest, at least as expressed in the article cited, is in category (b) of the Lutz classification—"measures of government intervention for purposes of modifying specific aspects of the pattern of production, consumption or distribution." I do not propose to discuss planning in this sense. There are and will be cases of specific government intervention. Each such case involves a number of considerations that are peculiar to it. To discuss all possible interventions, or even any large number of them, in terms of their own specific features, would be far beyond the limits of this paper and this author. It would, moreover, not deal with the distinctive feature of the planning proposal being considered here—which is a comprehensive system for intervention or at least for deciding where and how to intervene.

Planning as Improved Decision-Making

Related to the identification of all government interventions as "planning" is the tendency to identify any improvement in the government decision-making process as "planning." This identification often seems to run in both directions. "Planning," without further specification, is assumed to yield better decisions, and anything that is suggested to improve decisions is immediately labelled "planning." To be concerned with improving decisions is to be labelled a "planner."

This easy slide from "planning" in the sense of the application of intelligence, foresight and information to any decision to "economic planning" in the sense of the control or guidance of economic decisions by a comprehensive, centrally determined program is a source of great confusion. Witness a discussion that occurred in the same hearings of the JEC already cited on the subject of the troubles of real estate investment trusts (REITs): Mr. Leif Olsen, senior vice president, First National City Bank of New York, said that some of these troubles were due to tax incentives given by the government. Congressman Henry Reuss moved from there to the conclusion that the troubles were due to lack of planning—''I am darned if I can figure out who made the plan on that''—and that they would have been prevented by planning—''And would not an overall planning agency have marked out the implications of this, and so perhaps have induced the Congress and the banking industry and the REITs industry to build more intelligently?'' But there is no reason to think that the errors of the REITs could have been avoided by a decision made in the context of a plan for the economy as a whole. Nor is there any reason to think that if the Department of the Treasury and the Department of Housing and Urban Development and the Federal Reserve Board and the Federal Home Loan Bank Board and the House Ways and Means Committee and the Senate Finance Committee and the Congress and the White House made a mistake about REITs, an ''overall planning agency'' would not have made the same mistake.[6]

Improving the government's decision-making process is important and I will return to that subject. However, it is only confusing to define that as identical with ''planning.'' One of the main questions about ''planning'' is whether it does in fact improve decision-making, and there may be other steps not included within ''planning'' that would be helpful to that end.

Planning as Comprehensive, Centralized Guidance

I shall mean by economic planning here either concept (a) or concept (c) of the Lutz classification, that is, either the formulation of a comprehensive, centralized plan by which the whole economy is to be guided or the formulation of such a plan for guiding the totality of government actions. Each of these kinds of planning, or some combination of them, would be consistent with the proposed legislation. Which of these, or what combination, the sponsors have in mind is unclear. Senator Humphrey's repeated references to the need for coordination of government policy, to the government's left hand not knowing what the right hand is doing, and so on, suggest a great interest in planning to guide government in doing the kind of thing it does now without planning. However, he also expresses interest in guiding what has heretofore been the private sector and, indeed, makes no distinction between planning for the public sector and planning for the private sector. In general, statements originating with the Initiative Committee for National Economic Planning place more emphasis on planning for the private sector. Myron Sharpe has described the kind of planning the Initiative Committee has in mind as follows:

> This kind of planning consists neither in making elaborate forecasts spiced with wishful thinking, nor in giving detailed orders to businesses about how to run their affairs. The detailed decisions about purchases sales, production, employment, prices, and investment remain private. All the virtues of decentralized decision-making are kept intact. Undoubtedly many sectors of the economy which are in a state of good health, where projections look favorable, will not call for any planning action at all. But in a modern industrial economy, a collection of private decisions does not necessarily guarantee that private and social needs are met automatically. The purpose of planning is to provide, where it is lacking, the mechanism to relate needs to available labor, plant, and materials. The plan is a guide to the market.[7]

This description of planning includes no limitation in principle on government intervention in the private sector. The only limitation is pragmatic. The government will not interfere, there will be no "planning action," when the private sector spontaneously conforms to the plan—in other words, when the sector is in "good health" and the "projections look favorable." In such cases the "detailed" decisions will be left private. Conceivably such a planning system could involve little intervention in the private economy, if the standards of "good health" and projections looking "favorable" are permissively interpreted so that the conditions justifying "planning action" are quite exceptional. But the system described here obviously amounts to giving a blank check whose magnitude will depend on who fills in the numbers.

The basic fact is that the proponents of planning have told us little about what they mean: What are the objectives at which the plan should aim? What activities would be planned—governmental only or private also? In what detail would the plan be drawn? By what instruments would it be carried out or enforced on the private sector?

GOALS AND OBJECTIVES

The nature and implication of the planning process would depend, more than anything else, on the goals and objectives set for it. It is one thing to say that the government has certain goals and instruments, derived from past legislation, community sentiment, or other sources, and that we want to acquire more information and look farther ahead in order to rationalize the process by which these instruments are to be used to achieve our goals. It is quite a different thing to say that we now want to discover new goals and then develop the instruments with which to achieve them. The more the process is one of creating goals, the more ambitious these goals are, and the more they depart from the spontaneous outcome of market forces, the more "planning" will lead to government intervention and force.

Vagueness of Goals in the Bill

The bill does not start with any operational specification of the goals which are to be more effectively achieved by improved procedures which might be called planning. The proposed planning process is to include the identification of goals, and the bill and the discussion of it are silent about whether this means only to recognize the goals we have or to declare new goals. The bill seems to list goals, but what it really does is list a number of areas or subjects about which the government might have goals. It does not tell what the goals are.

The goals listed are things like "full employment, price stability, balanced economic growth, an equitable distribution of income, the efficient utilization of both private and public resources," et cetera. These are not goals from which one can deduce any necessary policies. It is not only that they are expressed without quantities, whereas the policy question is almost always one of how much. They are not even described qualitatively in a way that indicates what kind of thing the planner is supposed to be looking for and aiming the plan at. For example, what is "balanced growth," a goal of such importance that is named in the title of the bill? Is that simply rapid economic growth, with the word rapid replaced by balanced as a sop to the generation that does not think growth is such a great thing after all? Does it mean sustainable growth, or would that be too much of a concession to the conservatives who are always warning that rapid expansions will not be sustainable? Does it imply some particular pattern of output and, if so, what? What kind of thing is meant by "equitable distribution of income?" One in which everyone gets the value of his product, or his just deserts, or 3 percent more than he got last year? Or is it a more equal distribution, or one with fewer people in poverty, or fewer people "obscenely" rich, to use a favorite current adverb? Similar questions can be asked about the other goals mentioned in the bill.

Recognizing that the goals mentioned are not useful as a starting point for planning, the bill relies upon another concept, "economic objectives," which are to be the operational content of the goals. These objectives are to be determined in the planning process. That is, the developers of the economic Plan not only are to devise a program for achieving objectives specified for them by legislation, but also are directed to specify objectives with respect to employment, the price level, growth, income distribution, and other categories.

Planning as a Way of Creating Goals

Why is the proposed act so vague in describing the goals to which the planning would be directed? The argument for planning is that the present "unplanned" public and private processes fail to meet the goals of the nation or of the American people. Why then does not the bill state the goals that the planning process is to achieve? Perhaps it is haste, or loose drafting. But another explanation, at least as plausible, is that a proposal which specifies goals in the fields mentioned could not possible be passed. Suppose the bill said that the goals were 4 percent unemployment, 3 percent inflation, business plant and equipment expenditure equal to 15 percent of gross national product, the poorest fifth of the population earning 15 percent of the national income, et cetera. Could this be enacted? Probably not. In the course of the debate, it would become clear that the American people did not share the goals of the planners and were unwilling to pay the costs, financial and other, of achieving them.

The proposed planning system is an invitation for the planners to invent goals that the American people do not have, or at least do not have in a form that can be a starting point for planning. It is probably true that the American people do have an interest in "balanced economic growth, an equitable distribution of income, the efficient utilization of both private and public resources" and the other goals listed in the bill. But that interest may be satisfied by the outcomes that emerge from spontaneous private processes, requiring government intervention only in exceptional cases. If this is the nature of the goals, they do not, by definition, require government plans and policies to achieve them.

This dilemma was illustrated by the attempts to draft a Report on National Growth Policy, something the Administration is now required to do every two years. It was clear from the legislation requiring this report that national growth policy meant policy about the geographical location of people and economic activity. However, a great deal of thought turned up no better objective for the location of people and for economic activity than that people should live and work where they wanted, given their own tastes and the opportunities afforded by the market. This naturally provided little basis for recommending new government programs.

The bill, of course, implies that the economic Plan should specify objectives in fairly precise, substantive, and probably quantitative terms, and not as conditions arising from the market process. If the objectives were not specified in those terms it would be hard to make sense of the other provisions of the bill which call for action to achieve the objectives.

Can Goals Be Created?

Whether the processes set forth in the bill can create objectives that will serve to control government policy and guide government action is a question. The example of the Employment Act of 1946 is sometimes used to show the effectiveness of the declaration of a goal. However, the goal of avoiding mass unemployment evolved in the course of a decade of bitter experience during the 1930s. It was not invented by a government agency and a congressional committee. There are, it should be noted, a number of examples of efforts to identify or develop national goals that have proved to be sterile, because the goals did not emanate from needs felt by the public. One of these efforts was the work of the Commission on National Goals set up by President Dwight Eisenhower. Another was the work of the National Goals Research Staff, set up by President Richard Nixon in 1969 with the intention of producing a report every year on the 4th of July. The first report, published in 1970, was so remote from anyone's interest that it was also the last. Even a quite specific goal enshrined in legislation can be inoperative if it does not reflect a real interest. This was the case with the goal contained in the Housing Act of 1968, namely, that 20 million housing units should be built in a decade.

The Escalation of Goals

Nevertheless, it is not certain that the goal-setting process would be entirely vain or harmless. If the proposed act were adopted, and if some government officials, especially members of Congress, retained an interest in it, there might be a continuing effort to specify goals. Goals legitimized by the process of the act would not be conclusive for either executive or congressional policy, but they would have some influence in debate.

There would also be a tendency for goals to escalate as a result of the political process. Whatever goals the President proposed, there would be a great temptation for others, in and out of Congress, to bid higher by demanding or offering more ambitious goals—3 percent unemployment rather than 4 percent, 5 percent growth rather than 4 percent, Ph.Ds for all rather than BAs for all. The temptation or pressure for the Administration to get into this competition would be hard to resist. The escalation would be natural because the setting of the goal would not necessarily require any immediate action to achieve it. But once set, the goal would exercise an influence on policy decisions relating to it. It would become an argument for the expenditures or regulations necessary to achieve it.

FORECASTING THE PRIVATE SECTOR

The implications of the Plan for the relations between government and the private sector would be largely determined by the meaning of the rather mysterious Section 208 (a) (2), which says that the Plan shall "identify the resources required for achieving the economic objectives of the Plan by forecasting the level of production and investment by major industrial, agricultural, and other sectors. . . . "

The Use of Forecasts

Presumably what is intended is a forecast of what production and investment would be, by major sectors, if the objectives of the Plan were met. Otherwise the forecast would not identify the resources required by the Plan. But even if the forecast assumed that the Plan was achieved, most of the forecast production would not be a requirement of the Plan. That is, unless the objectives of the Plan were exceptionally comprehensive and specific, there would be few, if any, major sectors of the economy whose production would be largely absorbed by the Plan's objectives. Even in wartime there were only very few industries in which explicitly recognized national objectives took most of the production.

It is hard to see what the use of this forecast would be. If the forecast was both an estimate of requirements and a forecast of production, assumed to be equal, there would be no possibility of a gap and no need for any policy. If the forecast was really an estimate of requirements, no policy could be deduced from it without also having a estimate of supply, and if it was a forecast of supply no policy could be deduced without an independent estimate of requirements.

A Self-Fulfilling Forecast

A possible exception to this argument is that the forecast might be basically a forecast of requirements, and would turn out to be a forecast of supply also only because the forecast was made and published. It would be the publication of the forecast which brought supply into line with requirements. Producers in industry A, seeing the forecast production of their own industry and the forecast production of industries B, C, and D which were its customers, would plan to produce the forecast volume of output.

This feature is an element of the French planning process and explains its name, "indicative planning." It might be expected to be more effective in France than here since French policy is more tolerant than American of agreement among firms to divide up an agreed level of production. But even there the gaps between plan and forecast are large. The forecasting record of the federal government here is not so impressive that private industry is likely to regard the forecasts by themselves as compelling evidence of what the market will be. In fact, the federal government now publishes both short-run and long-run forecasts of production, employment, and related variables, in great industrial detail. The long-run forecasts, made in the Department of Labor, are done by the input-output method developed by Professor Wassily Leontief, one of the leaders of the planning movement in the United States today. It is hard to see any influence of these forecasts on economic activity in the United States. The planners do not refer to them, and apparently do not regard them as bringing about consistency in the pattern of production.

Forecasts as Requirements

The forecast would undoubtedly be more influential if there were a general understanding that the government would enforce conformity with it. Then private businesses would give more weight to the forecast as an indication of what was going to happen. It seems extremely likely that the forecasting process would move in this direction. For some industries at least, the forecast would be regarded as a statement of requirements which it is the function of the planning process to meet. The subsection of the bill which calls for the forecast is followed by one which requires the Plan to recommend legislative and administrative actions necessary or desirable to achieve the Plan's objectives. At another point the President is directed to take appropriate actions to ''encourage State and local governments and the private sector to carry out their programs and activities in such a manner as to further the objectives of the Plan''

For all its ambiguities, it seems reasonable to interpret the bill as calling for a specification of private activities that would be consistent with the Plan and for government measures, whether of law, regulation, or encouragement, to bring about conformity. How far this would go, how widespread the government's activity in managing private production and investment would be, how detailed, and with what combination of sanctions and ''voluntarism,'' cannot be told from the bill. The outcome would depend largely on the attitudes of the people in the Administration and in the Congress who would be interpreting and executing the act, and of the public at large.

One very likely outcome would be that an important barrier to selective interventions in the economy would have been removed. There have been repeated suggestions, for example, that the government should allocate credit, or that it should give differential tax credits for essential investment or, more recently, that it should allocate energy to its highest uses. A contrary argument has always been that the government does not know the essential purposes to which credit, or tax privileges, or energy should be directed. The forecasts made in the Plan would not change that situation but would seem to have done so. Under the Plan, there would be a pattern of private production and investment, validated by the government, which could guide selective credit, tax, or allocation policy. In fact, it would be hard to explain why the forecasts were made if not for that purpose.

DEMOCRACY AND FREEDOM IN THE PLAN

The modern planning movement, reacting against Soviet-style planning, emphasizes its desire to preserve freedom by relying on democratic and voluntary processes. However, both the democracy and the voluntariness of the processes proposed are illusory, and the democracy, even if real, would be no assurance of freedom.

Can Everyone Plan at Once?

The bill's approach to democracy is to get "everyone" involved, both in and out of the federal government. In the executive branch, the Plan developed by the Economic Planning Board would be reviewed and approved by a council of seventeen people including all members of the Cabinet and some other officers. In the Congress, every committee would be invited to submit views, and the final decision to approve or disapprove would be made by the whole Congress.

That a council of seventeen Cabinet-level officials could review the proposed Plan substantively is improbable. Each member of the council would have competence and responsibility for only a small fraction of the information, analysis, forecasting and policy proposals contained in the Plan. Cabinet members do not typically engage in serious discussion of "their" problems with others who have neither competence nor responsibility. And each member respects the jurisdiction of the others, in the expectation of reciprocal respect. Many recent experiences with inclusive Cabinet-level committees formed to discuss and recommend economic policy have shown how ineffective such committees are. The relation of the cabinet members to Plan would almost certainly be trilateral, as their relation to the budget is. The Cabinet member would negotiate his part of the Plan with the Economic Planning Board, and have a right of recourse to the President in case of major disagreement.

To expect the committees of Congress to report on the aspects of the Plan which concern them within sixty days of its receipt, is unrealistic. Even if all the committees took their responsibility to report to the Joint Economic Committee seriously, which for jurisdictional reasons they might not do, they could not agree on a position in so complicated an area within the allotted time, or even a much longer time. Certainly, the two Houses could not have a useful debate on the whole Plan and reach a decision, except a decision to pass, in the fifteen days provided. A congressional decision would have to be the product of staff efforts, backed by strong party leadership.

The bill seeks to make the planning process still more democratic by bringing forces outside the federal government into it. These forces include state and local governments, which would comment on the Plan and participate voluntarily in its implementation. This raises no particular questions other than of competence and feasibility; these governments are at least selected by some democratic, constitutional method. A more serious question is raised by the provision for participation of private citizens in both the development and execution of the Plan. No doubt there are many private people who could give expert advice on the Plan. However, the Advisory Committee and its subcommittees that would be established by the act are envisaged not as expert bodies but as representatives of the views and opinions of broad segments of the public. Typically, and inevitably, such committees are composed of officials, often not democratically chosen, and representatives of organizations that have designated themselves as spokesmen of this or that segment of the public. For example, in dozens of such committees it has never been possible to find any representative of "workers" except an officer of a union—this in a country where the large majority of workers are not organized—and surely there must be many consumers who do not regard Ralph Nader as their representative. Committees of private citizens may be less representative than our duly elected government officials, and influence given to advisory committees may make the whole process less, rather than more, democratic.

The fact is that comprehensive, detailed, "scientific" economic planning is an inherently undemocratic process. Because of its technical complexity, its demanding time schedule, and the difficulty of finding consensus, it cannot be done in a town meeting.

Democratic Coercion

In any case, the question of whether a planning process is democratic is quite different from the question of its effect on individual freedom. A plan that is coercive, even if adopted by a quite deliberate and informed choice of a majority of the people, will coerce at least a minority in ways with which they do not agree. And since the planning process spelled out in the proposed act is complex and has numerous requirements, even the majority that approved the Plan as a whole might be involuntarily coerced in some respects. The argument for freedom is not an argument for coercion by the majority. It is an argument for minimizing coercion.

Advocates of planning maintain that their proposals are voluntary, not coercive. However, it is hard to be sure. The bill as such would give the federal government no power it does not now have over private citizens. However, it calls upon the government to spell out goals, including goals which do not now exist, and to recommend legislative and administrative actions to achieve those goals. Once the goals have been legitimized, the way would be opened to give the government powers necessary to achieve them. The bill contains no inhibitions against this. It does not even contain the common ritual

language about achieving the goals of the act by means consistent with the free enterprise system.

Discussion of the coerciveness of planning is often confused
by the notion that government action is coercive only if it imposes the possibility of fine or imprisonment. In that light,
systems which provide tax benefits, or allocate credit, or give
preferences in government procurement, and so on, to individuals or businesses that conform to a plan are considered non-
coercive. That is a mistake. As Gustavo Velasco asked:

> But what coercive means will be more powerful and effective
> against a businessman, that of spending some days in jail or of
> paying a fine, or that of being deprived of advantages which,
> depending upon conditions in the branch of business in which he
> is engaged, the harshness of competition, and the general
> economic situation, can determine that his business does not
> expand or is not modernized, may not distribute dividends, or
> may even be displaced by those who enjoy official favors and
> assistance?[8]

In other words, if the government can make a private citizen an
offer he cannot refuse, it can exercise coercion. If the Balanced
Economic Growth Plan led to increasing use of these "conventional" instruments of governmental policy, as seems likely, it
would increase coercion. Even the provision of the bill which
directs the President to "encourage" the private sector to act in
a way that is consistent with the Plan could be coercive since it
involves a relation between the President of the United States
and enterprises that are heavily dependent on good relations
with the government and a favorable public image.

WHAT CAN WE EXPECT?

The bill, like the discussion of planning in general, is too vague
to tell us just what would happen if it were to become law. Even
if it were much more precise and specific than it is, the outcome
would be hard to predict, because it would depend inevitably on
the understandings and wishes of those who manage it and upon
its evolution in the future.

Nevertheless, some speculation may be offered about the direction in which the process would move if the bill were passed and a serious effort made to operate within its spirit.

(1) Goals for government policy that do not now exist, or more ambitious goals than now exist, would be increasingly advanced. These goals would represent the views of the politicized experts who would run the Economic Planning Board, the relevant congressional staffs, and the staffs of the private national organizations that would constitute the advisory layer. The goals would not determine policy. But they would lead policy in the direction of more government spending and more government controls to achieve the added goals.

(2) Management of the existing economic instruments of government would be increasingly supervised by the Executive Office, to the derogation of the departments and agencies, and would be addressed to the central goals, rather than to the more limited objectives which may have originally led to the creation of the instruments.

(3) Estimates would be made of required production and investment in some "key" sectors of the economy (meaning sectors in which the firms are large, because it is easiest for government to deal with them) and these requirements would be compared with forecasts. The government would try to correct the deficiencies that the comparison revealed. Initially it would do this by talking to the firms involved, but increasingly it would rely on incentives of various kinds to achieve the results.

(4) The high-pressure goals for employment, growth, and public services would cause more and more inflation, leading to repeated efforts at incomes policies, which would seem more congenial to the system as it became more planned. However, the incomes policies would yield no durable results.

(5) Uncertainties about government policy increasingly would depress private investment, requiring more and more government incentives to stimulate it. At some point the government would become unwilling to pay private businesses to do what it could order them to do. The system of incentives would yield to the system of command.

(6) So the economy would become more inflationary, less

free, and less efficient. Meanwhile, the unemployment problem would not have been solved, because we would not have ended the rise of inflationary expectations which make full employment impossible without intolerably accelerating inflation. And we would not have solved the problem of shortages because we would have suppressed the free movement of prices which, by attracting production and discouraging use, would help to cure shortages.

Passage of the bill would not lead us rapidly and irreversibly to the end of this line. There would still be opportunities to turn back. Other countries have started in this direction and then stopped, or converted their planning into an academic exercise. However, even if the bill does not determine that we go all the way, the road down which it would point us seems clear.[9]

PART II
NATIONAL EXPERIENCES
WITH ECONOMIC PLANNING

GREAT BRITAIN: THE LESSONS OF SOCIALIST PLANNING

RALPH HARRIS
General Director, The Institute of Economic Affairs, London

The United Nations study *Economic Planning in Europe*[1] made the useful distinction between the pursuit by government of broad "policy objectives" and their setting specific "plan targets" for such simple-seeming aggregates as production, investment, consumption, foreign trade. It is hardly conceivable that a modern government should refrain from the first kind of liberal* planning, if only because its responsibility for the national money implies some view about the desired course of domestic prices, and (in open economies) their impact via foreign trade on exchange rates. Even in "monetary planning," a government must take heed to ensure its price objective is consistent with other broad goals it may have concerning the acceptable levels (or range) of unemployment and interest rates, to say nothing of the relationship between government expenditure, taxation and borrowing. Thus, even the simplest hierarchy of "policy objectives," requires that priorities be established on the best estimates of the relevant "trade-offs."

---

*"Liberal" is used in its classical European sense as confining government to strategic measures necessary to maximize freedom, which appears to be roughly the opposite of its American usage.

With more ambitious forms of planning, incorporating specific "targets" for the size and detailed composition of national output, the need for consistency between broad objectives and specific elements hardly needs emphasising. And yet successive governments have failed by ignoring such an obvious requirement. This verdict is inescapable if we review the 30 years of British planning since the end of World War II, during which governments of both major parties have experimented with most varieties of central planning short of the command economies familiar in Eastern Europe.

SOCIALIST PLANNING

The record starts with the replacement of Churchill's coalition in 1945 by a Labor Government pledged to "plan the peace" on the analogy of successful wartime planning. Economists like Ely Devons[2] warned in vain that planning even in the closed war economy had been marked by appalling problems and waste, despite both coercive enforcement powers and the single, overriding objective of military victory. And neither special circumstance was applicable to the diverse, dispersed individual purposes of an open society in times of peace.

The socialists acknowledged that planning must serve a number of broad policy objectives, including stable prices, full employment, increasing welfare and living standards, not to mention a strong balance of payments to bolster the pound. "Plan targets" for such crude categories as investment, consumption, exports, were to be advanced by retaining war-time controls of rationing, allocation of materials, and the licensing of imports, building, capital issues, and bank credit. The transformation of the out-dated basic industries was to be accomplished by the outright nationalization of coal, gas, electricity, railways and steel.

The outcome can be briefly told. Despite the negotiation by Lord Keynes of an American loan for £1,000 million (equal to about one-eighth of the British national income) and appeals for wage restraint, prices rose annually by 5%, the pound was devalued by the ''Iron Chancellor'' Sir Stafford Cripps, and the Labor Party went down to defeat in 1951 amidst shortages, austerity and restrictions from which Churchill promised to ''set the people free.'' The full analysis of that progression from socialist planning towards planned chaos can be found in the brilliant academic polemic by Professor John Jewkes, who did not need to wait until 1951 to pronounce the funeral oration.[3]

LIBERAL PLANNING

The next phase of liberal economic planning under the Conservatives ran from 1951 to 1960, first under Churchill and then Macmillan. Churchill's ministers threw themselves with increasing confidence into dismantling restrictions and rationing. Price and wage controls were scrapped, despite Labor Party predictions of disaster, and the Bank Rate, held at 2% since 1939 in deference to the Keynesian panacea of ''cheap money,'' was allowed to rise as evidence that monetary and market mechanisms had a larger part to play. The success of this sharp repudiation of socialist planning was widely acknowledged by independent commentators no less than by the electorate, which in 1955 voted the Conservatives back with an increased majority. Churchill was succeeded by Sir Anthony Eden, whose breakdown after the Suez adventure gave Harold Macmillan the opportunity to justify the slogan that ''Conservative freedom works.'' At the subsequent election in 1959 the Conservatives broke a Parliamentary record by winning for the third time running with an increased majority. This was the heyday of ''Super-Mac,'' whose boast ''you have never had it so good'' was only later used to mock him in defeat.

INCONSISTENCY OF OBJECTIVES

Yet already, the shrewd observer could detect signs of troubles to come. Even in Churchill's time, his Chancellor, R. A. Butler, was sufficiently committed to the ''full employment'' and welfare state objectives of Labor's Hugh Gaitskell, that the term ''Butskellism'' was coined to describe the conservative government's Keynesian fiscal policies. Those policies pursued two conflicting, inconsistent objectives: full employment and a stable currency. Their pursuit has haunted both British policy-makers and the British economy since that time, and has been at least indirectly responsible for most of the disastrous planning efforts during that period.

By pursuing the conflicting objectives of full employment and a stable currency, the government was compelled every two or three years to produce emergency budgets adjusting the level of effective demand to the over-riding imperatives first of moderating prices, and then unemployment. American readers may be surprised to know that at this period British politicians interpreted ''full employment'' as setting a target of around 350,000 (1% of the labor force) for the tolerable level of unemployment. And since the official statistics include people unemployed for a few days as well as many unemployables who are on the register as a qualification for drawing social benefits, the objective of full employment meant for practical purposes that there were throughout the post-war years invariably more unfilled vacancies than unemployed people genuinely seeking work.

It was not necessary for the robust British trade union leaders to swot [sic] up elementary market analysis to discover that what passed as ''free industrial bargaining''[4] empowered them to extract increased money wages from employers without worrying about the unemployment effect which Keynesian fiscal policies would in effect buy off.

Nor was it necessary to master the subtleties of Friedman's concept of the ''natural rate of unemployment'' to grasp the truism that the determined pursuit of full employment in a world of powerful trade unions must put in jeopardy the further objective of stable prices. This basic conflict of aims in post-war economic policy was exposed in the endless exhortation for ''pay pauses'' and appeals for ''price stability.'' But the inconsistency in practice comes home to roost most quickly in a country like Britain which exports about a quarter of its domestic output to buy essential foods and raw materials. So long as the fixed exchange rate for sterling was upheld as a further objective, the rise in British prices at a rate higher than in countries with which we trade was bound to stimulate imports and reduce exports. The resulting trade deficit must weaken the pound and throw the strain on the gold and foreign currency reserves that stood between the Bank of England and devaluation.

The central analysis explains why Conservative governments were destined to fail in their effort to shift planning away from socialist conceptions to one more compatible with a liberal market economy. Their broad policy objectives were drawn in terms that were bound to prove mutually frustrating. In particular, the full employment target was set as a level which theory suggested and practice proved destructive of anything approaching a stable value of money.

INSTABILITY OF OUTCOME

Since it was the inevitable failure of pursuing these inconsistent objectives which carried planning back in a socialist direction, we may recall how the conflict manifested itself with mounting political irritation in the 1950s. To hit the full employment target, governments began by pushing effective demand to a level that drove wages and other costs upwards. Prices then began to rise, and as imports rose faster than exports, the resulting pressure on reserves provided a swift warning against "over-heating." The simultaneous commitment to maintain the exchange rate of the pound compelled Chancellors to reduce the pressure of domestic demand by such orthodox Keynesian measures as cutting government spending or raising taxes to achieve a revenue surplus, later supplemented by monetary restraint via Bank Rate and credit restriction.

The result of curbing excessive demand had its first impact, as Friedman for long taught unheeded, on unemployment and output, with the check on rising prices coming later. So that before the monetary medicine could affect inflation, political pressures developed for a renewed stimulus to stop unemployment rising further. In this way, successive governments alternated abruptly between expansion and contraction,[5] all in the name of "stabilizing" the economy. Since the favorite "regulators" were taxes on consumer durables and variations in the terms of installment credit, the result was to disrupt the forward planning of business investment to the maximum degree. The outcome was a swelling chorus of protest against what was characterized as "stop-go." However, since the initial error was in pushing the "go" phase too hard, a more correct description would have been "go-stop." But so long as "stop-go" was seen as the enemy, the obvious remedy seemed to be to tackle the "stop," rather than ask whether the "go" could be sustained. It was on this unsubstantial foundation that the case was born for more socialist planning after 1960.

PLANNING BY TARGETS

Just when politicians were looking for some escape from the dilemma of inflation under full employment, leading economists and publicists discovered French "indicative planning." Ignoring the spirit of the liberalizing measures following the 1958 Rueff-Armand reforms, the discussion concentrated on the Monnet-Massé Commissariat du Plan, which was credited with having engineered a growth rate averaging 4.6% in the decade since 1951, compared with 2.8% in Britain.[6]

The distinctive feature of indicative planning was for government to involve private enterprise and trade unions in the formulation of agreed targets for the major sectors of the economy so that all felt committed to their fulfillment. According to M. Massé, the Plan "having once been drawn up, as it were, carries itself out," although the French government retained powerful sanctions, particularly over the extensive public sector and the supply of capital for private investment.

It was on this model that a Conservative Chancellor in 1961 set up the National Economic Development Council, whose 20 members were roughly evenly divided between "representatives" of business, trade unions and government. Its terms of reference were to consider the obstacles to quicker growth and seek agreement on ways of improving Britain's economic performance. Liberal supporters hoped the Council would spotlight such institutional impediments to market efficiency and flexibility as trade union (and professional) restrictions, national wage fixing, differential taxation of dividends, protective tariffs and subsidies, rent control, resale price maintenance, indiscriminate welfare benefits. Others hoped the Council might question Keynesian high-pressure "demand management" which threw the burden of compensating adjustment onto the private sector while government spending moved only upwards.

Alas, it was not to be expected that representatives of the contending interests would opt for such a bracing route to growth. Instead, after searching in vain for a wages-profits-prices pact to keep inflation at bay without a repetition of "stop-go," in 1963 the Council launched a blueprint for growth at 4% a year from 1961 to 1966. While its authors denied this "program" was "a plan," *Growth of the United Kingdom to 1966* ran to 150 pages and 100 tables which set out the "implications" of the growth target for investment, manpower, imports, exports, consumption and 17 major industries covering half of industrial production. The central aim was nothing less than "sustained expansion," and the National Institute of Economic and Social Research, which had led the "growth" school from the start, provided the pretence of intellectual underpinning with the declaration that "a necessary and almost sufficient condition for rapid growth is for businessmen in general to expect that demand for their products will continue to grow rapidly."

Emboldened by this highly-statistical, scientific-looking program, the Chancellor, Mr. Reginald Maudling, played his part by maintaining expansionary monetary and fiscal policies appropriate to full employment. In 1963 public investment was stepped up, and taxes on income and consumer durables sharply reduced. With a euphoric degree of enthusiasm to crown the consensus—which superficially united businessmen, unions, all parties, most commentators and too many economists—

everything seemed set to ensure the best prospect of success. Yet Table 1 documents the complete failure by 1966 to approach the 4% growth target or the associated key objectives for investment, exports, imports, and GDP per head.

From an improvement in the performance of the British economy on the balance of foreign trade, which the planners regarded as critical, Table 1 shows that the increase in exports lagged well behind imports. Instead of improving, the balance of trade moved the wrong way over the 5-year period. This uncovenanted gain from the viewpoint of resources available for use in the domestic economy did not, however, help achieve the planned steady increase in investment—despite more favorable tax and subsidy provisions. Table II shows the patchy perversity of results in forecasting total output for half a dozen of the major ''industries.'' (In fact, the forecasting errors would be still wider if these targets were subdivided into the product groups lumped together in such heterogeneous totals.) The four components of fuel illustrate the ''domino fallibility'' of forecasting the supply or demand for products that are direct substitutes for one another, or are markedly interrelated in other ways.[7] Thus the central planners overstated the rise in electricity because they underrated the prospects for gas. A further vulnerability is shown in the optimistic target for steel, which was based in part on exaggerated hopes for an increase in the market for motor vehicles.

Charts comparing the course of output, unemployment and the balance of payments for the period of 1961–66 with the pre-planning period of 1957–62 would show a closely parallel cycle of initial expansion during the ''go'' phase, followed by a collapse of hopes for ''sustained growth'' as the inevitable ''stop'' was applied from the end of 1964 (as in 1960).

In October 1964, Mr. Wilson's Government took over; and, despite their earlier support for planned growth, the new ministers made much propaganda about the sharply worsening balance of payments position they inherited. Before the end of 1964, the new Labor Chancellor began to resort to the familiar

TABLE I   Plan Comparisons

Annual Rates of increase % at constant prices

	GDP		Investment		Exports		Imports		GDP per head	
	Plan	Actual	Plan	Actual	Plan	Actual	Plan	Actual	Plan	Actual
1958–9	—	2.0	—	7.5	—	4.2	—	7.0	—	
1959–60	—	4.4	—	9.9	—	5.2	—	12.8		2.5
1960–61	—	3.7	—	9.5	—	2.6	—	-2.2	—	
1961–62	4	0.8	5.3	-0.6	5	2.3	4	3.4		
1962–63	4	4.0	5.3	1.7	5	3.9	4	3.9		
1963–64	4	5.8	5.3	16.9	5	2.8	4	11.2	3.2	2.2
1964–65	4	2.6	5.3	3.5	5	5.4	4	0.8		
1965–66	4	1.6	5.3	0.6	5	3.4	4	2.5		
Average 1961–66	4%	2.9%	5.3%	4.4%	5%	3.6%	4%	4.3%		

TABLE II   Comparisons in Selected Industries

| | Annual increases for 1961–66 | |
	NEDC target	Actual
Coal	0.9%	−1.6%
Electricity	10.0%	7.0%
Gas	2.8%	6.8%
Petroleum	7.6%	7.8%
Steel	5.5%	1.9%
Motor vehicles	11.0%	6.6%

package of fiscal and credit restraint, which he dignified as "fingertip control of the economy." Because Conservatives still believed in such naivete, they did not, in Opposition, mock Mr. James Callaghan for this boast in 1967, when he (honorably) resigned for devaluing the pound, after confidently declaring that he would hold the parity at $2.80.

THE FIVE-YEAR PLAN

But we must go back to 1965 for the next stage in the saga of British economic planning. The new Labor Government had their own remedy for what they persisted in mis-describing as "stop-go." The trouble was, they thought, that the Treasury was less committed to economic growth than to such orthodox objectives as safeguarding the balance of payments. Accordingly, a new fully-fledged Department of Economic Affairs was established, under the ebullient Mr. George Brown, to take charge of planning for growth. (American readers would be surprised how closely the purposes of this now defunct Department corresponded to the aspirations for an Economic Planning Board set out in the draft Bill of Senators Humphrey and Javits in 1975.)

A comprehensive enquiry invited firms to supply detailed information on their present and estimated production, exports, imports, employment (in categories and regions), and their investment in buildings, plants, vehicles, ships, aircraft . . . all answers to be "on the assumption of a 25% increase in gross domestic product between 1964 and 1970." (The convenient round figure represented an average annual growth rate of 3.8% compared with NEDC's 4%.) From this meaningless assortment of mostly subjective, speculative data, *The National Plan* was collated and published with massive publicity in September 1965. It ran to 470 closely-packed pages and literally unnumbered tables and charts. It did not equivocate: it was a 5-year Plan and represented "a statement of Government policy and a commitment to action by the Government."

Happily from the viewpoint of this exposition, we do not need to examine the swamping morass of statistical targets incorporated in *The National Plan* which Mr. George Brown earnestly hoped in his foreword would be "widely read and discussed throughout the country." After a gestation period of one year in preparation, this portentous document mocked nature by passing within nine months from teething troubles to the death rattles, without the usual interval of hopeful life. In short, the Plan was formally and officially declared at an end in July, 1966. Mr. Brown retired and Mr. Wilson as Prime Minister announced the most severe credit squeeze yet, including a freeze on all incomes and control over prices. It was a desperate effort to combat the latest sterling crisis provoked by the worsening balance of payments and a collapse of confidence in the pound at its fixed parity.

The epitaph on *The National Plan*, which was explicitly aimed at solving "the most serious problem facing us . . . the balance of payment," came with the devaluation of the pound from $2.80 to $2.40 in November, 1967. The irony was that by the end of 1966, when the earlier NEDC program was to have yielded its full benefits, a second and still more ambitious effort to plan Britain into faster growth had already come and gone. If we cast forward to 1970, we find that instead of a 25% increase in output, the economy achieved 12%, or little over 2% a year, which was where the growthmen had come in. By 1975, it can be reported that the 1965 target increase of 25% in five years had not been reached even after a full decade.

"TOOTHLESS" PLANNING?

Defenders of control planning like Thomas (Lord) Balogh were prompt to blame failure on the absence of sanctions to enforce targets, descending to the level of the individual firm, with subsidies for those that collaborated and the threat of nationalisation against recalcitrants. Such an alibi was unconvincing for two major reasons. First, by the 1960s governments had a massive armory of devices to influence industrial investment and development, or even to control it outright. Tax discrimination, subsidies, government contracts, and building and development controls have long been available to guide private investment into favored activities or regions. And through nationalization and public utilities, governments have come to account for nearly half of all fixed investment.

Yet achievement in planning this governmental sector was as erratically at variance with the targets as it was elsewhere. In public housing, National Health Service, and nationalised industries wholly under government control, performance has continued to fall behind repeated promises.

The second fallacy in the Balogh alibi that planning lacked "teeth" can be seen from Table II. The three fuel industries of coal, electricity and gas were nationalised, and yet their outputs in 1966 departed from the NEDC targets far more than petroleum, which is produced by the wholly-private enterprise oil companies. If the Balogh view was that the targets based upon fallible forecasts should have been enforced on all producers, they would also have had to be imposed on the consumers, since it was their wayward preferences that helped explain why the pattern of output diverged from the plan.

The result of controlling output without rationing consumption of fuels was seen in electricity, where the nationalized industry took the NEDC projections seriously and launched a massive program of investment in new generating plant, thereafter left idle or run for years below capacity. It was fortunate that most businessmen, whilst often paying lip-service to government planning, took less notice of the official targets than of demand as indicated in the markets for their products. One private industry that allowed itself to be misled by government appeals for increased capacity was bricks. In response to a house-building target which was never reached, over-capacity in brick production was created in 1965, thereby causing an unmanageable accumulation of stocks and prompting firms to appeal for financial help to reduce excess plant.

On this and other occasions, as Professor Jewkes has observed, "The Government was called upon to act as saviour of the economic system it had disrupted." It is clear that "planning with teeth" would simply have made general the sporadic dislocations caused by the descrepancy between the inflexible forecasts of fallible planners and the changing kaleidoscope of consumers' demand.

SOME LESSONS FROM BRITISH EXPERIENCE

The total failure of central planning to achieve any of its objectives hardly calls for emphasis: the plight of the British economy in 1975 tells its own story. Given that the declared objectives of post-war planning were internally inconsistent, it remains a remarkable testimony to the impotence of government intervention that none of its aims has been achieved.

Cumulatively, since 1960, record levels of unemployment and inflation have come to coexist with flagging growth and a sinking pound, whilst a standard of living overtaken by most European countries is now prevented from falling further only by massive foreign borrowing. Indeed, the single striking success has been the resilience of the residual private enterprise element which has sustained a rapidly-increasing governmental sector, in spite of the burdens and the almost continuous disturbance imposed on industry by changing policies as successive plans have come to grief.

The distant onlooker may conclude that since economic planning was so completely ineffective, it can hardly be blamed for Britain's relative decline. In this respect, no doubt, there are deep-seated structural weaknesses in the British economy going back to our early lead in the industrial revolution. These include, among others, the cushioning against foreign competition wherever trade followed the imperial flag, and the consequent conservatism of British institutions, nowhere more firmly entrenched than in the bristling Maginot line of trade union resistance to change. So far from helping overcome such handicaps, however, post-war planning has invariably reinforced them and added fresh rigidities.

The essential appeal of planning to politicians is that it promises an escape from the ineluctable real world choice for a nation either to live within its income or to face the risks and adjustments that must come from fostering a more dynamic economy. Planning appears the soft option. While directing attention away from the structural changes that would help a market economy function more efficiently, it holds out hopes of rising standards of living by manipulating such apparently simple variables as the level of investment or employment.

The electorate is naturally in favor of such painless enrichment and, as workers and beneficiaries of state welfare, they promptly step up their demands for higher incomes at least to match the well-publicised growth target. When the aggravated demands on the economy inevitably exceed flagging supplies, the ruling politicians persist in hoping the plan will somehow deliver the goods. Thus, again and again, the existence of a plan delayed corrective action and intensified its eventual impact.

At the same time, politicians have their own ambitions for spending more. Accordingly, each phase of planning has been the pretext for enlarging the government's claims on the planned increase in output. When the growth failed to materialise, the economy was left with a bigger burden of unproductive, and often counter-productive, government expenditure. It is no accident that in the period since 1961, which saw the return to planning targets, the total government disposal of resources has risen from 42% of the national income to about 60%, while public employment (excluding the armed services) rose by one-quarter, to account for 26% of the (civil) labor force. We see here how swiftly the beguiling concept of a "mixed economy" can degenerate through ineffective planning towards an increasingly socialised system.

A besetting weakness of planners is the ability to allow their hopes to triumph afresh over every set-back. Nowhere is this more plainly seen than in their reliance on incomes and price policies to combat inflation caused by monetary laxity. There has hardly been a year since 1945 when Ministers have not called for "a standstill," "a pause," "a plateau," "a ceiling," or "a solemn and binding undertaking." When exhortation was finally seen to be ineffective, Mr. Wilson's government in 1966 overturned its election pledge by abandoning "free collective bargaining" and imposing a statutory standstill on wages and prices. In the past ten years, Conservative and Labor politicians have devoted endless ingenuity to refining these paper fortifications against inflation while the rate of price increases has escalated from around 5% in the late 1960s, to 10% in 1971, 15% in 1974 and 25% in 1975. Thus, negative planning directed specifically against inflation has proved as complete a failure as positive planning for growth.

Another characteristic shared by British planners, irrespective of party, is an overwhelming faith in their own judgment of industrial potentialities. As part of its plan to "restructure" British industry, the Labor Government after 1964 set up the Industrial Reorganisation Commission. Based this time on the model of IRI in Italy, the IRC was to apply state finance to encourage mergers of private enterprise companies into larger units. The assumption was, of course, that "bigger would be better," and the Government would receive a good political and pecuniary return on its efforts. It is painful for a British taxpayer to recall that two of the major amalgamations IRC brought about were British Leyland and the Upper Clyde Shipbuilders. Both rapidly degenerated into "lame ducks" and look like surviving only as permanent pensioners on public funds. The significant truth is that this humiliating failure has not prevented the present Labor Government from allowing Mr. Wedgewood Benn to establish the National Enterprise Board, with even more grandiose ideas about taking an equity in the "winners" it confidently expects to pick.

Confronted by such past follies, the planners' sublime response is that "it will be different this time." Thus, we are reassured, the NEB has been put under the charge of a captain of industry, who was promptly elevated to the peerage as Lord Ryder. But is it forgotten that the National Economic Development Council was one-third packed with private businessmen who believed they could bring off the 4% growth program? The sad truth is that the best entrepreneur may prove the most incompetent planner, once he is removed from the milieu of competitive business. But suppose Lord Ryder's judgment in picking winners were infallible. He would certainly come under pressure to succour failing businesses, whose collapse would upset the unions. The further fallacy here is that even if some plan were sensibly devised, governmental agencies will not resist the call of political expediency when the going gets rough.

Planning has not only proved an escape from reality; it has invariably operated to weaken competition. Some commentators have long expressed concern about the corporativist possibilities of running an economy by private collusion between powerful "representatives" of labor, management and government. The more immediate danger is that firms in the same industry which come together to put up a common front to government departments (with discretionary subsidies and privileges to disburse) may preserve a common front against the consumer, the importer, or the new entrant into their industry. If such tendencies prevail, the perverse planners will be given a further pretext for intervening against "monopolistic" developments that past planning has facilitated, if not actively encouraged.

Even where planners deny hostility to private enterprise, their belief in prescribed targets for output or investment is at odds with the operation of competitive markets, because it springs from a misconception of how a market economy works—a misconception, it may be added, from which businessmen are not always exempt. Thus, when the authors of the 1965 *Na-*

tional Plan sent out their questionnaire to firms, they asked for future output, investment, exports, to be given in physical quantities or at constant prices. But as Hayek has frequently emphasised, the essence of problems posed by economic development arises from the unforeseen changes in relative prices—the very changes which rapid growth would intensify, yet which the planners of rapid growth would ignore.

How can producers of coal, gas, electricity, oil, or of paper, plastics, tins, bottles, forecast[8] their production five years hence, unless they form some view of the likely range of changes in relative costs and prices, reflecting variations in techniques, availability of raw materials, and consumer demand? The absurdity of such planning would have been seen more clearly if the planners had been able to impose the erroneous targets on the firms that supplied the meaningless statistics.

CONCLUSION

The myth of planning has survived because each failure is met by its advocates shifting their ground to argue for "better planning." The concept is so elusive that Professor Jewkes has offered the definition: "Planning is what planners think and do."

Nevertheless, the weight of empirical evidence against all variants of socialist planning is now stronger than ever before. It should not be impossible to teach politicians that such endeavors to escape from scarcity and find shortcuts to prosperity are vain and doomed to bring deeper disappointment to their voters, and still further discredit upon themselves. If their craving for certainty and order is permitted to find an outlet in economic planning, the outcome can only be the spread of uncertainty and disorder.

The simple truth, confirmed by British post-war experience, is that there exists no science or dependable art of economic planning in the ambitious form most democratic governments are increasingly tempted to indulge. What passes as planning is in practice nothing more than a hotchpotch of ad hoc interventions connected by specious words that conceal an intellectual vacuum.

In anything but the most primitive and static economy, neither the information nor the criteria exist for planners to select a consistent set of targets for outputs, investments, techniques, employments that would form a coherent, operational system. And to use an Irishism, even if such a comprehensive plan were conceivable, there would still be no way of enforcing it in a society that allowed significant freedom for consumers and therefore, ultimately, for voters.

The Achilles' heel of the planner is ultimately what Hayek called in his Nobel Lecture "The Pretence of Knowledge."[10] Comprehensive information about the economic present (let alone the future), which would be a necessary starting point for control planning, can never be assembled in any centralised form. The merit of competitive markets is that they engage through the price mechanism all the scattered knowledge of producers, consumers, traders, to produce a spontaneous and harmonious order which can never be fabricated. In a devastating critique entitled *Galbraith and the Planners*,[11] Professor Frank McFadzean referred to the USSR, where 10 million Soviet citizens were estimated in 1962 to be engaged in collecting and processing data. He quoted Academician Glushkov's warning that if the Russians attempted to extend planning to every economic activity, "several quintillion relationships would have to be examined and appraised," and that would take several years even with "a million computers processing 30,000 operations a second."

The reality is even more adverse to planning than such a far-fetched illustration would suggest. The ceaseless changes in conditions affecting the daily demand and supply of countless goods and services must render the best statistics out-of-date before they can be collected. In contrast, markets operate like a linked network of computers, which supply each individual with the information he needs for his particular purposes through the changing signals of relative prices. Yet the planner boasts of sophistication in deploying a computable input-output model, fed on a comparative spoonful of stale statistics, to guide a complex and ever-changing economy. To watch British planners in practice falling back on ad hoc interventions interspersed with endless exhortation "in the public interest" is to see the substitution of a hand-and-mouth operated economy for the impersonal computer of competitive markets.

When theory reinforces the evidence that planning provides no solution to our economic problems, the conscientious planner's last refuge is in the familiar retort that markets are fine in theory, but imperfect in practice. It is in meeting this misconception that the Institute of Economic Affairs is having increasing success in Britain.[12] The need is to show that imperfections in the operation of free markets are manageable by reform of the monetary, fiscal and legal framework, whereas the limitations and contradictions of planning are inherent in its Frankenstein "nature."

The most hopeful portent I can offer from Britain is in the words of one of our outstanding economic journalists, Mr. Samuel Brittan, who left the *Financial Times* to help Mr. George Brown launch the National Plan in 1965. He learned the right lessons from its failure, and in an effort to rescue the basically neutral word "planning" from those who had perverted it for ideological purposes, he subsequently commended the idea of "a plan to set Britain free."

It would be a happy outcome of our travails if we can now switch the debate on "planning" to a livelier discussion of ways to improve the operation of the competitive market economy by reducing government to the more modest role befitting its limited capabilities. It was the Cambridge economist Alfred Marshall who used to meet suggestions for extending government functions by the rhetorical question: "Do you mean Government all wise, all just, all powerful; or Government as it now is?" If every would-be planner had first to overcome that doubt, we should be less troubled in future by their naive claims for the perfectibility of government economic planning.

PLANNING IN WEST GERMANY: THE SOCIAL MARKET ECONOMY

HANS WILLGERODT
Professor of Economics, University of Cologne

I

In the twenty years prior to the West German economic reforms of 1948, Germany experimented with a number of approaches to central economic planning and government intervention in the economy. Beginning in the final days of the Weimar Republic, the Germany economy was gradually transformed from an imperfect market economy into a centrally-administered economy in a totalitarian state.

It is difficult to say exactly when the "march into socialism," to use Schumpeter's phrase, began. But Chancellor Brüning's decision in 1931 to impose exchange controls for capital exports instead of devaluing the Reichsmark was a fatal step. For Brüning's decision began and made necessary a whole series of additional government controls of the economy.

Control of foreign trade, which resulted from the exchange controls, became complete in the "New Plan" of 1934. Principal features of the new policy were bilateralism and monopolistic price discrimination in foreign markets, to improve the terms of trade. To make the system work, it became necessary to establish a comprehensive licensing apparatus, to regulate all economic transactions with foreigners, and finally even to control and censor the private mails.

This system was praised even by non-German authors[1] as an intelligent way to improve trade results and to insulate the German economy from international disturbances. However, it did not work out quite that way. Germany's trading partners proceeded to copy what were rather antique mercantilist techniques of international discrimination and economic warfare, and therefore whatever gains Germany might have hoped for from its new foreign economic policy vanished by imitation.

But the controls on foreign trade caused serious and increasing damage to Germany's internal economy. Imports were no longer selected by the price mechanism, but were planned and distributed according to so-called public needs, which could not be measured reliably. Therefore, resource allocation in Germany became increasingly irrational. The situation deteriorated for several years, until the imposition of comprehensive price controls in 1936 destroyed the market mechanism.

Fiscal and monetary expansion, undertaken behind the wall of exchange controls, created inflationary pressures, which the government tried to reduce with price controls. Following a program designed by Germany economists long before the publication of Keynes' *General Theory* (but in some important ways similar to his proposals), the government stimulated employment by increasing public expenditures, combined with rapid growth in the money supply. By 1936, prices were beginning to rise at a rate that the public, remembering the great inflation of 1919–1923, would not tolerate.

In place of monetary and fiscal restraint, the government imposed a ceiling on prices and wages. Then, as shortages appeared almost immediately, they took some first steps toward rationing consumer goods. From that time on, Germany was exposed to repressed inflation, and as shortages increased, the country experienced increasing government controls on the economy.

The inflationary pressures resulting from rapid monetary expansion continued until the end of World War II and even after the war, as the Allied occupation powers added their military banknotes to an already-inflated money stock. The National-Socialist government maintained the strict control system of price fixing and rationing by techniques familiar to a police state. These included concentration camps and even death to people caught dealing in the black market.

After 1945, neither the new democratic German government nor the allied military governments were prepared to employ such brutality, at least in the three Western occupation zones. At the same time, they inherited an incredible morass of economic confusion—the breakdown of an economy that had been one of the most advanced industrial economies in Europe. The task of administering the misery fell to a mixture of military bureaucracies and decentralized German institutions, which tried to cope with the situation by the techniques of government planning, mainly production orders, licensing, price controls and rationing.

At the end of the war, the German economy was in a state of confusion. More than 10 million refugees had pressed from the eastern parts of Germany into the western occupation zones, which were separated economically not only from the East, but also for the most part from each other. Allied monopolies controlled and manipulated German foreign trade, and except in cases where they had a special interest in securing access to German resources, they seemed primarily interested in blocking German exports of industrial products. This was accomplished by absurd formalities and unending red tape. In the end, at least right after the war, industrialized West Germany was forced to export primarily coal, timber and scrap iron—which raw materials she badly needed, but either lacked opportunity or was not allowed to use in her own factories.

Under the prevailing political conditions, centralized economic planning could not work at all, and a system of free markets was not permitted. As a result, the labor markets lost their flexibility and responsiveness to changing conditions, thereby preventing an efficient division of labor, and the economic process degenerated into a system of isolated production in self-sustaining subsistence units, primitive barter, black market activities, and allocations of goods officially regulated at starvation levels. In short, during this period the entire population of the country was fully employed in an unproductive struggle for survival.

In the midst of this chaos, the three Western military governments had little idea of what to do following the currency reform they instituted. Perhaps partly from inertia, partly because of political tendencies in their own countries, they had a strong, general inclination to perpetuate the discredited and chaotic system of central planning. In this context, it is interesting to recall the sentiments of the then Chief of the Division of Occupied Areas in the U.S. State Department, Mr. J. K. Galbraith, who had this to say in March 1948 about the economic policy to be recommended for Germany:

> During the past two years it has been asserted with increasing frequency and vehemence that if, somehow, the German economy could be freed from materials and manpower regulations, price controls and other bureaucratic paraphernalia then recovery would be expedited. . . . Yet there never has been the slightest possibility of getting German recovery by this wholesale repeal, and it is quite possible that its reiteration has delayed German recovery. The question is not whether there must be planning—the assignment of priorities to industries for reconstruction and rehabilitation, the allocation of materials and manpower, the supplying of incentive goods and all the rest—but whether that planning has been forthright and effective.[2]

There is no doubt that the West German central economic planning, as administered by the Allied military governments, was one of the most ineffective systems of planning ever devised. Even a wholly centralized system could have been far more rational. But although this point must be conceded, Galbraith's 1948 planning proposal remains deplorably weak. After the reforms of 1948, the incentives given for economic activity by free markets proved to be superior to all premiums and bonuses granted by bureaucratic apportionment. No centralized government planning could provide the rationalizing effect of the price mechanism. Moreover, the central authority necessary for comprehensive planning of the West German economy as a whole did not exist in 1948.

East Germany, on the other hand, fulfilled the political pre-conditions for centralized economic planning and tried to achieve competitive results by political force. But over time, by almost every standard, the West German market economy has outperformed the planned East German economy, for reasons of the lost efficiency and productivity that go hand-in-hand with centrally-administered economies.[3] This explains why, before the erection of the Berlin Wall, millions fled East Germany for not only political, but also economic reasons.

West Germany, however, chose another way. Even before and during the war, a small group of German economists had analyzed the problems of the centrally-planned system and had developed a theory of comparative economic systems which even today is largely unknown outside of Germany. One of the centers of this school was the University of Freiburg, where economist Walter Eucken and lawyer Franz Böhm, among others, worked together.[4] The new theory, apart from its theoretical aspirations, tried to find an economic and social framework that would encourage both a productive economy and personal freedom in a socially-balanced order.

The framework they developed meant not only the abolition of central economic planning and a return to free markets, but also the establishment of what Müller-Armack[5] called a "Soziale Marktwirtschaft"—a social market economy. Despite the sophistication of the theory, it became an extremely successful political slogan. The concept was put into practice by Ludwig Erhard, who became Director of the Department for Economic Affairs of the United Economic Territory (the combined American and British occupation zones) in 1948, Federal Minister for Economic Affairs in 1949, and Federal Chancellor in 1963.[6]

II

On June 20, 1948, the currency reform established a new West German currency, the "Deutsche Mark." Immediately after the reform, Erhard had the courage to lift at one stroke most of the price and rationing controls without asking the military government for approval.[7] The success of the measure became immediately apparent: Almost overnight the general public could buy commodities which had disappeared from the markets for years. The result was a strong incentive to work and to raise productivity. Despite many difficulties and imperfections, the classical medicine of free markets, competition, and a stable currency had a result completely unexpected by the adherents of "modern" economics and central planning.

With the currency reform and conservative monetary policy, inflation was brought under control. As a result, the formerly disguised unemployment of the control and planning era was revealed as open unemployment. The then-fashionable post-Keynesian orthodoxy prescribed a policy of "aggressive credit expansion and public investment measures"[8] to absorb the unemployed, which equaled about 10% of the labor force in early 1950.

But unemployment at that time was predominantly a structural problem, with the highest rates prevailing in the agricultural districts of West Germany, which had absorbed a great many refugees from more industrialized districts. In the more industrialized districts, problems of housing and a shortage of working capital could not be solved immediately.

The government did assist correction of structural problems, but only through non-inflationary techniques: tax incentives for investment and house-building, numerous interventions to widen bottlenecks, directing counterpart funds of foreign aid into high priority projects. At the same time, Erhard normally refused to stimulate demand by fiscal and monetary expansion when incompatible with price stability, which Germany had done after 1936, and which had led to totalitarian central planning of the economy. On the other hand, the same critics who blamed him for refusing to employ monetary and fiscal expansion to reduce unemployment at the same time eagerly denounced him for rising prices. They demanded reimposition of price controls and rationing, especially during the Korean crisis.

Disregarding this advice, German economic policy relied on circumstances peculiar to a country impoverished by war: a high propensity to consume, a low liquidity preference, and investment opportunities good enough to guarantee a high rate of growth. No austerity programs such as rationing or licensing were initiated to repress "undesirable" consumption. Consumption was restrained indirectly: those with high incomes had to choose between the advantages offered by numerous tax exemptions for investment, or pay high taxes. Expenditures in general, that is for investment *and* consumption, were not restricted by direct controls but by the scarcity of the stable currency.

The price level remained remarkably stable from 1950 to 1960. The average increase in the price index during that period was 1.9% per year—including the irregular price boom that occurred during the Korean war.

During the same period, the real gross national product index rose from 100 to 212,[9] and employment increased without interruption, while unemployment fell below 5% in 1954, despite continuous immigration from East Germany. Consumption and real wages also expanded considerably.

A balance of payments crisis appeared in 1950–1951, but it was turned into a surplus within two years. Henceforth the Federal Republic of Germany could afford to become a champion of freer trade and lower tariffs. Exchange controls were gradually dismantled, and the Deutsche Mark was made convertible during the fifties, even for capital transactions for both non-residents and residents.

The remarkable and well-known accomplishments and also some defects of West Germany's social market economy cannot be detailed in a paper of this length. At the same time, they are also very well-known. However, several additional points should be made.

First of all, it is important to say something about the levels of social services in the context of West Germany's relatively free market, post-war economy. Since the end of the 19th century, Germany had developed a rather extensive network of social security and social service programs, which in fact made Germany the first real welfare state. This system had many shortcomings and even irrationalities, but in general it proved not only useful, but even essential in implementing the post-war social market economy. Without it, and without additional programs added to it after the war, the market economy almost certainly would not have been acceptable to the masses of refugees, victims of war destruction, and persons deprived by inflation. In the first decade of the Germany social market economy and even afterwards, the percentages of gross national product spent for social service programs was (and still is) one of the highest in the world.

A second point relates to problems of information and forecasting. The effectiveness of central planning depends on the accuracy of planners' diagnoses and predictions. In a market economy, those predictions are less important, as reliance is made on the market mechanism, reacting to changing prices, to correct and adjust economic decisions to fit changing economic circumstances. On the other hand, as inevitably happens in a planned economy, West German planners' predictions proved to be wrong so many times that effective economic policies could not be built upon them: Some experts assumed that the partition of Germany would prevent a revival of the West German economy.[10] But West Germany compensated for the loss of her Eastern markets by increased trading with the West. Opportunities for West German exports to Western Europe and the United States were estimated with great pessimism.[11] But it was not long before German exports had increased so much that the Federal Republic of Germany became the great creditor of the European Payments Union. This outcome had been forecast as early as 1950 by Wilhelm Röpke, a friend and adviser of minister Erhard.[12]

Planners regarded the shortage of coal and steel as limiting factors for industrial production. As a result, prices for these basic materials were controlled for a considerable period after the economic reform. But despite the pessimism, real production of the other sectors rose even in the face of shortages of coal and steel, which continued price controls only perpetuated. In 1952, another planning operation was undertaken to correct the first mistake: other parts of industry were forced to give investment credits to the coal and steel industry. Five years later, over-production and huge surpluses of coal had become the great problem.

Forecasting of demand and supply for energy has been no more successful since those days, despite the greatly increased sophistication of hardware (including computers) available to econometric prophets.[13] Many other examples of faulty predictions for the West German economy could be mentioned;[14] and more often than not they persuaded the government to postpone integration of special sectors (such as capital markets and housing) within the market system.

On the other hand, Erhard and the advocates of the social market economy had to forecast how the economy would react when controls were abolished or certain signals and incentives were given by economic policy. With undeniable success the government applied "pattern predictions" (to use Hayek's term) and relied on the market system to respond by continuous adjustment when new information became available and economic facts and circumstances changed. In many cases, the direction of development could be predicted without excessive concern about exact magnitudes.

"Modern" economists could only look with bewilderment at the "hazardous" German experiment. To avoid revisions of established modern theories, they have advanced various special explanations for the German "miracle":

The large number of refugees—once widely accepted as an excuse for the failure of planning before 1948—are now presented as a decisive factor of economic growth. No explanation is given why they were such a factor only in the market economy after 1948, and why not before that time in the system of central planning.

Foreign aid is also mentioned. But while foreign aid was

certainly important, it could not explain the better performance of the West Germany economy as compared with similar countries receiving the same or even more aid.

Even government planning itself has been adduced to explain West German economic development. In some senses not intended by its advocates, this thesis might have some validity, and we will analyze it presently.

Another argument has been that the surplus of labor undermined the bargaining power of the trade unions. Although this is true to some extent, real wages increased rapidly, often more rapidly than in other countries.[15]

Some critics predicted that Germany would face "the familiar 'British' problem of excess demand,"[16] when the country reached full employment and the inflow of labor from the East had dropped (which happened after the completion of the Berlin Wall in 1961). Again the prophecy turned out to be ill-founded: West Germany managed to sustain high growth rates and extremely low rates of unemployment for another decade from 1960 to 1970 (interrupted only briefly by the recession of 1967). During this period, the price index rose at a rate which, although high by recent German standards, was idyllic in comparison with other countries. Increased inflation, however, did not result from rising internal costs, but from inflation imported from abroad through a large export surplus—an inflation which Germany tried to avoid by several revaluations of the DM. The inflation did not change its imported character before 1970, at which time the social market economy was gradually replaced by another style of economic policy.

III

No single factor can be identified as responsible for the whole. The economic revival of West Germany was the result of a number of factors. The government did reestablish a system of relatively free markets, but government expenditures as a percentage of gross national product (including social service programs) was already 37% in 1950, 39% in 1962, 38% in 1971, and 44.5% in 1973.

Socialists and other proponents of central economic planning, feeling uneasy about the West German economic success, even tried to explain it by the stabilizing influence of the State. Thus, they argued that economic disaster in the "mixed economy" of West Germany could only be avoided because large public expenditures and other state interventions were able to neutralize the "irrationalities of free markets and capitalism." The doomsday of the market economy, inescapable nevertheless, is thus said to be postponed for a time. This theory is now quite common with the communists, who invented the term "state-monopolistic capitalism" to describe West Germany's economic system: The activities of the State, they claim, are guided by the interests of monopolies and "the capital."[17] The theory—in some ways similar to Galbraith's "New Industrial State"—was also accepted by some left-wing segments of the ruling Social Democratic Party of Germany (SPD), to the great embarrassment of those party leaders and officeholders of the SPD who administer the federal and many State and local governments.[18]

There is no doubt that government activities had a significant impact on the West German economy. A closer look at the details of those activities nevertheless shows that in most cases the State could not control the markets by its large share of the gross national product:

State consumption as a percentage of Gross National Product was comparatively small (about 15%) and comparatively stable.

Government investment was important, but especially in the reconstruction period, there was little room for discretionary investment by the State: roads, bridges, railways (which are owned by the State), schools, and so on had to be rebuilt and expanded.

A large portion of the budget went for transfer payments, including subsidies, loans for housing-building, and so on; even here the opportunities for discretionary planning and steering were rather limited, because most recipients of the payments were entitled to them by laws that could not be changed on short notice. Transfer payment programs were sufficiently stable to permit private business to plan its affairs around them.

Another factor limiting central planning was the constitutionally-created and protected federal structure of the republic. Under the West German federal system State and local authorities could act more or less independently of the Federal government, which was otherwise dominant. This independence had the effect of hampering concerted public action even when it was badly needed. Sometimes, for instance, the anticyclical policy of the Federal government was thwarted by procyclical behavior of State and local authorities.

At the same time, certain planned government influences and even controls were maintained on both macroeconomic quantities and the microeconomic structure of the economy:

1. The doctrine of the social market economy includes stabilizing and anticyclical devices.[19] The instruments employed for these purposes were rather conservative (primarily monetary policy) or long-term in character with careful consideration for timing (for instance, tariff reductions in boom periods).

2. On the other hand, fiscal policy encountered serious problems, which only by chance did not endanger the whole system: High unemployment in 1949 created political pressures for investment stimulation and monetary expansion, which the government reluctantly started. The fiscal and monetary expansion exploded in 1950 during the inflationary Korean boom and aggravated the balance of payments deficit that followed. To correct the nearly unavoidable mistake, the monetary authorities instituted rigid credit restrictions.

In the years after 1952 a large deflationary cash surplus in the Federal budget was deposited with the central bank, thereby improving prospects for price stability. The surplus did not result, however, from sound economic caluculations but was, rather, a by-product of difficulties paying out as much money for defense as planned. The seven billion DM accumulated at the end of 1955 encouraged politicians in parliament to spend with inflationary effect what they regarded as "free" money around the election of the Federal parliament in 1957. For this purpose, they set up a special committee, which got the nickname "Kuchenausschuss" (committee to distribute the cake).[20] German textbooks of public finance present this example to demonstrate the political precariousness of anti-inflationary fiscal policy.

The West German economy absorbed the consequences of this behavior, which was irrational economically. But German economists questioned the qualifications of politicians[21] who, according to now-fashionable proposals, are to be entrusted with a decisive role in a system of comprehensive and democratic national planning.

After several unfortunate experiences, no further important attempts were made to use fiscal policy for "fine-tuning" business fluctuations before Erhard's resignation. But many times he exhorted the different groups to act as required by the equilibrium of the economy as a whole. During this period, however, the Federal Bank lost much of its influence on money supply, as its policy of defending the fixed exchange rate in the face of mounting trade surpluses forced it to buy large amounts of foreign currency. Maintaining a stable price level in a world of inflation became more and more difficult without revaluation of the DM. Finally, in 1961, the government revalued the Mark for the first time and although mounting balance of payments surpluses were not altogether removed by this measure, the situation eased. Perhaps more importantly, the taboo that currencies can only be inflated and devalued had been destroyed.

3. A variety of subsidies, prohibitions, and other state interventions had their impact on the economy:

—For instance, the ministry for agriculture pursued a policy of strict protection for agriculture, by market regulations, high guaranteed prices, and subsidies. Nevertheless, the dynamic growth of the whole economy induced enormous changes in the structure of agriculture, even in the face of the official protectionist policy. This result had been predicted by agricultural economists—most of them adherents of the market economy—in a report prepared for the government. Their prognosis was absolutely correct in direction and only slightly less accurate in the magnitudes they estimated.[22] The report aroused a predictable storm of protest from agricultural organizations, but had little effect on agricultural policy.

—The ministry for transportation was occupied with the protection of the Federal Railways against competition primarily from small trucking enterprises. Nevertheless, the ministry could not prevent immense deficits of the railways, as market forces, though distorted and slowed by government planning, moved away from rail to other modes of transportation.

—Government regulations and interventions in many other sectors of the economy produced the same results. We have noted interventions in the coal and steel industries. Following patterns observable in other countries, these interferences were and for the most part still are self-defeating or in conflict with other government activities and programs.

Nevertheless, on the whole, these interventions did not do as much damage as might appear. Some of them were even helpful in permitting decontrol of certain sections of the economy, by smoothing the adaptation of industries to new market conditions. The most striking example of this were the subsidies for home-building, which encouraged such high rates of growth in this industry that rents could be decontrolled without unbearable consequences. At the present time, rents are again indirectly limited primarily for "political" and ideological reasons.

The post-war success of the West German economy cannot be attributed either to microeconomic state intervention or direct government regulation of macroeconomic quantities. In the first decade of the social market economy, there were no comprehensive national budgets or consistent national economic plans at all. On the other hand, there has been a persistent will to regulate the quantity of money to avoid inflation. Money certainly had to be planned. Easy money, endangering price stability, was never accepted as a normal and permanent method to encourage investment and growth.

Investment and growth were encouraged by other means, particularly by fiscal and tax policy. The most important factors supporting investment and growth were a relatively stable and trustworthy government, pursuing a stable and predictable economic policy—not changing its attitudes from one day or one budget to the next. Private business was thus not discouraged from long-term commitments by unpredictable political risks.

During this period, government undertook planning of a very different nature than the planning promoted by the socialists. This different kind of planning may have been the decisive element in West Germany's economic recovery, for this planning was concerned with re-establishing free markets and new rules of the game. For the first years after the currency reform, a gradual dismantling of the remaining quantitative controls and price regulations had to be planned, taking into account the high irritability of the new political system and of an economy without sufficient capital reserves. The population had been greatly disillusioned by the war and its aftermath, and they were highly critical and sensitive to mismanagement by any government. In short, the transition from chaotic planning to a new market economy required careful planning.

But the authors of the social market economy had also long-term objectives. They were resolved not to repeat the errors of unrestricted laissez-faire, and they were convinced that the rules of conduct in a market economy could not and cannot be left entirely at the mercy of market agents, whose own self-interest would often encourage them to harm the new system.

—In this respect, the most important task was the protection of workable competition. Apart from the concrete market structures established, a new spirit of competition was certainly one of the most important features of the West German economy in its first decade. The antimonopoly and deconcentration laws of the military governments, followed by the rather imperfect German law against restraints of competition, all had some effect in this direction. However, the most important influences encouraging competition were West Germany's policy of freer trade, European economic integration, convertibility of the DM, and open doors for international capital movements.

—In addition to measures favoring workable competition, other institutional changes have had important influences, some involving government intervention and others not. One of them, involving labor relations, had strategic importance. The system of labor relations and trade unions in West Germany is quite different from the system prevailing in the Weimar Republic before 1933. Trade unions and employers are organized on an industry-wide scale. Although originally it was intended that there would be only one trade union in each industry, this objective was not fully attained. At the same time, demarcation disputes between different trade unions are unknown in West Germany. Collective agreements between trade unions and employers' organizations fix only minimum wages, thereby permitting actual wages to be higher than formally-negotiated levels. This system has thereby secured some upward, as well as downward, flexibility for wage payments.

Most important is the German tradition of regulating and containing labor disputes by legal action and by the special labor courts. When strikes cannot be avoided, they must be conducted in a strict legal context and according to rules that have the effect of restricting the bitterness of the strike. These rules are comparable to the Hague Land Warfare Convention, although much more effective. Special laws protect the rights of single workers, and a special Law on the Constitution of Enterprises (Bertriebsverfassungsgesetz) defines the rights of employee representation in an enterprise. Since the Weimar Republic, workers' representatives have seats with the same rights as the representatives of the shareholders in the supervisory boards of joint stock companies ("Mitbestimmung"—codetermination). This system was expanded after 1945. Trade unions and socialists now demand "parity" in the number of seats for "labor" and "capital" in all industries—a scheme already prevailing in the coal and steel industry.

The value of some of these new laws is debatable. Nevertheless, the laws reflect a situation which diminishes the reasons a German worker might feel a hostile or adversary relationship with the enterprise in which he is working. In this system, strikes are normally unpopular.

IV

At the end of 1966, Erhard resigned as Federal Chancellor. His economic policies were no longer accepted wholeheartedly by the parties of his coalition government. Monetary and fiscal mismanagement, together with some lack of concern for the principles of the social market economy, were responsible for the ensuing recession of 1967. As is frequently the case in times of uneasiness, increased State planning was seen as the best device to overcome the difficulties.

As early as 1962, President Hallstein of the European Economic Community had called for medium-term forecasting, more planning of quantitative economic policy, and more "presence of the State" in the economy—all of which Erhard rejected. The subsequent discussion about the merits of economic planning was confused, because the advocates of government planning failed to distinguish sufficiently between prognosis and planning, and between different kinds of planning, including planning of traditional government activities which even Adam Smith acknowledged, consistent planning of the order and rules of the economic system (a major tenet of the social market economy), planning for the stability of money and a stable economic process, and numerical government planning of the quantities of private business transactions.[23] Subsequent development of West German economic policy reflects this confusion.

To improve economic forecasting, an independent expert council for investigation of the economic development (Sachverständigenrat zur Begutachtung der gesamtwirtschaftlichen Entwicklung) was established in 1962. As a rule, the council's annual reports gave excellent explanations for past events, and its principal recommendations for shaping the economic order were usually of the same high quality. Its conditional short-term forecasts, however, were not reliable as guidelines for quantitative planning.

In 1967 further steps for planning and stabilizing the economic process were enacted when Parliament passed a law to Promote Stability and Growth of the Economy (stabilization law). According to the new Minister of Economic Affairs, Karl Schiller, the new law was intended to unite in an "enlightened market economy" the "Keynesian message" (which means global steering of macroeconomic quantities) with the "Freiburg imperative" (the doctrine of Erhard and his friends). The law obscured the priority of a stable currency by endorsing both price stability and high employment, external equilibrium, and adequate growth as more or less equivalent goals for economic and financial policy.

—Price stability could have been defined rather precisely as stability of the purchasing power of money for the consumer. But the politicians were uncomfortable with this and they proclaimed instead a "relative" price stability as a guideline to be defined at will. In 1971, West Germany's rate of inflation rose to 7.9%, the highest rate since the currency reform. The "planning" of the price stability has thus been carried out by adapting the definition of "stability" to inflationary developments which the government could not, or did not want to, control.

—After the recession of 1967, high employment continued to exist until 1974, but since then unemployment has increased. The problem is cyclical only in part: In the same period, the climate for investment deteriorated, and profits were squeezed to make room for various "reforms" enacted by the new government after 1969.

—External equilibrium could not be attained as long as fixed exchange rates prevailed. The leaders of the Christian Democratic Party after Erhard decided against revaluation of the DM (they were not trained economists and accepted the wrong advice, which contributed to their defeat in the 1969 elections). The successor government, a coalition of the SPD and the Free Democrats, however, also made mistakes: Disregarding the lessons provided by exchange controls during the 1930s, they introduced new controls—this time for capital imports—after 1971.[24] These controls were gradually tightened; and when all capital imports were finally licensed, Finance Minister Schiller resigned in protest against these and other irrational actions—all of which were the result of a government led by Chancellor Willy Brandt and the SPD, whose ambition it was to reform society by "rational planning." It was not long before market forces prevailed: Fixed exchange rates gave way to flexible rates, which solved the problem and restored the ability of the central bank to control the supply of money. Once again controls on capital imports were abolished.

—Including the goal of "adequate growth" in the stabilization law might suggest that the government is able to induce a steady growth rate of some specific magnitude by using the modern tools of macroeconomic policy. However, since 1968, when the law was passed, the West German economic growth rate has shown a conspicuously unforeseen instability, and in 1975, the growth rate was actually negative.[25]

To achieve the stabilization law objectives and put macroeconomic planning into practice, several new instruments were provided:

—The financial policy of different public authorities is to be coordinated at the federal level. Medium-term finance planning is prescribed for the Federal Government to bring about increased stability.[26] But this objective failed. An expensive and in some respects romantic program of "internal reforms" proclaimed in 1969 and put into practice during the following years, produced a financial crisis in 1975, which was reinforced by the cyclical downswing of the economy and thereby declining tax revenues.[27] A procyclical correction in the growth rate of public expenditure thereby became inevitable after 1974.

—To make fiscal policy more effective, the stabilization law also provides that private expenditures and investment may be regulated by changing tax rates. In addition, private business organizations are required to cooperate in an institutionalized "concerted action" with trade unions and public authorities. This was initiated to give them the opportunity to participate in government macroeconomic decision-making. Except to inform the partners of each others' opinions, this institution gained little influence. If it had, it would have been appropriate to inquire about the compatibility of this procedure with the federal constitution.

Despite the new law and its high ambitions to plan stabilizing activities more rationally, it is impossible to avoid the conclusion that the government achieved worse rather than better results than those achieved without planning during the Erhard era. This is not to say the new instruments are entirely useless; it is only to say their inventors did not take into account either the impossibility of predicting the future with any accuracy, or the imperfections in the process of decision-making.

Planning euphoria is immune from counter-argument by practical experience. The last ten years have bred all kinds of long-term plans for different parts of the economy and society, some of them reasonable, many of them irrational, but most of them containing special provisions for increased government spending. One of the most striking examples of unsuitable State planning involves plans to expand the educational system, which in Germany is dominated by the State. These plans for expansion responded to predictions made some years ago by a professor (Picht), with a flair for publicity, that West Germany faced an educational catastrophy, because he asserted the country was not producing enough high school and university graduates. At the present time, the number of high school graduations is much greater than expected, and the universities cannot cope with them. At the same time, the State ordered "reforms" of the universities through "democratization," which included surrendering the administration of universities to representatives of students, non-scientific personnel, assistants, and professors, and had the effect of reducing their capacity and standards. As a result, some universities deteriorated and even became dominated by left-wing extremists and communists. Official plans for expanding the educational system have been so grandiose that they would have absorbed the entire increase of public revenues for many years. So the plans have had to be scaled down and returned to reality by painful recision.

It is little wonder that so many specialists in public administration try to streamline the planning organization of the State. The stabilization law established a new planning council to coordinate anticyclical behavior of various public authorities. In some ways, the already-existing Finance Planning Council had been entrusted with the same task. Later on, a planning department in the office of the Federal Chancellor was set up to coordinate in a mild form the planning activities of the federal ministries.[28] Planners regard the federal and decentralized West German political system as an impediment to efficient and comprehensive planning. They agree on the necessity of simplifying the complexities of expanded and differentiated government activities. But they never consider the possibility of improving government effectiveness by governing less and by concentrating government decisions on strategic issues.

On the contrary, they advocate increased planning and government interference, and they can find considerable support, especially in a significant element of the ruling SPD. In contrast to these demands for increased state responsibility, the State is often unable even to fulfill its ordinary responsibilities; and at some State-owned universities public authority is disappearing. Nevertheless, the State continues to be seen by many people as the great hope for eliminating disturbances of economic life: The State, it is hoped, in its unlimited wisdom, distilled by democratic voting, will achieve a new and improved society of equity and equality with a higher ''quality of life.'' According to this view, the State can do no harm, so long as it is governed by the enlightened persons who are elected by democratic procedures. Nothing in German history has been sufficiently bad to prevent the resurrection of these authoritarian dreams.

The most recent product of such thinking is a proposal to control private investment and even certain trade union circles are demanding central planning of investment, while pretending they are unaware that investment controls will inevitably, sooner or later, lead to controls on the movement of labor. They would probably be prepared to tolerate such controls as long as the controls are executed by democratic trade unions. The answer to this is nowhere better given than by Adam Smith:[29]

> The Statesman, who should attempt to direct private people in what manner they ought to employ their capitals, would not only load himself with a most unnecessary attention, but assume an authority which could safely be trusted, not only to no single person, but to no council or senate whatever, and which would nowhere be so dangerous as in the hands of a man who had folly and presumption enough to fancy himself fit to exercise it.

PLANNING IN FRANCE*

JOHN SHEAHAN
Professor of Economics, Williams College

The appeal of French planning is that it attempts to combine the dynamic forces of a market system with explicit consideration of the ways in which markets can be used to serve collectively determined social goals. It does not operate by giving orders to firms but by shaping the framework of incentives. At least in principle, it should create the sense of direction that would make economic growth more constructive.

In practice, the results have been modest, possibly even negative in some respects. This is partly a matter of political choice. Recent presidents have been on the conservative side, and democratic planning tends to go the way the country votes. But it also reflects conflict among alternative ideas of what planning can mean. Through successive plans, at least four different conceptions of the purpose of planning have been mixed together in varying combinations:

(1) to give the country a sense of the alternatives open with respect to the uses of national income, the division of income, the balance between private consumption and social services such as education and health, and to some degree the composition of private consumption;

(2) to determine the structure of production, the development of particular industries and occupations, and thus the supply

*Reprinted with permission of *Challenge*, 1975.

characteristics of the economy as distinct from the uses of income;

(3) on a more partial basis, to define corrective programs for particular problem areas such as energy or transportation;

(4) to clarify the conditions necessary for a stable economy consistent with full employment and external balance.

The First Plan in 1946 was based on supply-specific planning of the second type. The Seventh Plan, which will take effect in 1976, is likely to combine the third and fourth types. However, if the general approach to planning has a significant future, it will probably have to be based on the first concept.

FROM PLAN ONE TO PLAN SEVEN

At the beginning of the postwar period, the feelings of release and hope common to the peoples of France and the United States enabled them to break through old political restraints and try new methods of economic management. In the United States, the productive capacity of the economic system was scarcely in doubt; the problem was generally seen to be one of managing aggregate demand to ensure full employment. The Council of Economic Advisers was a sensible answer to this particular problem, with a scope of activities limited to economic stabilization.

France, however, chose the second way, and created a Planning Commission to reorganize the structure of production. French capitalism had proven unable to cope with change. To be dynamic, capitalism requires two basic elements: entrepreneurs willing to take risks; and an economic system in which entrepreneurs are free to act even when the changes they set in motion undermine established positions. Prewar France certainly had some capable entrepreneurs, but, compared with the United States, French business preferred safety and it operated in a social milieu that tended toward rigidity.

In artistic and intellectual domains, France was ahead of its times. Yet the country failed to develop an economic and social system that would accommodate necessary change. An unusually defensive structure of regulation and trade restrictions held back the transition from agriculture to industry, sheltered smaller producers and older techniques of production, and, in the process, helped keep social classes in fixed positions. France gradually lost its earlier ability to provide scientific and technological leadership, proved increasingly unable to compete in new industries, fell behind in income growth, and clung to an extremely unequal division of income and opportunities. The one significant attempt at social reform by the Popular Front government in 1936 was swept away in less than two years by a conservative reaction.

After France's defeat in 1940, the Vichy government instituted a corporate state subservient to those who had clung to the status quo in prewar France. Conservatism became identified with collaboration. As a result, the immediate postwar governments were dominated by men identified with the Resistance. Even though their individual political views were far apart, the new leaders were able to agree on what then seemed to be drastic changes: establishment of a thorough system of social security, nationalization of the leading banks and much of the country's infra-structure, and creation of a Planning Commission to revitalize the economy.

Jean Monnet and the members of the first Planning Commission did not have any clear authority to force firms to accept the Commission's plans, but they could count on many of the new people in government financial and regulatory agencies to use their positions to support industrial modernization. Further, a significant fraction of private business management accepted the concept of planning as long as its goal was modernization of the economy. The Commission adopted a form of planning suited to these circumstances: consultation with all interested parties, technical review of proposals which originated in both the nationalized firms and private companies within the industries selected for attention, and then a bargaining process in which financial incentives and regulatory favors were traded for cooperation. The approach succeeded. The French economy reached and then maintained a high rate of growth, even though individual firms paid only as much attention to the plans as they wished.

As the economy moved from reconstruction to sustained growth, new pressures forced policymakers to give attention to inflation and sectors of the economy other than industry. The Second Plan (1954–57) responded by shifting somewhat toward the fourth concept of planning, giving less emphasis to expansion and more to economic stabilization. Targets for production were set so low that most were quickly exceeded. Perhaps the greatest achievement of the period was the virtual halt of inflation without the creation of significant unemployment or a break in the momentum of growth.

The Third Plan was considerably bolder. It was prepared under a government led by the Socialists and other moderately left parties and clearly reflected their preferences with respect to the content of growth. The plan, intended for the period 1958–61, called for a reorientation of national economic goals that would place less emphasis on private consumption and more on social investment. It moved firmly toward the first concept of planning—managing the uses of productive capacity. It would not have entailed any increased control of producers but would have worked instead by shaping the composition of government expenditures and credit. Sector planning then filled in the gaps between the new composition of final demand and the structure of investment.

Whether or not the Third Plan might have led to a real change in the course of growth is a matter of conjecture, for the government made the tragic mistake of intensifying a futile war to prevent Algerian independence. Federal spending changed in the wrong directions and the plan ceased to matter. Support for the government disintegrated and the country turned to de Gaulle. The Left has not won a presidential since.

The Gaullist government, which wrote the Fourth and Fifth plans in the 1960s, and that government's direct descendent, which prepared the Sixth for 1971–75, continued to support the idea of planning and added some interesting themes. But the

Gaullists retreated from the attempt to restructure growth for social purposes and concentrated more narrowly on industrial expansion and the development of new technology. And even these more limited objectives were compromised by the increasing concern over inflation. The Fourth Plan was an activist program, particularly intended to stimulate research and the development of advanced technology, but it was undercut by a policy of monetary restriction. The Fifth Plan sought to combat inflation with a coherent incomes policy—a program which might have reconciled high growth with less inflation—but the plan got very little support from the government as a whole and even less from labor and private business. The government stressed fiscal and monetary restraint instead, in spite of rising unemployment, until the popular explosion of May 1968 broke through this atavistic fixation.

Recent plans have backed away from production targets for industry and have turned more to particular problem areas and even to individual companies considered to be especially important to the export and high technology sectors. With respect to social planning, perhaps most notably for health care, the plans have become more detailed and more pragmatic. By the Sixth Plan, health planning had gone well past its earlier preoccupation with investment in equipment to stress policies of prevention and programs to aid groups most subject to illness and accident. Again, it turned out that the planning process produced excellent ideas, but the government failed to carry them out. For all forms of social investment combined, the rate of actual to planned expenditure was only 83 percent for the Fifth Plan (1966–70), and, through 1974, was approximately 87 percent for the Sixth Plan (1971–75).

The pattern now being passed on to the Seventh Plan is thus fairly discouraging, if one thinks of planning as a means for achieving basic change in the future course of events. But it still has two positive elements. One is that the consulting process allows many interests to be expressed, creating pressure on the government to widen its concern beyond inflation and the crises of the moment. The other is that the formulation of corrective programs for particular areas is encouraged, especially, at present, in health planning. Even though there is no assurance that the programs will be enacted, the planning process provides a progressively better understanding of these specific problems.

PLANNING BY CONSULTATION AND ITS EFFECT ON OBJECTIVES

Among the many explanations as to why the planning process in France evolved as it did, two are particularly relevant for any other country interested in the possibilities of such planning. One argues that planning by consultation and negotiation drives the planners into such close alliance with business interests that it chokes off concern for social reform. The other maintains that planning requires a significant degree of control over international trade and capital movements. According to this view, planning is futile in an economy with a large trade sector.

There can be little doubt that the consultation and negotiation process has fostered a community of interest between the planners and those groups within management who cooperate with them. The Planning Commission has been a consistent advocate of high rates of industrial investment and it probably has nudged government policy toward low corporate tax rates and regulatory favors for cooperating firms. This bias has its good side in that it encourages strong aggregate demand and high employment. Moreover, the development of productive capacity is a fundamental social concern. But it also has negative implications in that excessive emphasis on industrial investment restricts the amount of resources available for other objectives.

Cooperation has not involved anything like the narrow subservience to particular industry interests that has characterized some of the American regulatory commissions. The economy-wide interests of the Planning Commission and the high quality of its staff have saved it from that. But it is still true that a method which requires the Commission to grant favors to corporations in return for cooperation is tantamount to making the commission a spokesman for business within government. In particular, the Commission acts as a representative for the firms which it finds easiest to deal with: these are the largest companies with professional managements best able to understand and influence the plans. The Commission has almost automatically favored greater industrial concentration. This attitude has led to increased concentration both where it may mean greater efficiency and where it may entail disfunctional size. It has weakened any change of significant domestic competition. If ITT were a French corporation, the Planning Commission would be its natural ally.

Was it inevitable that planning based on consultation and cooperation with business would lead to a reduction of social concerns? Probably not. The Planning Commission does not dominate the policies of the government. The proposals incorporated in the Third Plan give a clear indication of what might be done if the country elected governments with greater social concerns. The Planning Commission may alter the balance toward business interests in those conservative governments that already lean in this direction, but, within a more socially oriented government, it might provide a healthy shield for genuine investment requirements. The Commission would certainly be able, and probably would prefer, to fit investment plans into a more equalitarian framework of social reform if the country elected a government that wanted to move this way.

The tendency of French planning to favor the business community could be minimized by getting away from supply-specific planning of the second type mentioned earlier. It is this particular version of planning which, by requiring business cooperation at the level of detailed enterprise decisions, stacks the cards against social reform. Plans of the first type, which define the goals of society rather than the actions of individual firms or industries, would free the system from the need to bargain with producers. It would not be possible to drop supply-specific planning in an economy which does not have a major trade sector, but it should be feasible with the more open system France has now. That raises the second set of issues central to the evolution of French planning: In what ways does an economy—one with a large trade sector—limit, and in what ways does it liberate, the kinds of planning that are possible?

PLANNING IN A RELATIVELY OPEN ECONOMY

Monnet and the members of the first Planning Commission directed postwar policy toward a more open economy in order to end the self-perpetuating stagnation of the prewar system, to force French industry to modernize and keep up with the rest of the world. This choice has been fundamental for the character of French planning because it dissolves the connection between socially determined goals with respect to the composition of final demand and the actual structure of domestic production.

In an open economy, objectives in the sphere of final demand may be achieved by importing goods rather than producing them. Investment programs for particular firms or industries may turn out to be mistakes either because costs are too high to meet import competition or because producers are able to find export markets and need to expand production beyond domestic targets. Both export markets and import supplies can diverge from expectations for reasons beyond national control. Any plan which entails a fixed program for production would therefore be a costly one. Plans may be oriented toward improving the flexibility of supply, but they should not set specific production targets or attempt to ensure markets.

Breaking the connections between final demand and the structure of production does not preclude a form of planning centered on the *uses* of national income. The decision of a country to devote more of its income to prevention of disease, to improvement of the environment, or to mass transportation instead of private automobiles can be implemented more readily in an open economy. International trade frees the pattern of demand from the limits of domestic production. It widens the choices of supply and lessens pressures to use the plans as a form of market support for producers. Planning must match the size of total demand to total productive capacity, but it need not make the investment and production decisions of individual firms.

For those who view French planning as a means of altering the structure of production, emphasis on the flexibility gained from foreign trade appears to be a loss of control. If the nation's goal is not just to have a certain amount of hospital equipment and data-processing services available, but to produce them as well, then international trade gets in the way. A completely open economy allows supply-specific planning for human skills and nontradable goods and services, but it rules out application of the same approach to tradable industrial products.

Naturally, these conflicting views of planning have resulted in a series of compromises. In the 1950s pressure led the Planning Commission to propose postponing entry into the Common Market. The de Gaulle government ruled the other way in 1958 but soon reversed course to shelter national development in computers and atomic energy. Attention thus came to center on advanced technology, which received considerable support through government purchases and research contracts, while more open policies were followed in less sensitive fields such as consumer nondurables. Consequently, there are still important industrial sectors in which supply-specific planning can be applied. And in crucial nonindustrial sectors such as health planning, the main issues relate to training and use of human skills, not to international trade. So supply-specific planning is not ruled out by any means. An open economy works against supply-specific planning for most industrial fields. But this is not a disaster which weakens planning but a saving grace, for it frees planners from dependence on private business decisions.

WHAT REMAINS THAT IS USEFUL?

Planning as practiced in France is an instrument of economic management that has real potential. But most of that potential is being wasted. Not because of any fatal limitations imposed by the market system or by a relatively open economy. The waste exists because recent governments have been preoccupied with manipulating aggregates to fight inflation or with salient problems of the moment. But they have failed to develop long-range goals that might help shape the future of society.

American economists who have come to despair of the Council of Economic Advisors are probably wrong to think that the direction of the American economy would have been greatly different had there been a planning commission instead. They are wrong in two ways at once: the Council could still be a constructive force if any administration wanted to make it so; and a planning commission would not have helped much given the kinds of planners and ideals that would have been likely under the current president and his predecessor.

It is nevertheless a sound instinct that makes many people in France want to retain planning and some in the United States to propose it. All noncommunist countries will have to change their style of economic management in fundamental ways if they are to cope with problems that now go far beyond questions of aggregate demand. Economic growth in the sense of material output must be slowed down without generating the high unemployment that would almost automatically result under present conditions. France needs to recover some of its earlier ability to serve human values in a society with slower economic growth, while avoiding the rigidities and extreme inequality that characterized its prewar system. Inflation, international capital flows, and the behavior of multinational firms all require that the world economy be taken fully into account when national policy is determined. And national policy should not be based on narrow self-interest; it must be a policy which the rest of the world can accept as a basis for cooperation.

The last innovative Council of Economic Advisors, in the Kennedy administration, recognized the need for a broader frame of reference and began to create one. It went beyond demand management to include corrective measures, notably wage and price policies and at least the beginnings of programs to correct supply deficiencies in medicine and construction.

These were potentially crucial innovations, designed to meet needs that could not be adequately dealt with in the existing American framework of economic management. Planning would offer a more appropriate institutional structure for such efforts. It need not, and probably should not, give any major role to the directive planning of individual supply decisions with which French planning started. What is required most of all—and this is something France needs to recover—is the kind of planning that considers explicitly the *purposes* of economic growth and offers a coherent sense of direction for social change.

THE END OF PLANNING: THE SOVIET UNION AND EAST EUROPEAN EXPERIENCES*

SVETOZAR PEJOVICH
Professor of Economics, University of Dallas

General Background

In 1918, Lenin and his followers dissolved the Constitutional Assembly, abolished private property in land (without compensation to landowners), nationalized financial institutions and large firms, placed small private businesses under strict governmental controls, and dis-franchized clergy, merchants and other "undesirable" elements. The result was complete economic chaos and famine. The first priority of the Party was to save the new regime from collapse. Ironically, in 1921 Lenin accomplished this by introducing a set of market-oriented policies into the system. Those policies that came to be called NEP represented a retreat from the regime's policy of nationalization and confiscation of private assets.

Within a few years, the economy recovered from war and famine, and signs of general prosperity became quite evident. Importantly, the Communist Party was able to use this period of relative prosperity to consolidate its hold over the country. When this was accomplished, Lenin turned his attention to the problem of political power *within* the Party. A number of deci-

*The writing of this paper was facilitated by grants from the Earhart Foundation and the National Science Foundation.

sions were announced clarifying the relationships within the
Party. It was decreed that the rank and file of the Party must
accept the leaders' decisions, must not criticize or question
those decisions, nor criticize the leaders themselves. Quickly,
the Party became a hierarchical and monolithic institution as
the dictatorship of the proletariat became the dictatorship of the
top Party leadership.

It was not long before Lenin turned the Soviet Union into a
totalitarian state, run by the Politburo which is a small, self-
perpetuating elite. G. Warren Nutter summarized the early
evolution of the Soviet political system as follows:

> It was Lenin's genius to recognize the importance of embellish-
> ing the Soviet system with all the trappings of democracy. If the
> people want a constitution, give them one, and even include the
> bill of rights. If they want a parliament, give them that, too. And
> a system of courts. If they want a federal system, create that myth
> as well. Above all, let them have elections, for the act of voting is
> what the common man most clearly associates with democracy.
> Give them all these, but make sure that they have no effect on
> how things are run.[1]

Next, the Party leadership turned to the problem of controlling the character and level of economic activity in the country.
The Soviet leadership has always considered that the regime's
security depends on the Party's controlling every aspect of life
in the country. Predictably, soon after Lenin's death in 1924
NEP was abolished, in favor of "scientific planning" of the
national economy. The Russian people were told that "scientific planning" would improve the standard of living, eliminate
the exploitation of man by man, strengthen the first land of
socialism vis-a-vis the capitalist states, and perform a number of
other miracles that children in the West often associate with
Santa Claus. References to Marx and Engels provided an
ideological basis for economic planning. However, the rhetoric
about the advantages of planning must not deter us from going
behind the words to identify its real purpose both in the Soviet
Union and elsewhere. Economic planning is ingenious cam-
ouflage for attempts to extend governmental control over the
character and level of economic life in a community.

The enactment of the First Five Year Plan in 1928 signaled the beginning of economic planning in the Soviet Union. The first plan called for the nationalization of private businesses that had prospered (and had helped the economy to prosper) during NEP, liquidation of kulaks (all peasants who had land and were disliked by local party officials were eligible), construction of new plants, and quadrupling the manufacturing output of the economy.

During the first five-year plan, the Soviet leaders began to force peasants into collective farms. Collectivization of land was an effective way of tightening the Party's political control over not-too-reliable peasantry, while economically enabling the Party to determine the allocation of the food supply. Control over the supply of food was essential to the Party's objective of speedy and ruthless transformation of the Soviet Union into an industrial state.

The peasants' resistance to nationalization of their land was stubborn, long, and costly to the state. The precise number of peasants arrested, exiled or shot will probably never be known. One major result of the forced collectivization of peasants was the famine of 1932–33. Unsurprisingly, the famine caused more sufferings and starvation in rural areas than in the cities, as the government opted to feed industrial workers at the expense of starving peasants.

Until the early 1960s Soviet intellectuals were only allowed to praise Soviet planning. But in the early sixties Khrushchev allowed them to criticize Soviet economic planning, and from that criticism various proposals for economic reform were subsequently born. In the meantime, Khrushchev fell from grace, and the new leadership slowly reversed the trend. Subsequent changes in Soviet planning were quite correctly identified by James Blackman as "New Wine in Old Bottles."[2]

The Soviet Plan

The basic features of the Soviet economic system are state ownership of non-human resources, central administrative planning of the allocation and use of resources, and emphasis on the development of heavy industry. Within the constraints of those basic characteristics, Soviet leaders have always been interested in improving the performance of the nation's economy.

The Soviet government allocates resources and assigns productive targets to all industries and firms in the economy. All decisions concerning the level and character of the economy flow from the top leadership through various bureaucratic channels down to productive units. The sum total of these administrative orders is the economic plan. The plan is a law of the land; and individuals who are caught interfering with the plan might be taken to court.

The central Soviet planning agency, Gosplan, is an executive agency. It provides economic and technical solutions for decisions, directives and instructions issued by the top leadership in the Politburo. Operationally, the Politburo controls Gosplan through administrative sections of the Party's Central Committee concerned with economic matters. In addition, Gosplan is also supervised by the Council of Ministers, which is the highest executive agency of the Soviet Government. But since the director of Gosplan is also a vice-chairman in the Council of Ministers, the decision-making powers wielded by Gosplan are fewer than one might expect for an institution responsible for economic planning. In the Soviet hierarchy of political and economic institutions, Gosplan is restricted to technical expertise in preparation, modification, and execution of the plan. It prepares both current (annual) and long-range plans, sets and controls prices, and rations the use of raw materials and intermediary goods (the goods in process).

The long-range plan is a blueprint of the economic program for a five-year period. It identifies a number of targets that economic units will be expected to attain. G. Warren Nutter defined the long-range plan as a hazy vision of things that it would be nice to have—something for the planners to shoot at, and the ministry of propaganda to shout about.[3] The current annual plan is an *operational* document that specifies production assignments, sources of supplies, and delivery dates for economic units.

The Party leadership sets objectives for the economy. Gosplan then translates those objectives into production targets for business firms, state farms, and collective farms. The planning procedure is not unlike preparation of the budget in the U.S.A. Gosplan sends preliminary targets via bureaucratic channels to various regions, industries and firms. Those preliminary figures are related to the past performance of productive units, new capacities, new priorities, changes in productivity, and so on. Productive units must then send back their comments and suggestions. Of course, they tend to understate what they can do and overstate what they need. In short, Soviet planners and the managers of productive units meet with fixed bayonets.[4]

The most pressing problem facing Gosplan is that production targets must not, in the aggregate, exceed the economy's productive capacity. The target plans must be balanced, and balancing creates an enormous problem for Soviet planners For example, the machine tool industry is turning out about 125,000 products. Thus, in that industry alone, Soviet planners have to take into consideration about 15,000,000,000 possible relationships.

In the Soviet's centrally-planned economy, each firm's output depends on the availability of raw materials and intermediary goods produced by other firms. Thus, the economic plan must prescribe not only outputs of individual firms, but also the allocation of inputs. Assuring a regular and adequate flow of raw materials and intermediary goods to productive units is thus the central problem in the Soviet system of economic planning. And the supply plan is therefore the core of the Soviet economic plan.

The supply problem is peculiar to a planned economy. In a market economy, business firms bid for supplies in the market. To allow firms to do the same in a planned economy could easily (would almost certainly) disturb the plan's objective and frustrate the will of the ruling elite. Thus, economic planning must eventually lead to the planning of supplies. In the Soviet Union, Gosplan controls the allocation of about 2,000 inputs, while

various ministries and lower level bureaucracies allocate
another 38,000 inputs. In total, Soviet bureaucracy thus controls the allocation and use of about 40,000 inputs.

Sizeable bureaucracies have been established to administer
supply planning. In theory, firms are told what inputs they will
get, in what quantities, from whom and when to expect deliveries. In practice, supplies arrive late or never. They also
come in wrong quantities and specifications. The result is that
even a small deviation from the supply plan can easily cause a
chain-reaction throughout the system. Suppose that a firm that
produces screws and bolts fails to deliver them on time to other
firms. The rate of output of those firms is immediately affected.
And in turn, enterprises that depend on those firms' output then
become affected. And so on.

So-called material balances play a key role in preparation of
the supply plan. Soviet planners draw material balances for all
products in physical units. The balance for each input shows its
sources (inventory, current production, imports) and uses (inventory, current production, exports). On the basis of material
balances and production targets, the supply plan determines the
allocation of inputs to individual enterprises. Again, several
layers of bureaucracy are involved in the process.

Business enterprises provide information to their administrative supervisors about technical coefficients that relate inputs to
outputs. On the basis of those *reported* production functions of
business firms, past performances of enterprises, some expected (planned) changes in productivity, and the knowledge
that the managers of business firms never tell the whole truth,
the Soviet planning bureaucracy develops the supply plan. The
final figures, however, are far from perfect, because the number
of inter-dependent relationships that must be integrated into the
plan is too great. Soviet planners can neither generate information about those relationships nor produce a computer to handle
them all.

After investing tremendous human and non-human resources
in producing the all-embracing economic plan, economic planners, one would hope, could relax, enjoy the fruits of "scientific

planning,'' and occasionally feel pity for their brothers in non-planned, chaotic economies.

Unfortunately, the job of correcting even a minor mistake in the plan is enormous. Suppose that planners detect that production of screws is lagging behind the planned rate. Clearly, they must increase the allocation of coal, steel, iron, and so on to the firms producing screws. But to do that, they must reduce the allocation of coal, steel, iron, and so on to other firms. And they must then reduce the planned rate of output of these firms, as well as other firms that depend on them, and on and on. Every time a mistake in the plan is noticed, the supply and production plans for a number of industries must be revised. As an example, the 1961 plan for the Tartar Autonomous Republic was modified five hundred times. When these modifications occur, in effect, the plan is constantly revised and brought in line with the business firms' actual performance. Thus, in the course of the year, the plan and the economy's actual performance eventually converge and at the end of each year the Soviet press can therefore honestly report that the annual plan has been fulfilled.

For example, the average rate of growth of total industrial output was set at about 8 percent per year in the 1971–75 plan. The actual rate of growth in 1971 and 1972 fell to 6.1 and 5.4 respectively. Then, the Soviet government simply reduced the planned rate of growth to 5.8 percent per year.

It is clear that revisions and adjustments in the plan must result in lower output targets for many firms and industries. To take care of this, the ruling elite designates certain sectors of the economy as low-priority areas. And for this purpose consumer goods industries have consistently been assigned the task of bearing the cost of miscalculations, inadequacies and inconsistencies in the plan. Put another way, centrally-planned systems need a buffer to absorb mistakes in the plans. In the Soviet Union, the consumer serves that function.

Preserving the environment is an important economic value, but like all scarce goods, it is expensive. To produce a better environment, therefore, something else must be given up. Massive environmental disruption has occurred in the Soviet Union in part because the growth-oriented Soviet government is not willing to give up other goods for environmental values such as clear air and water, but also because the absence of private property rights in air and water place no private cost on polluting activities.[5] Without some governmental effort to impose such a cost, environmental problems will persist.

The Soviet government is genuinely interested in improving the performance of the nation's economy within a given set of political constraints. To this end, the government has consistently relied on material incentives to reward the managers and employees of business enterprises for meeting and exceeding their planned targets. The so-called success indicators (gross value of output, labor productivity, cost per unit of output) are used to evaluate the performance of business enterprises. In effect, success indicators are simply a form of control over the management of firms. They evaluate each firm's performance in relation to its plan. The number of success indicators has changed frequently. From as many as 40 indicators in the 1950s, the number was reduced to 9 in the 1960s, and raised to about 15 in the 1970s.

For at least two reasons, Soviet planners must closely monitor the performance of productive units. First, to make adjustments in the plan, Soviet planners must have information about its shortcomings, miscalculations, bottlenecks, supply problems, and so on. Second, planning without control could easily frustrate the Party's objectives. It would be like planning a candy-free diet for a six-year-old. Unless his parents take on the cost of controlling him, the boy's real diet will almost certainly frustrate the parents' "plan." One important device for monitoring execution of the plan in the Soviet Union is the financial plan.

The Soviet firm's financial plan is the monetary equivalent of its production plan. Like the budget of a government bureau in the U.S., the financial plan of the Soviet firm identifies its receipts and expenditures by categories. Unlike the budget, it specifies both the firm's contractual partners and terms of exchange. Suppose that a firm is told to produce 1,000 television sets per month and deliver them to specified retail stores at $100 each. Assume also that the firm's supply plan allocates to it 1,000 wooden boxes at $30 each, 10,000 screws at 25 cents each, $20,000 for wages, and a total of $40,000 for other inputs. The firm's planned revenue is $100,000, planned expenditures are $92,500, and planned profits inclusive of turnover tax are $7,500. Depending on the Party's priorities, the firm's planned receipts are equal to, greater than, or less than its planned expenditures. In our case, the surplus is $7,500, and it is used to subsidize other (higher-priority) firms and governmental activities.

All transactions of Soviet business firms are done through the bank, which transfers funds from one account to another. As all payments must be made through the bank, the bank checks those payments against the firm's financial plan. The Soviet firm cannot withdraw cash to make payments to its contractual partners. For such payments would escape the planners' control over the firm's transactions and could interfere with fulfillment of the plan by other firms.

The financial plan thus serves two major functions. By controlling the flow of receipts and expenditures of business firms, the bank can deduct miscalculations and bottlenecks in the plan, and alert the appropriate planning bureaus. Also, the bank serves the function of watchdog. It helps the government reduce if not eliminate deviations from the plan by business firms.

The financial plan could, under some circumstances, complicate the planners' job. Suppose that the price of screws rose from 25 cents to 35 cents. The firm's budget of $2,500 would then not be sufficient to purchase 10,000 screws. The firm's payment of $2,500 to its suppliers would give no assurance to the bank that the firm has received all the screws it needs to produce 1,000 television sets. The planners' cost of monitoring the execution of the plan would therefore increase.

Because stable *relative* prices are important to Soviet planners, planners make them stable by administrative decisions. With few exceptions, most prices in the Soviet Union are set by the government and rarely changed. Soviet prices are not meant to determine *who gets what* and *who does what*. They do not, as in a market economy, reflect relative scarcities. No Soviet citizen or institution can raise his money offer to bid a good away from other claimants.

For obvious reasons, major features of Soviet economic life are long lines of people waiting to purchase consumer goods, and shortages of supplies needed by business managers to meet production targets. Inflation therefore takes on a different form in the Soviet system than it does in the West. In the Soviet Union, inflation does not appear in the form of rising money prices, but rather by changes in the time needed to seek and obtain various goods. For example, whenever the Soviet housewife discovers that it takes an additional hour to find and obtain a pound of meat, she has one hour less to seek other goods. And the price of meat has therefore risen.*

The Soviet Consumer

The contemporary folklore has created two myths. It says that economic planning will save the consumer from exploitation by for-profit corporations. It also claims that economic planning reduces inequalities in a community. In this section of the chapter we shall consider what economic planning has done for the Soviet consumer.

The Soviet system of economic planning rules out what has come to be known in the West as consumer sovereignty. As we have seen, the Soviet consumer has little influence on the allocation of resources and the composition of output. Soviet planners give his preferences and income a very low priority. Given the planned assortments of consumer goods and their relative prices (money prices set by the state and search costs determined by

---

*The precise amount of the price rise depends on how much the individual housewife values her own time: the greater her personal valuation of time, the greater the price increase. The same phenomenon occurs in reverse in other countries: where inflation is reflected entirely in increased money prices, people who value leisure in relation to other goods will suffer relatively less from inflation than those who care more about the goods.

the market) the Soviet consumer is free to choose how and when to spend his real income.

Economic planning obviously places a low value on consumers' sovereignty. On the other hand, popular folklore has it that substitution of careful planning by publicly-spirited civil servants for those non-planned, profit-motivated decisions by private corporations must and will benefit the consumer. Unfortunately, the facts of life here at home as well as in the Soviet Union suggest otherwise. Two prominent economists offer an important observation in this regard:

> Food is grown, harvested, sorted, processed, packed, transported, assembled in appropriately small bundles and offered to consumers every day by individuals pursuing personal interests. No authority is responsible for seeing that these functions are performed and that the right amount of food is produced. Yet food is available every day. On the other hand especially appointed authorities are responsible for seeing that such things as water, education and electricity are made available. Is it not paradoxical that in the very areas where we consciously plan and control social output, we often find shortages and failure of service? References to classroom and water shortages are rife; but who has heard of a shortage of restaurants, churches, beers, shoes or paper? Even further, is it not surprising that privately owned businesses, operating for the private gain of the owners, provide as good, if not better, service to customers as do the post office, schools, and other publicly owned enterprises?[6]

One could, of course, dismiss this observation by suggesting that public organizations must have hired the wrong people. Their supporters in the West often suggest that there is nothing wrong with Soviet institutions that a more saintly team won't solve. Unfortunately, the personal traits of decision-makers are only marginally important in determining the behavior of their institutions. The real explanation for the differences in the behavior of various types of organization lies in the penalty-reward system (survival traits) they generate. The survival of a for-profit firm is much more dependent on the consumer's likes and dislikes than that of a not-for-profit firm or a government bureau. Thus, the former has *more* and the latter *less* incentive to satisfy the consumer's preference.

The Soviet ruling elite lives on the strength of its political power; Soviet planners live on their service to the ruling elite; Soviet managers prosper as they can fulfill their plans. Regardless who runs Soviet institutions, the Soviet consumer will lose out. But he is not ignored because the system is run by wicked men. The consumer's misfortune lies in the fact that the system offers no rewards for decisions that take into account his preference.

The Soviet leadership might occasionally feel that its objectives require improvements in the consumer's well-being. The consumer then gets a break. This situation seems to have occurred in the 1960s. From 1967–70, the growth rate in the output of consumer goods for the first time exceeded the growth rate of intermediary goods and equipment. In the early 1970s conditions returned to "normal." In fact, the five year plan for 1971–75 actually reduced the growth rate in the output of consumer goods. The plight of the Soviet consumer is shown in figures 1 to 3. Figure 1 indicates the difference in the Soviet leadership attitude toward the consumer in the 1960s and 1970s. Figure 2 compares private consumption in the USA in 1890 and in the Soviet Union in 1968. Figure 3 shows the number of work-hours it took the average wage earner in Moscow and New York to earn enough to purchase various consumer goods in 1970.

In the Soviet Union there is one market, the so-called collective farm market, in which goods are sold at market-clearing prices and for private gains. Two sources supply this market: (i) agricultural products grown by collective farmers on their individual plots, and (ii) the food produced on collective farms over and above their own consumption and planned (compulsory) deliveries to the state. A casual observation quickly establishes the difference in the quality of various foods sold by greedy farmers in the collective farm markets and by public servants in state stores. The quality of goods sold in the farm markets is clearly superior to anything that is available in the government

FIGURE 1 Consumer gains in the USSR, 1966–70 and 1971–75 (in percent)

	Growth Plan	
	1966–70	1971–75
Indicators*		
Real income per capita	33	31
Average wages	26	22
Real income of collective farmers	54	40
Social consumption funds per capita	44	34
Retail trade per capita	37	35
Per capita consumption of food		
Meat and meat products	17	23
Milk and milk products	22	11
Eggs	28	21
Fish	22	43
Vegetables	14	33
Per Capita consumption of non-food goods		
Cloth	15	15
Knitwear	26	43
Leather shoes	25	20
Household stocks of consumer durables@		
Television sets	112	41
Refrigerators	191	100
Washing machines	148	29
Radios	22	30
Sewing machines	8	9
Housing		
Urban living space per capita	10	8

*Calculated from Soviet data and based on Soviet definitions of these indicators.
@Derived from Soviet statistics on stocks per 100 families.

stores. Money prices are higher, too. Yet, there are no waiting lines in the farm markets, and for many consumers (those who place a high valuation on their own time), real prices, including search costs, will actually be lower in the farm markets than in state stores.

The private sector of Soviet agriculture consists of small subsidiary plots (about an acre per household). Collective and

FIGURE 2   USSR and US: Comparison of Selected Indicators of Consumption: USSR, 1968; US, 1890

	USSR 1968	United States 1890
Flour	1,474	922
Potatoes	255	163
Meat and poultry	204	530
Milk	353	575
Fish	20	16
Sugar	354	229
Fats and oils including water	346	408
Cotton fabrics (linear meters)	31.8	42.9
Wool Fabrics (linear meters)	1.9	6.4
Shoes (pairs)	2.5	2.7

FIGURE 3   Comparison of Real Purchasing Power of an Average Wage Earner in the United States and the USSR

Item	Worktime	
	Moscow*	New York
Bread lb.	17.0 min.	5.4 min.
Potatoes lb.	3.9 min.	2.1 min.
Beef lb.	62.6 min.	18.7 min.
Butter lb.	140.0 min.	16.4 min.
Sugar lb.	40.3 min.	2.5 min.
Milk qt.	24.0 min.	5.6 min.
Eggs doz.	92.6 min.	12.2 min.
Man's shirt	11.4 hrs.	1.7 hrs.
Man's suit	157.0 hrs.	26.3 hrs.
Man's shoes	35.0 hrs.	6.0 hrs.
Woman's dress	42.0 hrs.	6.0 hrs.
Woman's shoes	33.0 hrs.	5.3 hrs.
Nylon hose	2.9 hrs.	17.5 min.
Soap	16.3 min.	2.0 min.
Cigarettes	15.1 min.	8.5 min.
Vodka fifth	6.6 hrs.	1.36 hrs.

(Copyright 1971, Field Enterprises, Inc.)

*exclusive of search costs (author's comment).

state farm households are entitled to hold such plots. They do not own them but have the right to use them to grow food for their own consumption or for sale. In addition, households are entitled to have a cow, two pigs and as many chickens as they want (but no horses). Those lots account for about three percent of the total agricultural area in the Soviet Union. Yet, they are responsible for about one-third of the total agricultural output in that country.

Undoubtedly, the performance of this small, but for-private-gain, sector of the economy is a source of embarrassment to economic planners. Yet, the government has no choice but to tolerate it. The collective farm markets, where these gains are captured, serve two vital functions in the Soviet economy. They allocate a significant percentage of the total supply of food. Also, the collective farm markets help to absorb the excess purchasing power of the population.

The popular folklore also has it that regulated, welfare-oriented, planned economies assure their people of more equal distribution of income. While it is not clear what ethical norms are violated when incomes are unequal, the claim itself is refuted by real world observations. Lowell Galloway has recently shown that income distribution in the USA, Sweden and Russia are much the same.[7] Data on the distribution of income in the

FIGURE 4   Families of Workers and Employees
by Annual Income

Annual Income Per Person In Rubles	Percentage of Total
less than 600	32.6
601–900	31.2
901–1,200	17.7
1,201–1,500	9.1
1,501–2,100	7.1
more than 2,100	2.3

(Source: Korzhenevskiy, *Osnovnyye,* 1971, p. 112.)

Soviet Union are hard to get. Figure 4 provides income distribution data for an unspecified region of the Soviet Union published in 1971. From the information in this figure it appears that about one-third of the population in this region had less than 600 rubles per year. Soviet authorities consider the income of 600 rubles a year as providing only the basic living minimum.[8]

The average wage in the Soviet Union in the early 1970s was about 130 rubles a month. The minimum wage was set at 70 rubles a month in 1972.[9] Directors of large enterprises, high officials and top scientists, earn more than 1,000 rubles a month. Compared to the minimum wage of 70 rubles, it is a big salary. Moreoever, the wage differentials do not fully explain the differences between income groups in the Soviet Union. The upper income groups (high Party and government officials, high-ranking military personnel, scientists, engineers, managers of enterprises) have access to special stores where they can buy goods that are not available to ordinary Russians. In addition, they receive a number of valuable benefits such as better housing, a summer house, an official car, among other things. If we include those things into our measure of income distribution in the Soviet Union, the differences between the upper and lower income groups would be much larger. What does the average wage of 130 rubles a month buy? Following are some prices from department stores in Leningrad in the summer of 1974: stockings, 7 rubles; pajamas, 70 rubles; chocolate, 1.50 rubles; slip 40–50 rubles. Meat was priced at 1.5–2 rubles per pound, while a pearl in the collective farm costs .80 rubles.

The effects of economic planning on the Soviet consumer are self-evident. He needs help. One must wonder if the market had failed as badly as the Soviet plan in protecting the consumer, would the market have received as sympathetic a hearing as Soviet planning has received.

Economic Reforms

In the 1950s and early 1960s, economic planning in the East European countries (except Yugoslavia) was similar to the

Soviet system. Some differences did exist between individual countries, but they were differences in form rather than in substance. During that period, East European leaders exercised their survival skills by showing devotion to the first land of socialism, and there were few more effective ways of showing devotion than by "learning" from the Soviet "experience" with scientific planning.

In the mid-1960s, the Soviet Union and East European countries began to feel strong pressures to substitute economic relations for rigid administrative planning in the allocation and use of resources. At the same time, it would have been embarrassing for the Soviet government to admit after forty years of scientific planning that a scientific plan is still to be developed. Therefore, Soviet propaganda explained that as production becomes more varied and sophisticated, planning systems must be adjusted to changing economic conditions.

In fact, in the mid-1960s, Party leaders recognized and implicitly admitted that their totally authoritarian economic system had failed to devise an incentive and control system able to induce productive units to increase productivity and efficiency. The economic "reforms" of the mid-1960s, as the changes became known, gave the appearance of a marked change in the Communist belief that administrative planning is superior to the market-oriented allocation of resources. However, the real purpose of what turned out to be very modest reforms in the U.S.S.R. and Eastern Europe appeared more likely to be a search for an institutional structure that would direct production efficiently in a world where non-human resources cannot be privately owned.

The *announcement* of economic reforms must not be confused with their *actual implementation*. As a rule, all economic reforms announced in the East in the mid-1960s were either quietly rescinded or implemented slowly and reluctantly. For in a planned economy the bureaucracy will have no trouble understanding that all genuine reforms are contrary to its self-interest. Thus, the bureaucracy will have every incentive to sabotage reforms, to misinterpret their intent, to stall them, and even to try and convince the leadership that economic reforms are con-

trary to the "public interest." As a result, actual implementation of economic reforms tends to depend on the strength of the
"establishment." Of all East European bureaucracies, the
Soviet bureaucracy is the oldest, best developed, and certainly
the most powerful. And as such, the Soviet bureaucracy has
succeeded in bringing economic reforms in Russia to a virtual
halt, while it has also succeeded in slowing down economic
changes in Czechoslovakia and (with some help from the military) East Germany, and in bringing about the retrenchment of
some reforms in Bulgaria and Poland. Only the reforms in Hungary and semi-independent Rumania have continued on or near
schedule into the seventies. It is important to note that economic
reforms in the Soviet Union and most East European countries
(except Hungary and Czechoslovakia before April 1968) were
directed primarily toward improving the operation of the centrally planned system—that is, toward administrative stream-
lining.

By the early 1970s, the Soviet economic reforms became
"mini-reforms." The vast majority of supplies in Russia continues to be allocated administratively; prices still play no al-
locative role; and the reluctance of administrative agencies to
relinquish control over the enterprises remains strong. In fact,
the Soviet bureaucracy seems to be growing stronger. Keith
Bush reveals the magnitude of Soviet problems with the following observation:

> Early in 1970, one plant director wrote of two years' delay in
> obtaining certain material inputs, while another director dwelt
> bitterly on the lack of supplies. Over 40,000 basic producer
> goods are still administratively allocated . . . if the rates of re-
> cruitment achieved in 1966 and 1967 are maintained, the
> material-technical supply branch will have grown by 250,000–
> 300,000 bureaucrats during the eighth five-year plan.[10]

And Gertrude E. Schroeder added this comment:

> Although there is still much talk in the Soviet press about
> economic reform, the phrase now has come to mean simply all
> changes in economic management procedures that are made to

improve the existing system. There is little mention of spontaneity, except to condemn it, or for granting more decision-making authority to enterprises.[11]

The announcement of economic reforms in the Soviet Union and East European countries triggered a lively debate in the U.S. on the consequences of these reforms *if they were implemented*. But it was an empty debate, because it failed to raise the question of the nature and difficulties of reforming fundamental legal and contractual relations as a necessary condition for implementing economic reforms. To consider the consequences of economic reforms without considering the cost of changing the country's institutional environment reveals rather naive assumptions about the ruling elite's willingness to make fundamental legal changes. But as I have argued elsewhere, in a totalitarian state run by a huge bureaucracy, it is much easier to announce economic reforms than to implement them.[12]

The proponents of centralized economic planning obviously hope that central planning will solve social and economic problems that they believe inhere in a market economy. However, both economic analysis and all available historical evidence indicate a wide gap between the *intended* purposes of planning and its *unintended* effects. Under the circumstances, one might expect that those countries that practice economic planning will almost certainly try to talk us out of it.

They need someone to feed them.

PART III
ECONOMIC PLANNING
IN AMERICA

THE HISTORICAL ROOTS OF AMERICAN PLANNING

PETER P. WITONSKI

I

In *Henry IV* (Part I, Act II, Scene I), Gendower boasts, "I can call spirits from the vasty deep." To which the pragmatic Hotspur replies, "Why, so can I; or so can any man; but will they come when you do call to them?" Glendower's illusion remains seductive, especially in an age as gullible as our own.

One need only examine the vast corpus of literature devoted to economic planning—produced over the past thirty years— to have this fact brought home. Like the necromancers of old, contemporary economists have stood on the precipice of common-sense, oblivious to the primal chaos of the abyss below, and endeavored to summon spirits from the vasty deep. The modern-day Hotspurs have been consigned to Coventry, relegated, as it were, to the dustbin of history; and the planned economy, with its deceptive promise of *scientific* progress, has been proclaimed as the answer to all our economic woes. "There seemed to be but one god in economics—state planning and interventionism—and Keynes was his prophet," the London *Economist* wryly observed in 1971. Lord Keynes even made a belated appearance on the cover of *Time* magazine (December 31, 1965); and in America the votaries of *dirigisme* dusted off their deity and rechristened "Keynesian planning" as the "New Economics"—a vulgarization that would have caused more pain than amusement for the Bloomsbury sage, who was never one to suffer foolish jargon gladly.[1]

II

An understanding of the forces behind the rise of economic planning requires some understanding both of the history of economic ideas and of entrepreneurial history since the early 19th century. As Professor Jewkes has written, "Fashions in economic thinking are notoriously infectious and fickle. They run through communities with the speed of forest fires."[2] In America, it is often noted by *aficionados* of the planned economy, the free economy, or *laissez-faire* capitalism, reached its intellectual and political zenith at the very moment when its doom as a system of economic organization was already clear—during the so-called Gilded Age.[3] "Paradox as it is," Max Lerner has written, "it is not unusual in history that an idea-system should reach its 'triumph' exactly when its base of social reality is crumbling away."[4] Certainly a large number of significant intellectuals at the beginning of the twentieth century, in both Europe and America, believed capitalism to be doomed both as a system and an ideology.[5] In his visionary novel, *Looking Backward* (1888), Edward Bellamy predicted what the America of the future would be like—a harmoniously planned and logical society, devoid of poverty and suffering. "Our children will surely see it," he wrote of his utopian America.

The liberty and profound sense of individualism advocated by Adam Smith and his followers seemed to men such as Bellamy to be both unjust and irrelevant of the needs of the 19th century. The good society advocated by Smith in his *Wealth of Nations*, they argued, was essentially an anti-egalitarian society, favoring a tiny minority of property holders. The emerging proletariat class—deprived of goods and political influence—possessed nothing but its own labor to sell. The earliest defenders of the proletariat anticipated many of the concepts of Social

Darwinism, and predicted that the new economic freedom would be the undoing of the impoverished common man. Only the fit would survive, only those individuals with a stake in the free economy could hope to profit from it. The concepts of economic liberalism and social democracy were held, almost from the beginning, to be contradictory, since it was clear—the early critics of liberal capitalism argued—that all members of society were not equally endowed with property or the opportunity to acquire property. Even in frontier societies, such as the United States and Canada, South Africa, and Australia—where land was cheap and, in some cases, free—economic liberalism was the enemy of social democracy.[6]

There were also those, including many religious leaders, who questioned the morality of economic liberalism. A concept, they argued, that championed the cause of individual self-interest was a concept predicated upon selfish and un-Christian instincts, instincts that, therefore, threatened to undermine the social order of Christian civilization. By the beginning of the industrial revolution, the economic and social doctrines of the liberal economists were under attack from many important sectors of society, including proto-socialists, romantic conservatives, and church leaders; and the defenders of the free economy, then as now, were reduced to mouthing naive platitudes about the liberating virtues of private initiative and economic freedom—the first qualities of true social harmony.

III

Since the principles of the modern free economy were first expounded by the leaders of the Scottish Enlightenment, they have been under attack for a multitude of reasons. The early critics of economic liberalism discovered, almost from the beginning, that the free economy was relatively easy to attack and rather difficult to defend—at least politically (as opposed to intellectually). One of the first writers to recognize this point was the French sociologist Emile Durkheim in his treatise *Le*

Socialisme. [7] Durkheim recognized that the planned, socialized economy was predicated upon concepts that were almost magical in their appeal, whereas the capitalist economy was mired in the imperfections of the real world. Adam Smith's "utopia," governed by the caprice of an invisible hand, could never match Karl Marx's classless society when it came to utopianization.

The early members of the Austrian school of economics, such as Eugen von Böhm-Bawerk, had, Durkheim maintained, endeavored to defend the free economy in a negative and futile manner by attacking the critics of the free economy instead of defending the principles of economic freedom themselves. Böhm-Bawerk's almost scholastic critique of Marxism was, Durkheim argued, like Penelope's labor "constantly in need of renewal." The planned economy was impervious to this kind of criticism. Durkheim understood that ideologies could not be attacked, as Böhm-Bawerk had attacked Marxism, abstractly.

Ideological criticism had to be based on concrete facts and specific arguments. When Marx propounded his communist doctrines, he did not attack the abstract theories of capitalism (indeed, he praised them); he attacked the poverty and squalor of the industrial revolution. As a citizen of *fin de siècle* France Durkheim could understand the appeal of that kind of criticism. France, after all, was a capitalist society, and any French citizen could see that it was a society afflicted with severe social and economic problems. The fact that early 20th century France was not the kind of abstract capitalist society that the champions of economic liberalism advocated was of little importance from an ideological point-of-view. The imperfect nature of European capitalism was, Durkheim rightly understood, the matrix of the socialist appeal.

The planned society as articulated by the various socialist denominations had a profound advantage over capitalism: it did not yet exist, it had nothing to do with the real world. It was a bold abstraction directed toward the future, toward utopian bliss, and Durkheim based both his analysis and his criticism of socialism upon this fact. Socialism was an eudaemonic concept, devoid of scientific validity. At the very best socialism was a kind of pseudo-scientific superstition, an eschatological fantasy with no grounding in the practicality of the real world. But those very weaknesses, Durkheim understood, were socialism's greatest ideological strengths. Its appeal for the masses was its unscientific nature. Durkheim perceived the strength of socialism to be its idealism, its *untried* idealism.

Socialists, including Durkheim's own socialist students, failed to recognize this fundamental weakness in their ideology,[8] just as libertarian critics of socialism could not bring themselves to accept that socialism's lack of empiricism was its greatest political strength. As a student of sociology, Durkheim was fascinated by the extent to which his fellow intellectuals were willing to accept the nostrums of an untried ideology like socialism; but as a rigorous positivist he was offended by the ideology's unscientific nature. How, he asked, can one fail to be struck by the enormous disproportion that exists between the scant documentation that socialism has borrowed from the sciences and the extent of the practical conclusions which it draws from them? Marx's *Das Kapital* was, for Durkheim, a classic example of pseudo-science in action. ''What a lot of statistical data,'' he exclaimed upon coming to the work of Marx. A true scientist, he cautioned, would discover his doctrine in the results of his research rather than the other way around, as Marx had done. Socialism, Durkheim concluded, is inspired by passion instead of science. Socialism is, in the last resort, nothing more than ''a cry of pain.''

''Marx,'' he noted, ''has one very clear idea—that of class conflict; it is this idea that inspires all his practical action, and he subordinates to it all his theoretical researches.'' To understand Marx one had to recognize, first, that Marx was a brilliant sociologist, and second, that he did not understand the economic implications of his sociological conclusions. Specifically, Marx did not understand, as Adam Smith had understood, the ''logic'' of economic action. *Das Kapital* had, therefore, to be approached more like a holy book than a scientific treatise. Like all holy books, Pareto noted, it is full of vague and obscure dogmas, ''a happy mixture of passion and reason, calcu-

lated to satisfy the exegesis both of the vulgar and the learned.''
This conclusion, it is said, caused Lenin more worry than any
other anti-Marxist conclusion he had ever encountered.[9]

While Pareto may have, as he later joked, turned Marx on his
head, in much the same way that Marx thought he had turned
Hegel on his head, his critique did little to blunt the socialist
appeal. The non-logical character of the socialist appeal, which
Pareto would later examine with clinical brilliance in his
Treatise on General Sociology, was, by its very nature, immune
to criticism. Marx's nostrums about a classless society must be
accepted—if at all—on faith alone.* Beyond that, Marx, like
those social planners who followed in his wake, has virtually
nothing to say about such essential economic problems as *how*
his political society would actually work, how it would own and
operate the means of production, how it would be planned, how
it would choose its planners, and what the relationship would be
between the managers and the managed. As Robert Heilbroner
has written, ''*Das Kapital* is the Doomsday Book of capitalism,
and in all of Marx there is almost nothing which looks beyond
the Day of Judgement to see what the lineaments of paradise
may present.''[10] Would the Day of Judgement mark the end of
the class struggle, or would new kinds of class conflict arise, as
Pareto had predicted?

IV

During the first forty years of the present century socialism and
the quasi-socialist planned society remained merely untried
ideals, in Durkheim's sense. When juxtaposed to the poverty
and inequality that existed in the imperfect capitalist societies
of Europe and America their idealistic appeal became all the
more potent. To this one must add the fact that post-Marxist
socialists had succeeded, as Pareto noted, in investing their
doctrines with powerfully moral imperatives that rendered

---

*This is clear from reading his two most serious works, *Das Kapital* and the *Grun-drisse der Kritik der politischen Ökonomie.*

them almost religious in their force. Marx became a kind of prophet, and socialist theorists and politicians became secular saints—the noble defenders of the wretched and the oppressed.

Arrayed against socialism in an almost manichaean antithesis were the capitalists, depicted as "robber barons" and exploiters of the poor. The vast wealth of the new class of capitalists stood in vivid contrast against the idealized poverty of the new industrial working-man, and it was not very difficult to create an elaborate mythology of class conflict and opposition from these two caricatures. In America the so-called "muckraking" magazines, such as *McClure's, Munsey's, Cosmopolitan, Hearst's,* and *Everybody's,* took careful aim on the evils of American capitalism. The rhetoric of the social Darwinists, which capitalists such as Andrew Carnegie had used to defend their wealth, was turned upside-down by the muckrakers. Thorstein Veblen blasted the "conspicuous consumption" of the capitalist system, and such writers as Lincoln Steffens, Ida Tarbell, and Upton Sinclair publicized what they considered to be the most beastly and evil aspects of the system. The Progressive movement, the new industrial trade unions, and such groups as the Socialist Party all contributed to the general critique of American capitalism.

Commenting in 1914 on the general thrust of the muckraker's critique, the young Walter Lippmann wrote,

> There is in America today a distinct prejudice in favor of those who make accusations. Thus if you announce that John D. Rockefeller was going to vote the Republican ticket it would be regarded at once as a triumph for the Democrats . . . "Big Business," and its ruthless tentacles, have become the material for the feverish fantasy of illiterate thousands thrown out of kilter by the rack and strain of modern life. . . . all the friction of life is readily ascribed to a deliberate evil intelligence, and men like Morgan and Rockefeller take on attributes of omnipotence that ten minutes of cold sanity would reduce to a barbarous myth.[11]

At the same time, Lippmann observed, there had to be some reasons for the muckraker's success. "For America," he explained, "the willingness to believe the worst was a strange development in the face of its traditional optimism, a sign perhaps that the honeymoon was over.'' Muckraking, he noted, had flared up shortly after the closing of the frontier, when land was no longer freely available as it had been in the past, and when ''large scale industry had begun to throw vast questions across the horizon.''

The industrial revolution in America, as in Europe, had helped to transform the American character. When the muckrakers and other critics of American capitalism spoke, they spoke to a public that was prepared to listen to their charges, a public that recognized that America had problems. ''Muckraking,'' Lippmann concluded, ''is full of the voices of the beaten, of the bewildered . . . It has pointed to a revolution in business motives; it has hinted at the emerging power of labor and the consumer.'' As Lippmann looked into the future from the vantage point of 1914, he became convinced that the free society of liberal capitalism was finished or near to being finished. Marx and socialism would, he believed, succeed only in appealing to a tiny minority, since his ideas were as inadequate for the modern world as were the ideas of Adam Smith. Lippmann found both liberal economists and orthodox Marxists to be out of touch with ''the latent forces of this age.'' Both groups ''have built a dialectic . . . upon the texts of their masters; they have lost their command over change, and so they have become apologetic, and eager to save their faces in the wreck of their creed.'' What Lippmann saw with great clarity in 1914 was the rise of the planned, capitalist society in America, a kind of halfwayhouse, standing, as it were, at the crossroads and confronting both capitalist and socialist nostrums. Lippmann saw, more clearly than his other contemporaries, the inexorability of the mixed economy.

V

Frederick Jackson Turner had raised similar points in his essay ''The Significance of the Frontier in American History''

(1893). It was Turner's thesis that the ever-expanding frontier was the main source of American democracy and social peace. The frontier had acted as a kind of "safety valve" for the pent-up industrial and social problems existing in the cities of the East. A worker in one of Carnegie's steel mills could dream of heading west, where there was free or cheap land, new opportunities, a second chance on life. On the frontier all men were equal, there were no social classes, and all were judged according to their abilities. But according to the United States Census of 1890, the frontier had been closed by the time Turner began to speculate on its significance, and to many the closing of the frontier was an event of greater significance than all the evils of the industrial revolution combined. The safety valve had been closed in 1890, Turner lamented, and its closing did not bode well for the future of the Republic. Turner and Lippmann were joined by other thinkers who began to question the American political tradition in the wake of the industrial revolution. Henry Adams' autobiography, *The Education of Henry Adams,* was full of dour prognostications about the future; Herbert Croly's *The Promise of American Life* questioned the viability of the Jacksonian-Jeffersonian forms of democracy; and Charles Beard wondered about the wisdom of our founding fathers.

The early years of the twentieth century in America were for some a time of questioning about the future of American political and economic institutions; but the capitalists of this period still believed in what the late Louis Hacker called "triumphant American capitalism." Men such as Charles M. Schwab,[12] the first president of United States Steel, believed in the boundless capacity of *American* capitalism to "get the job done" however difficult the job might be. For the American entrepreneur of the period, capitalism was the *new* American frontier, and industrial growth was the new version of Westward expansion. Horatio Alger came to stand for the American virtues of the day in much the same way that the frontiersman had stood for the virtues of preindustrial America.

To those who questioned the morality of the social arrangement that had produced the kind of inequality that seemed to exist in America following the industrial revolution, the new millionaires could respond with quotations from William Graham Sumner. "Let it be understood," Sumner had written, "that we cannot go outside of this alternative: liberty, equality, survival of the fittest; not-liberty, equality, survival of the unfittest. The former carries society forward and favors all its best members; the latter carries society downwards and favors its worst members."[13] The new multimillionaires at the top of American society were, for Sumner, products of natural selection. "It is because they are thus selected," he explained, "that wealth . . . aggregates under their hands . . . They get high wages and live in luxury, but the bargain is a good one for society."[14]

The critics of American capitalism in the late 19th and early 20th centuries failed, initially, to win out over the new capitalism for other reasons; however, Sumner's ideas, as the late Richard Hofstadter has noted, were not the stuff that mass movements are made of. Their influence was confined largely to the academy and to several pro-business newspapers that championed the ideas of social Darwinism. The great advantage that American business possessed at the turn of the century was, as Lippmann perceived, that its leaders understood the American political tradition better than the critics of American business did. In his introduction to the American edition of the *Fabian Essays*, the ardent socialist Edward Bellamy summed up the problem which he and his comrades confronted whenever they presented their ideas to the American people. The typical American, he lamented, "conceived of a socialist, when he considered him at all, as a mysterious type of desperado, reputed to infest the dark places of continental Europe and engaged with his fellows in a conspiracy as monstrous as it was futile, against civilization and all that is implied."[15]

Socialism, the most vehement opponent of American capitalism in those days, was an alien ideology for most Americans. Its leaders were mainly foreigners or Europeanized Americans who thought about America in foreign categories. The socialist literature of the period reveals, as Louis Hartz has noted, an irrelevance to American life, and the "persistent use of the European concepts of Marxism when the nation was ruling them out of its mind."[16] The most successful critics of American capitalism, the Progressives, called for reform rather than social revolution and thus appealed more to the moderate strain in the American political tradition. The socialists failed primarily because they did not truly understand the pragmatic nature of American individualism. Americans are realists, and, as Martin Diamond has noted, they perceived more readily than Europeans the untenability of socialism.[17] Capitalism, on the other hand, came much closer to the practical reality that Americans understood. Most turn of the century Americans accepted, without necessarily knowing it, the Smithian concept of the "invisible hand": i.e., that when an individual "intends only his own gain . . . he is . . . led by an invisible hand to promote an end which was no part of his intention. . . . pursuing his own interest he frequently promotes that of the society more effectively than when he really intends to promote it."[18]

Smith's individualism and libertarianism readily conformed to the ethos of the American liberal tradition, which since colonial times has stood as the nation's most powerful hedge against statism. From their very beginnings Americans have viewed their society in egalitarian terms. But egalitarianism in America was based upon equality of opportunity rather than equality of results. As children of the Glorious Revolution Americans have traditionally viewed the individual's place in society in Lockean terms. They have always thought of themselves as free men, capable of forging their own destinies. In America there was no feudal tradition, established church, aristocracy, or class system. The appeal of socialism in Europe, on the other hand, was predicated upon the existence of a rigid class system left over from feudal times. More than the industrial revolution, the remnants of this old system—which had received a short-lived infusion of new blood during the violent aftermath of the French Revolution—were to provide the European socialist with his main source of ideological ammunition. This was also the case in Latin America, where many of the feudal institutions of counter-Reformation Spain and Portugal had been transplanted during the colonial period.

But if Europeans and Latin Americans questioned the viability of their respective systems at the turn of the century, Americans continued to believe in their system. They harbored doubts about the future, they disliked many of the more sordid aspects of industrialization, but they continued to view their country as "God's country," the freest and most dynamic civilization in the world. And so, without many major defenders to champion their cause, the American capitalists—possessing an inarticulate understanding of the American political tradition—survived the anti-capitalist rhetoric of the industrial revolution without encountering the kinds of social problems that afflicted European and, to a lesser degree, Latin American capitalists of the day.

VI

There were, of course, other reasons for the failure of anti-capitalist rhetoric in America during and after the industrial revolution. One searches in vain throughout the folklore of American socialism for examples of the kind of severe social brutality that European socialists could attribute to European capitalism. There were, to be sure, examples of social inequities for the critics of capitalism to draw upon, but it was clear to most observers that the industrial revolution in America had been far more peaceful and just than it was in Europe.

Then too, the American worker had received greater profits from the industrial revolution than his European brothers had received. The German economist, Werner Sombart, writing in 1906, marveled at the fact that American workers were far better off in terms of material goods, standards of living, and working conditions, than their European counterparts.[19] For the American worker, Sombart noted, " 'freedom' and 'equality' (not only in the legal and political sense, but also in the material and social sense) are not empty concepts, or vague dreams, as they are to the proletariat in Europe. To a great extent they are realities.''

The superior position of the American worker Sombart understood to be due in large part to America's liberal tradition. He was most impressed by the lack of class consciousness among American workers, which he attributed to the absence of feudal traditions in American history. The American worker, he observed, ''seems neither oppressed, nor submissive. He treats everyone as 'his equal,' not just in theory, but practice.'' The social distance between the various levels of American society—thanks to the democratic Constitution, the general diffusion of education, and the workers' relatively high standard of living—did not seem very great to the worker at the bottom, Sombart concluded.

''The tone of 'equal treatment,''' Sombart declared, ''is . . . dominant within the capitalist enterprise [of the country] itself. . . . [The employer] does not treat the worker as if he [the employer] were a 'lord' who demands obedience. . . . From the beginning a purely business approach became the dominant one in dealing with wage contracts. Formal 'equalization' of employers and workers did not have to be won . . . in a long struggle. . . . The employer of labor takes care to adopt a polite, obliging attitude toward his workers.'' When Charles Schwab addressed the members of the radical International Workers of the World (the IWW) at the Skinner & Eddy Shipyards in Seattle during World War I, he began in a way that no European ''boss'' would have begun. ''Now boys,'' he declared, ''I am a very rich man . . .'' The Wobblies laughed and applauded and when Schwab had finished his talk the men made him an honorary member of the IWW.[20] Only in America could an event like that take place, and only in America could a man like Schwab, who had started at the bottom as a laborer, boast so openly about his vast wealth. The fact that many of the millionaire capitalists produced by the industrial revolution in America had started at the bottom was yet another factor that typified their business conduct. If men like Schwab and Carnegie could become millionaires any industri-

ous and imaginative person could also. The system was open
and there seemed to be plenty of room at the top.

In America, Sombart observed, socialist utopias had been
defeated by roast beef and apple pie. The high living standard
(compared to Europe) and the liberal tradition blunted the arguments of American socialists. Eugene V. Debs and Jack
London, for all their eloquence, never managed to get their
points across to the American worker.

VII

The statesmen of the industrial revolution in America had succeeded brilliantly in using the rhetoric of classical liberalism
to explain away the harsh vicissitudes of industrialization. Politicians, trade unionists, and business men used the language
of Adam Smith to explain the gospel of industry to the American
people, but it is clear that most of these self-styled champions of
economic liberalism had little use for laissez-faire. The industrial revolution in America was a time of high protective tariffs,
governmental intervention into the workings of the market, and
state planning. Lord Bryce, in pondering this fact in his *American Commonwealth*, declared that contrary to the American
mythology, the late 19th century was a time of massive governmental intervention into ever-widening fields of American
life. William Graham Sumner, who believed that the social
classes owed *nothing* to one another, was disgusted by the federal role in the building of the railroads.

By 1929 John Dewey could write, in his *Individualism Old
and New*, that the concept of liberal individualism propounded
by the social Darwinists had been corrupted by the marriage of
capitalism to the state. America, he declared, was already living
in a collectivist age, and the choice confronting Americans was
the choice between the unplanned "collectivism of profit" and
the idealistic "collectivism of planning." Only a popular collectivism, he argued, could help Americans to regain the
genuine individualism that was so vital a part of their cultural
and political tradition. Hitherto, Dewey argued, reforms in

American society had been made on a catch-as-catch-can basis. "Reforms that deal now with this abuse and now with that without having a social goal based upon an inclusive plan, differ entirely from effort at re-forming, in its literal sense, the institutional scheme of things." Central planning was, for Dewey and his growing army of followers, "the sole method of social action by which liberalism can realize its professed aims." Dewey was the first to argue that the word "liberal"—which once stood for liberal, free-market capitalism—could better serve the needs of social democracy in America than the word "socialism." The liberalism of Adam Smith was out-of-date, Dewey argued. The liberating goals of liberalism could be achieved in the 20th century "only by a reversal of the means to which early liberalism was committed."[21]

Dewey was not an economist or even a sociologist, and yet to many Americans there seemed to be a core of genuine logic and common sense in his views. The market economy, as propounded by Smith and his followers had begun to strike many as unscientific. The Great Depression had shaken the faith of many Americans in the benevolence of the invisible hand. Although America had not been living under laissez-faire since the Civil War, our business and political leaders, it was argued, had convinced the majority of Americans that we were. When times were good economically, chambers of commerce attributed the nation's bounty to the practice of laissez-faire capitalism. Now that times were hard it was only logical that many Americans would blame liberal capitalism for their economic misfortunes. The arguments of Veblen, who viewed the market model as a deliberate misrepresentation of economic action, began to manifest themselves in the pages of the popular press. Veblen hoped to free the productive sector of the economy (industry) from the embrace of "business," which was only concerned with profit. For Veblen the "price system" held back production and new technology. "In any community that is organized on the price system, . . ." he declared, "unemployment of the available industrial plant and workman . . . appears to be the indispensable condition."

Veblen proposed to exchange the price system with a central planning board. In his *Engineers and the Price System* (1921) he called for replacement of the market system with a board of experts who possessed the power to make direct allocation of available resources throughout the entire economy. By 1932 the arguments of the socialist central planners, combined with the implications of the Depression, served to create a debate among American intellectuals that reduced the available alternatives to socialism or the free economy. President Hoover's Secretary of Treasury, Ogden Mills, summed up the arguments when he declared, "We can have a free country or a socialist one. We cannot have both. Our economic system cannot be half free and half socialistic . . . There is no middle ground between governing and being governed, between absolute sovereignty and liberty, between tyranny and freedom."[22] *Business Week* editorialized in its July 9, 1930 number that the question "to plan or not to plan" was no longer important; the real question was, who is to do the planning.[23] Several significant financial journals, including *Fortune,* argued in favor of Mussolini's approach to planning. "The American businessman under Mr. Hoover had, when he needed succor, to sneak through the servant's quarters, . . ." *Fortune* lamented, "[but] the Italian businessman went in and goes in, proud and unashamed, through the front door."[24]

VIII

In the midst of the great debate over the future of the free enterprise system in America, one economist emerged to claim the middle ground between socialism and laissez-faire capitalism, John Maynard Keynes. As an advisor on economic policy to the British Liberal Party during the 1930s, Keynes had called for an expansionist policy based on massive spending on public works as a way out of the depression, but he was not listened to by the Socialist Prime Minister of the day, Ramsey MacDonald, who described the Keynesian proposals as a "patch-work of pettifogging neo-capitalism." In 1934, hoping to advance his ideas in America, Keynes penned a famous open letter to President Roosevelt. Keynes wrote to F.D.R.:

> You have made yourself the trustee for those in every country who seek to mend the evils of our condition . . . within the framework of the existing social system. If you fail, rational choice will be gravely prejudiced throughout the world, leaving orthodoxy and revolution to fight it out. But if you succeed, new and bolder methods will be tried everywhere, and we may date the first chapter of the new economic era from your accession to office.[25]

Keynes, as Harry Johnson has demonstrated, was fully conscious of the fact that he was propounding a revolutionary doctrine that might well shape the future course of economic theory.[26] At the same time, Alex Leijonhufvud had argued, he knew more than enough about economic history to realize that his ideas, as propounded in *The General Theory* (1936), were the products of a unique set of historical circumstances, and were therefore not necessarily applicable to other situations in future times.[27] Keynes called for a *via media* between socialism and laissez-faire capitalism. He attacked Say's Law (i.e., the theory that supply creates its own demand), and called upon his colleagues to study the business cycle in order to predict rises and declines in public spending. This would enable the planners to decide upon the ideal moment for state intervention into the workings of the economy. Unlike Dewey and Veblen, Keynes did not consider himself to be an advocate of planning on a socialist scale; he proposed, on the contrary, to intervene into the workings of the economy as little as possible.

Contrary to the popular assumption, Keynes did not picture himself as a social reformer, although he recognized that his ideas could easily be used by social reformers. As Alvin Hansen has written,

> Collective bargaining, trade unionism, minimum-wage laws, hours legislation, social security, a progressive income tax system, slum clearance and housing, urban redevelopment and planning, education reform—all these [Keynes] . . . accepted, but they were not among his preoccupations.[28]

Keynes preferred to think of himself as a kind of economic physician, dispensing cures—in the forms of monetary and fiscal care—rather than as an economic planner or reformer. In this context he considered Marx to be a quack and the British socialists who refused to heed his advice to be economic illiterates. How, he asked of Marxism, "can a doctrine so illogical and so dull [exercise] so powerful and enduring an influence over the minds of men, and through them, the events of history?" To his Marxist critics he asked, "How can I adopt a creed which, preferring the mud to the fish, exalts the boorish proletariat above the bourgeois intelligentsia?"[29]

It is not our purpose here to review the content of Keynesian thought. Rather, we are concerned with the manner in which the theories of Keynes—quite often in highly bastardized forms—came to influence economic policy in the United States, and with their development from mere theories of economics to their present status of established economic orthodoxy. By definition, as Harry Johnson has noted, an orthodoxy (in any field) is always vulnerable, since it tends to be elaborated from complex ideas beyond the ken of most practical people. "The essence of an orthodoxy," Johnson has written anent the Keynesian revolution, "is to reduce the subtle and sophisticated thoughts of great men to a set of simple principles and straightforward slogans that more mediocre brains can think they understand well enough to live by."[30] Hence former President Richard Nixon's willingness to affirm his loyalty to the doctrines of Keynes, or, rather, to a vulgarized version of those doctrines.

The principles and slogans of any economic revolution are invariably vulnerable, again in Professor Johnson's phrase, when their very orthodoxy places them in "conflict with the facts of everyday experience." This phenomenon is particularly dangerous in political economy, especially when the economic orthodoxy at hand is predicated upon prescriptions elaborated in another time and place. Keynes, in a famous phrase, recognized this problem, when he declared that

> the ideas of economists and political philosophers, both when they are right and when they are wrong, are more powerful than

is commonly understood. Indeed, the world is ruled by little else. Madmen in authority, who hear voices in the air, are distilling their frenzy from some academic scribbler of a few years back. I am sure that the power of vested interests is vastly exaggerated compared with the gradual encroachment of ideas. Not, indeed, immediately, but after a certain interval; . . . so that the ideas which civil servants and politicians and even agitators apply are not likely to be the newest. But, soon or late, it is ideas, not vested interests, which are dangerous for good and evil.[31]

There is no better explanation in recent political literature for Richard Nixon's tardy conversion to Keynesian economics. Indeed, there is no better argument against Keynesian economics than that quotation from the master himself.

When we talk about Keynesianism here, we are talking more about a political climate of opinion than the work of a real economist. Keynesianism as an ideology, like all ideologies, is based upon a distortion of the ideas of Keynes. When an idea or body of ideas becomes ideologized, Raymond Aron has written, it loses its intrinsic qualities of exactness.[32] When individuals or peoples come to accept an ideology without regard to the origin or nature of the ideas contained within it, the ideology becomes an orthodoxy. This can be seen, as Aron has demonstrated, in many scientific concepts that are accepted by large groups of people who do not understand science (one thinks of the general acceptance of Ptolemaic astronomy by the people of the Middle Ages and of quantum mechanics by contemporary people), and it can be clearly seen in Richard Nixon's acquiescence to Keynesian dogma.

Keynes was quick to recognize that the ideas he had advanced in the 1930s to deal with the Great Depression and to defend capitalism had been vulgarized and turned into dogmas by his disciples, and after World War II he began, much to the chagrin of his followers, to return to classical economic doctrine.[33]

IX

The vulgarized version of Keynes—the version accepted by Richard Nixon and a host of politicians and economists—was predicated on a belief that capitalism was doomed. The only way to save capitalism, according to this school, was to resort to massive economic intervention into various markets, and to various forms of state planning. In our time, the most convincing doomsayer on the subject of capitalism's future was the late Joseph Schumpeter, who believed that the "civilization of capitalism," as he called it, rested upon a series of social arrangements that were best expressed in the political sphere by the theories of classical liberalism.[34] The ideals of classical liberalism greatly appealed to Schumpeter (as they did to Keynes), but he viewed them, ultimately, as nothing more than ideals. They were, he sadly concluded, never put into practice. Classical liberalism remained, Schumpeter argued, the ideology of a small intellectual elite. Surveying the future, Schumpeter asked the question, "Can capitalism survive?" His answer was a firm "No!"[35]

Schumpeter's pessimism was based upon the deep conviction that the social arrangements upon which the "civilization of capitalism" rested had begun to rot with the rise of imperialism in the 19th century, when nationalist measures such as protective tariffs came into conflict with economic liberalism. By 1900 *classical* liberalism, he believed, for all intents and purposes, was dead in Britain and dying in the rest of the industrialized world. With the death of classical liberalism as a political expression of public policy, Schumpeter was convinced that capitalism's passing was the next event on the agenda.

Capitalists who never believed in the laissez-faire doctrines of classical liberalism shared Schumpeter's pessimism. And from the beginning of the industrial revolution in America businessmen have always been willing to avail themselves of the state's help. It was only on those occasions when the state did things they didn't like that American capitalists sounded the clarion of classical liberalism.

The interesting factor about the situation in America—as opposed to Europe—was that Americans in general, and American businessmen in particular, believed themselves to be living in a liberal society governed by a liberal form of capitalism. But almost from the beginnings of the Republic, the liberal tradition had lived side-by-side with a paternalistic tradition and a desire for social perfection that often completely out-weighed liberalism when it came to the conduct of public policy. It was out of this secondary strand in American culture that the first form of planning emerged.

The capitalist tradition in America, therefore, was not liberal in Adam Smith's sense of the word; but at the same time it was not illiberal. From the beginnings of our society Americans have been addicted to passionate and instant action, what Walter Bagehot described as the "menace of philanthropy." One need only go back as far as the Northwest Ordinance of 1787 for a vivid example of the kind of society the founding fathers envisaged in the new territories. That "new" society was planned from the top to the bottom, from the local economy to the place of the village school house. But the kind of planning our founding fathers mused upon was the benign planning of the country squire with his sense of *nobless oblige*. It was local in extent, and the early "planners" had no desire to "nationalize" their plans. The "national idea" did not really begin to establish itself in America until after the Civil War, and the attempts by *Ante Bellum* politicians—such as John Quincy Adams and Andrew Jackson—to foist national "plans" upon the rest of the country were invariably spoiled by the intervention of Congress and the Supreme Court.

By the time of the industrial revolution, the climate in America had begun to change. By 1884, in his *Congressional Government,* Woodrow Wilson could make the kind of argument for a strong presidency and a national government that would have shocked even Alexander Hamilton.[36] But even in the early years of this century, the American political climate was less hospitable to the kind of powerful state needed for economic and social planning than in Europe where a strong central government had been the rule in most places since the 16th century.[37] Such protoplans of the 19th century as the Morill Land Grant Act of 1862, which influenced both education and agriculture throughout the country, and the Homestead

Law of 1862, can hardly be called plans in the modern sense—and yet they were plans. The same can be said for the various forms of national banking legislation, protective tariffs, and other pieces of legislation designed to strengthen the federal government and help win the loyalty of various special interest groups in post-Civil War America.

In America planning and government control were introduced selectively and compartmentally. Specific sectors of society were chosen, and the federal role in those sectors gradually increased over a period of time. In order to promote the expension of railroads, during the 1870s, the federal government granted 134 million acres of land to aid railroad companies in their construction programs, and state governments provided millions of acres as well. The government also issued about $48 million in federal bonds to aid railroad construction, and state and local governments—under federal influence—lent $88 million and subscribed to about $125 million in railroad stock. The railroads were also given tax exemptions at both the federal and state levels. In the end, the various plans to stimulate railroad construction succeeded, but at a great cost to the free enterprise system, because with federal aid came federal control and regulation. By March 21, 1918, the relationship between the railroads and the federal government was such that Woodrow Wilson, with the backing of Congress, could push through the Railroad Control Act, which placed railroads under direct government control in order to aid the war effort.

By the time of America's entrance into World War I the political climate had begun to change. The liberal tradition was no longer the potent force it had been. To win the war, Wilson believed, would require "illiberalism at home to reinforce the men at the front . . . conformity would be the only virtue . . . and every man who refused to conform would have to pay the penalty." Such language was new in America. It ran counter to everything Americans had traditionally stood for. Yet Americans—or, rather, *most* Americans—went along not only with Wilson's policies but with his rhetoric.

X

The business of the 19th century, Albert Jay Nock wrote, had been the establishment of the individual's right to liberty and self-expression; the 20th century, he believed—as he wrote from the vantage point of Wilsonian America—would be devoted to creating circumstances for *improving* the collective lot of the newly emancipated and enfranchized masses. The latter, he feared, would be done at the expense of the former through the office of the state. The great fortunes of America, he observed at the beginning of the present century, were created by means that were unfair, at least if one thought in terms of classical liberalism. The owners of the new fortunes were, he wrote, "in control of the State's machinery, and were using it to their own advantage by way of land grants, tariffs, concessions, franchises and every other known form of law made privilege." America, which once valued liberty above all other virtues had, Nock lamented, succumbed to the ideology of "economism"—that is, an ideology that viewed "the whole sum of human life in terms of the production, acquisition and distribution of wealth." Such an ideology "must not conceive of the State as an instrument of justice"; it must, on the contrary, conceive the State as Voltaire did, as "a device for taking money out of one set of pockets and putting it into another."[38]

Nock saw little difference between the early capitalists and the avatars of social reform. Both groups were motivated by what he called "economism," and both groups viewed the state as the most important means to their respective ends. There was no talk at the beginning of the century about reducing the power of the state; on the contrary, Nock observed, both the capitalists and the reformers sought only to increase its power. In early 20th-century America, reformers and capitalists did not struggle against one another in Marxian terms, they struggled only for control of the state's machinery. It was in the midst of this historical *milieu* that modern planning began to take root.

While the roots of economic planning can be traced back to

the 18th century, the concept of scientific economic planning is
a relatively new one. As Jewkes notes, there are no references to
it in the works of Marx or of the Fabians or the late 19th century
American reformers.[39] Even in Britain, where it was to take
hold with a special force, there are no references to planning in
the various histories of British socialism until the end of the First
World War.[40] It seems to have started in Germany during that
war, and was later seized upon by German intellectuals "who
saw in it an endlessly fascinating set of problems in complex
administration and an irresistible opportunity of breaking individuals to the purpose of the state."[41] In Russia after the Revolution, Lenin, who was fully cognizant of the untried nature
of socialism, viewed planning as a means to socialization. In a
letter to Krzhizhanovsky, he wrote,

> Couldn't you produce a plan . . . which would be understood by
> the proletariat? For instance, in 10 years (or 5?) we shall build 20
> (or 30 or 50?) power stations covering the country with a network
> of such stations, each with a radius of operation of say 400 versts
> (or 200 if we are unable to achieve more) . . . We need such a
> plan at once to give the masses a shining unimpeded prospect to
> work for: and in 10 (or 20?) years we shall electrify Russia, the
> whole of it, both industrial and agricultural.[42]

In Lenin's letter, Jewkes notes, can be found the embryo of the
planning idea, "with its already well-established characteristics
of political cynicism, slap-dash economics and obsessions with
the spectacular." Planning on this scale was the apotheosis of
Glendower's illusion, and Lenin's request on the subject of
power stations is every bit as realistic as Glendower's call to the
spirits from the vasty deep.

But as Jewkes and others have demonstrated it is not so easy
to define real planning, especially in a nontotalitarian society
like America.[43] Lenin viewed the planned economy as an economy devoid of private enterprise and ownership in which the
entrepreneur working for a profit is replaced by a planning board
working for the good of society as a whole.[44] Hayek has defined
planning as the "central direction of all economic activity according to a single plan laying down how the resources of soci-

ety can be 'consciously directed' to serve particular ends in a particular way."[45]

Planning, however, can have many objectives, ranging from the equal distribution of income to a simple method of running the economy with nonegalitarian goals. There is a certain surface logic in planning that doesn't seem to exist in the uncontrolled environment of liberal capitalism. Planning seems to make sense, it is what every rational person does with his life and resources; and it logically follows that every rationally constructed society ought to plan.

If one argued the case for planning on the grounds of "common sense," leaving out the specific details of a given plan, the definition of planning becomes quite vague. And yet, as Hayek has argued, this is exactly what most planners do. The very vagueness of planning's meaning constitutes part of its appeal to rational individuals. If one leaves out the draconian aspects, the painful realities that invariably accompany economic planning, planning becomes all the more appealing. The historic appeal of planning, as its critics and defenders have both pointed out, is its idealism, its *untried* idealism. Of course, once the plan is put into action—and many plans have been put into action in many countries since the publication of Durkheim's book on socialism—there is always the possibility that it will fail to achieve its stated goals, that it may even cause unforeseen problems. Yet the ordeal of bad planning has not, as of 1975, damaged the enthusiasm of the planners. There remains an element of wishful thinking in political society that fuels the enthusiasm of the planner and inspires him to even greater plans. That element of wishful thinking remains the greatest strength of planning.

Today the kind of socialism that argued for state ownership of the means of production is dead. The socialist enthusiasm that Durkheim railed against towards the beginning of this century is today a thing of the past. Socialists, as the Polish Marxist Leszek Kolakowski has observed, no longer believe in the *future* of socialism, since socialism now has a past that is anything but glorious.[46] But planning, the adopted child of socialism, is in no such trouble. While socialism's legacy has ranged from the brutal totalitarianism of Russia and China to the benign rot of British Laborism and the Kafkaesque sterility of Scandinavian regimentation, planning has taken a more comfortable middle course. The results have been vague and difficult to evaluate. The striking failures of classical socialism are not to be found in planned economies that still allow for certain market forces to do their work.

Americans, with their Calvinist sense of order, have always been willing to accept various forms of moderate planning. The anti-socialist traits that Edward Bellamy noted in his fellow countrymen did not prevent them from embracing planning, which struck most Americans as a very natural and intelligent thing to do. When moderate American plans failed, they did not fail as disastrously as, say, the great socialist plans of Britain. To paraphrase Lord Acton, "moderate planning only corrupts, but absolute planning (i.e. socialism) corrupts absolutely." The wishful thinking that is so much a part of planning is also very much a part of the American tradition. Indeed, America, as the "land of the future," historically has possessed more wishful thinking than most other countries. The movement to ration the consumption of oil in the United States in the aftermath of the Arab oil embargo provides an excellent example of American wishful thinking in action. Many Americans remembered the confusion caused by gasoline rationing during World War II—a confusion that was partially assuaged by the patriotic intensity of the period—and many of those same Americans believed that rationing had nevertheless achieved something for the war effort. In 1974, after the embargo had caused Americans to recognize that our energy resources were finite, it seemed only logical to repeat what we had done during World War II. Several national opinion polls conducted at that time revealed that a majority of Americans favored some form of rationing plan. It seemed to most Americans—Republicans and Democrats alike —more rational to rely upon the good sense of the planners who would allocate oil where it was most needed than to rely upon the capricious forces of the market place. Rationing plans were called for by such disparate individuals as J. K. Galbraith and Melvin Laird. In the end, however, both Presidents Nixon and Ford refused to embrace rationing, and the decision was an unpopular one.

The rhetoric of laissez-faire capitalism remains a seductive force in American life. It is invoked even by social democrats in this country.[47] But there is little to the rhetoric, save for words which echo the liberalism of the American orthodoxy. Despite the fact that America continued as a capitalist society—perhaps the most purely capitalist society left in the world today—its capitalism is less free than it was ten years ago, and a good deal less free than it was before the advent of the New Deal. America has clearly begun to journey down the "road to serfdom," and the capitalist system, therefore, is on shakier ground than it has ever experienced before.

This does not mean that capitalism is doomed in America. There has been a renaissance of laissez-faire capitalist theory in the academy, and while it has had no real influence on the course of public policy, there is no reason to believe that its thrust will be blunted by the inexorable push of the controlled economy. On July 14th of 1975, Adam Smith followed Lord Keynes on the cover of *Time* magazine. *Time's* cover asked, "Can Capitalism Survive?" and a balloon emerging from Smith's famous profile answered, "Don't count me out, folks." *Time's* editors concluded optimistically that capitalism will indeed survive in America. "Despite its transitory woes and weaknesses," *Time* declared, "capitalism in the foreseeable future will not only survive but also stands to prosper and spread. Perhaps the most balanced judgement of Adam Smith's wondrous system is Winston Churchill's famous conclusion about democracy: It is the worst system—except for all those other systems that have been tried and failed."[48]

But, of course, *Time* was not really talking about the kind of capitalism that Adam Smith advocated. *Time* was talking about the watered-down Keynesian version, the mixed economy, planned so as to protect it from the very force Smith apotheosized—the free market. From the vantage of 1975 it seems unlikely that an American politician advocating free market solutions to America's economic problems could be elected to the Presidency. Americans still believe in the capitalist system, but they no longer trust it. It remains to be seen whether they will continue to believe in it as even greater controls are placed upon its operation. Most Americans believe that Franklin Roosevelt, with his massive planning, his WPA, CCC, and NRA, saved America from ruin during the Great Depression. And since 1932, American political life has been dominated by politicians who have won their offices by promising greater plans and greater controls. Planning appears to be a permanent fixture in American life, and for that reason the disciples of real capitalism will find it difficult to share *Time's* optimism. We can only pray that the spirits dwelling in the vasty deep are more benevolent than the claws of the invisible hand.

AMERICAN TRANSPORTATION PLANNING

GEORGE W. HILTON
Professor of Economics, University of California, Los Angeles

American transportation planning falls into two general categories: first, the allocation of resources in a public establishment either under public ownership or under a publicly controlled corporation of nominal private ownership; and second, regulation of facilities which actually remain under private ownership. Facilities under outright public ownership include roads of all sorts, airports, transit systems in most major metropolitan areas, dams, locks, and other navigation facilities on the inland rivers, and aerial navigation facilities. Governmental enterprises which operate as public authorities, though under nominal private ownership, are the National Railroad Passenger Corporation, customarily known as Amtrak, and the Consolidated Rail Corporation (ConRail). The supersonic transport program was an effort at governmental innovation for an industry which was to remain under private ownership though under governmental regulation. Government regulation of privately owned facilities encompasses auto safety and auto emission standards, but in addition to other programs, such as maritime safety and maintenance of aerial navigation, these are omitted in the interest of brevity. In all these, the pattern and results of planning and regulation are essentially the same.

ROADS

Roads provide the archetype for governmental planning behavior in transportation facilities. The provision of roads, including their building, allocation and maintenance, is by any ordinary standards an appropriate governmental activity. Access to and egress from ordinary roads are so ready that it would be excessively costly for the private sector of the economy to levy and collect prices for the use of facilities. While this logic does not apparently apply to roads of limited access, where prices can be collected at points of access or egress, in American practice roads of both sorts are nevertheless in the public sector.

Users are charged for roads, typically, by an annual license fee, by an excise on gasoline or other fuels, plus some miscellaneous excises on tires, recapping material, truck bodies, and so on. A few states charge a ton-mile fee for truck movements within their jurisdictions. Users are not charged for noxious emissions of their vehicles. The license fees are levied on the basis of the value of the vehicle or its horsepower, but not usually on the basis of its weight or the square footage of roads which it occupies. States vary in their relative reliance on license fees versus excises, but most states rely overwhelmingly on the proceeds of the gasoline excise.

The design of the American automobiles has adapted to this fee structure; the American automobile has been large in square footage and weight, profligate in its use of air, and not notably fuel-efficient relative to the automobiles of most foreign countries. Similarly, the American road system has been planned taking this fee structure as given. As economists have widely pointed out, the nature of American user charges does not give appropriate incentives to economize on the existing supply of roads. The gasoline excise, which is the principal user charge, usually amounted to about a third of the pump price of gasoline until the approximate doubling of the pump price in recent years. This is a small enough percentage of the total cost of operating an automobile that American drivers have manifested an extremely low price elasticity of demand and have, in fact, behaved almost as if the use of the roads were free to them.

Adversely, however, funds raised through this tax system have customarily been earmarked for further investments in roads. The federal Highway Trust Fund of 1956 receives the most publicity, but similar arrangements of earmarking user charges for the building and maintenance of roads, plus related facilities such as departments of motor vehicles, are common on the state level. The absolute rate of utilization of roads is so high that even though the user charges do not provide the usual function of a price of encouraging economization of the existing supply of the facility, the funds generated for building new facilities until recently have been abundant.

American road planning, then, has been carried on within this context. Highway departments have frequently attempted to quantify benefits of road building in relation to costs, but frequently they have proceeded simply by trying to remove bottlenecks, or upgrade portions with poor accident experiences. Nothing in this process seeks to equate marginal benefit and marginal cost and thus to assure that the resources go to their highest valued use. The process has been studied rigorously by Ann Friedlaender in an extensive benefit-cost analysis of the Interstate freeway system.[1] Professor Friedlaender concluded that the program was justified, that urban users cross-subsidize rural users, and that the investment is poorly allocated. Political considerations caused the system to contain a large mileage of lightly utilized freeway, especially in the plains states, whereas the investment would have given society a greater return in more populous areas of the country.

Although on the average, urban users cross-subsidize rural users, urban users in peak periods are thought not to pay the full marginal cost of their movements. The pricing system gives them no pecuniary disincentive from using the facilities in rush hours.[2] Accordingly, radial freeways from central business districts suffer a severe peaking problem which gives rise to a political demand for redundant facilities. These facilities may take the shape of freeways parallel to existing freeways to handle peak hour traffic, such as the Junipero Serra freeway south of San Francisco, or rail transit facilities such as the Bay Area Rapid Transit in the San Francisco East Bay. Because political resource allocation determines the building of these facilities, a political struggle over the direction of the investment is customary. However, all these facilities, whether redundant freeways or rail systems, are uniformly ineffective in dealing with peak-hour congestion, for they do nothing to make the use of existing facilities more costly.

Alternatively stated, the way roads are priced also fails to give society an accurate indication of the demand for new facilities. The congestion which the non-price rationing of roads creates causes planners of additional facilities to direct investment to radial facilities which serve a trip that is at best stagnant in demand, and frequently absolutely declining. The demand for additional trips is mainly between-suburbs and circumferential journeys of people who have no business in central business districts at all. Such trips are handled on facilities like the beltways around Washington and Baltimore, the San Diego freeway in Los Angeles, and routes 128 and 495 around Boston.

Apart from the fact that the system gives inadequate incentives to economize on existing facilities and erroneous impressions on demand for additional facilities, it provides excessive resources for investment and not enough for maintenance. Thus, the interstate freeway system at present is encountering budgetary stringency in maintenance facilities.

AIRPORTS

Airports provide possibly the best example of the nature of the planning and investment process in American transportation facilities. In this instance the facilities are in the public sector not because the private sector would find it impossible to price them, but rather for an historical reason: municipalities sought to advance the development of commercial aviation while this was considered a premature industry.

Until quite recently, little attention was paid to airport resource allocation, but in 1969 Professor Michael Levine of the University of Southern California Law School, produced an article in the *Journal of Law and Economics,* which conceptualized the behavior of airport authorities.[3] The trustees or other administrators of airports are entrusted with allocating something which is quite scarce and valuable, the time of airport runways. The cost may be as great as $4,000 per minute in the economist's usual sense of opportunity costs, the value of the resource for other purposes. One might under the circumstances expect airport authorities to begin their considerations with the pricing of runways, but instead, they customarily begin by auctioning off the monopoly rights to ancillary airport services: parking, auto rental, bars, restaurants, newsstands, souvenir shops, and the like. Having captured such monopoly gain as is available from these services, the authorities then proceed to price runways simply to make the airport break even. In some small airports the runways are thus provided at no price at all. At the larger airports airport authorities usually charge average-cost pricing; levying fees usually on the basis of aircraft weight undifferentiated by hour. This usually means a fee of under $25 for a private plane but several hundred dollars for a large commercial plane.

As could easily be predicted, the average level of charges for the use of the runways is so low that the fee does not encourage economic use of the facility. The fee is so low for general aviation aircraft that a major airport may prove to be the cheapest place to land a light plane. Even for commercial aircraft the fee is so low relative to the average total cost of operation that it amounts to a trivial discouragement. In the late 1960s it was estimated that it cost a major airline approximately $5,500 to fly a 707 from Los Angeles to New York, but then the landing fee at Kennedy Airport was only $75. Under the circumstances, the airline was rational in acting almost as if the fee did not exist. At the same time, Rand Corporation economists Park and Carlin have estimated opportunity cost of using the runway on such a facility in the vicinity of $1,800 to $2,000 at peak hours.

The airlines deal with the allocation of runways as one would expect, given the non-price rationing which prevails and given their own industrial organization in a cartel under the Civil Aeronautics Board. They typically meet to allot one another short periods, usually of thirty seconds, for taking off and landing. As usual in non-price rationing, there is no assurance that the runway goes to its highest valued use, as for example, it would tend to do if runway use were auctioned off. The problem is compounded by another normal consequence of cartelization, a low utilization of resources. This manifests itself in relatively low load factors of planes, historically around 50 percent. The C.A.B. has no powers over the size of aircraft or the frequency with which the airlines fly; and as a result provision of larger partially-filled planes and frequent departures is a major form of non-price rivalry in the industry.

As usual under non-price rationing, queuing occurs. This involves lines of planes forming waiting to take off and burning well over $25 of fuel per minute and also, a much more expensive form of queuing, flying around in plane stacks waiting to land. In such a queue, a full 747, including both its cost of operation and the value of passenger time, could result in queuing costs of more than $3,500 an hour—probably the most expensive form of queuing in society.

Inevitably under the circumstances, the organization of airports creates political demands for building additional airports. The Federal Airport Aid program since World War II has encouraged this process; since 1970 a trust fund analogous to the highway trust fund has financed the program. This policy has resulted first, in proliferation of airports in smaller communities such as the numerous medium-sized cities in central Indiana, and second, in construction of redundant airports at major cities. Medium-sized city airports, satisfying political interests in thinly-populated areas, are like misallocated mileage within the interstate freeway system, which responds to the same political interests. At the same time, redundant airports are the analog of parallel freeways.

The problem of redundant airports is perfectly illustrated by

Dulles Airport at Washington, D.C. This airport was built in a rural area twenty-six miles from downtown Washington, because of the congestion at National Airport—which in turn resulted from the normal airport pricing policy. Because National Airport is almost immediately adjacent to downtown Washington, the building of Dulles did not reduce the attraction of National to the majority of airline users in the area. Since air fares are the same to both airports, the Federal Aviation Administration, which operates both, uses a form of non-price rationing as between them. Larger jets plus all planes going farther than approximately St. Louis are required to use Dulles—with the result that too-small jets are used to serve National on some routes, and perverse passenger behavior is encouraged. Passengers can usually avoid the trip to Dulles by taking a flight from National to Chicago or other intermediate points, and then transferring to their destinations. This causes numerous unnecessary trips to O'Hare and other heavily utilized airports.

The arrangement does not reduce the congestion at National Airport in peak hours, and therefore, despite considerable funds spent on redundant airports, it appears to the public that the problem is insoluble.[5]

TRANSIT

Since the early 1960s, the federal government has subsidized and planned transit facilities under the Urban Mass Transportation Assistance Program and the experience is parallel on essentially all grounds to the highway and airport programs. Initiated in 1961 and separately funded in 1964, the program accepts the economic organization of transit in cities into monopolies with a strong labor union of bus drivers and other employees. Most large city transit monopolies are now publicly-owned.

The reasons for this organization are also entirely historical. When transit was provided by horsecar and cablecar, transit companies typically served an individual street or a limited area of a city. The development of the electric streetcar in 1888 introduced into transit a comprehensive economy of scale: A single generating system with a city-wide distribution network for electric power became the optimal organization of a street railway system. Virtually all cities issued city-wide franchises, in return for which the street railways were required to provide city-wide trips for a five-cent fare, with transfers between lines. This created a cross-subsidy of passengers who travelled more than approximately 2.5 miles by passengers who travelled less than that, a rather typical example of the cross-subsidy in regulated industries generally. The arrangement was popular with cities, whose governments approved the resulting geographical pattern of a strong central business district with relatively long home-to-work trips.

This organization, however, provided an incentive to develop a form of transportation with a comparative advantage for the short movements (of less than 2.5 miles) against which the discrimination was directed, but capable of moving passengers at higher speeds than streetcars' average 8 to 10 miles per hour, with a higher standard of comfort, greater flexibility in destinations and, finally, capable of competitive economic organization. This vehicle took shape in the form of the bus in the jitney movement of 1914–15. The jitneys were owner-operated vehicles which essentially provided a competitive market in urban transportation with the usual characteristics of rapid entry and exit, quick adaptation to changes in demand, and, in particular, excellent adaptation to peak load demands. Some 60 percent of the jitneymen were part-time operators, many of whom simply carried passengers for a nickel on trips between home and work. Consequently, cities were criss-crossed with an infinity of home-to-work routes every rush hour.[6]

The jitneys were put down in every American city to protect the street railways and, in particular, to perpetuate the cross subsidization of the street railways' city-wide fare structures. As a result, the public moved to automobiles as private rather than common carriers, and the conversion of electric streetcars to bus was made within the calculations of a monopoly. The transit monopolies converted from streetcar to bus mainly between 1935 and 1955, without modification of their linear route structures. Most had radial routes from a central business district, flat fares and strong unions. Consequently the industry continued to provide service of approximately the same kind and quality which the street car had. This form of service proved to have low responsiveness of ridership to fare changes, and usage tended to drop off as per-capita or family income rose. In economists' terms, the system had a low price elasticity, and except in the lowest income brackets, a negative income elasticity. Net receipts could be maximized by contracting the output and raising the fares. Accordingly, this was a rapidly declining industry. By the 1950s the private sector could no longer support most enterprises, and they were increasingly converted to public ownership. The conversion in general reduced the rate of decline, while increasing the cost of operation. There was no great effect on the quality of service.

The strength of the union causes transit enterprises to opt for a relatively large vehicle, a Diesel bus of 40 to 50-passenger capacity, stopping relatively frequently (usually every block), and to concentrate service on a small number of major routes. If organized competitively, as the jitneys were, the operators would likely opt for a smaller vehicle, probably of about 8-passenger capacity, would run longer distances without stopping, and have a greater variety of routes.

In addition to all this are the consequences of the road pricing system, described earlier, which does not encourage economical use of streets. As a result, the buses become mired in the congestion which follows from non-price rationing of roads. Thus buses are prevented from achieving their comparative advantage for providing home-to-work trips. At the same time, this system gives a superficial attractiveness to rapid transit and suburban rail systems, which have the advantage of separate rights of way and, therefore, freedom from the congestion produced by the non-price rationing of roads. Accordingly, both the economic organization of the transit industry and the nature of road pricing cause the industry to be overly capital intensive. It uses buses of 40 to 50 passenger capacity for urban collection and distribution for which buses of about 8-passenger capacity are appropriate, and it frequently uses rail systems for line haul functions that the buses of 40 to 50 passenger capacity could perform.[7]

The Urban Mass Transportation Assistance Program (UMTA) attempts to deal with the decline of the transit industry. Specifically, it tries to produce external benefits: reduced traffic congestion; reduced atmospheric pollution; increased mobility for the aged, the young, the poor and other groups thought to be disadvantaged by present dependence on the automobile; and preservation of urban patterns of the New York-Chicago-San Francisco-Boston type, reversing the movement toward Los Angeles-Houston-Indianapolis urban patterns. The program attempts to achieve these benefits within the present economic organization of the industry, in several respects even solidifying that organization. The program provides funds for the conversion of transit systems from private to public ownership. In several respects it tends to strengthen the union—directly, because approval of the union is required under Section 13(c) for major expenditures under the program, by assuring that the capital purchased with funds under the program will be used in complementarity to the union's members, rather than in substitution; indirectly, as the program makes the industry more capital-intensive, by reducing the elasticity of demand for the members' services.

Through most of its history, the program has been a series of capital grants, though funds have recently been available for subsidy of operating expenses. About two-thirds of the funds have been spent on building rail systems, primarily of conventional rapid transit character. This means multiple-unit cars and high-level platforms with spacing of stations from a quarter mile to two miles apart—a technology which, in general, ceased to be economic for new investment by the private sector of the economy at the time of the panic of 1907. By that time, most cities with the tributary population density to justify such capital-intensive technology had already been fitted with such systems. At the same time, the forces for diffusion of cities began with the development of the Model T Ford in 1908.

However, this was the technology that appeared most attractive in pursuit of the external benefits the program sought. As indicated earlier, such systems have the indisputable advantage of separate rights of way, free from the congestion of radial freeways from central cities in rush hours. The political movement to build these systems overstated the superiority of rail systems to buses and as a consequence grossly overestimated the ability of such systems to produce external benefits. The lines built under the Urban Mass Transportation Assistance Program in Chicago, Boston, and Cleveland have demonstrated an ability to attract a number of drivers approximately equal to six months' to one year's secular growth of traffic on parallel freeways. This is so low relative to the daily variance of vehicle counts on freeways that it cannot be perceived.

The Bay Area Rapid Transit in the San Francisco area has proved to have a similar experience. On the basis of its early history, it is apparently able to divert a number of drivers approximately equal to two percent of the daily vehicle counts on the San Francisco Bay Bridge and to reduce vehicular traffic on the bridge by about four percent in rush hour. The system cost $1.8 billion and is currently losing about $20 million per year. Its completion has inevitably reduced enthusiasm for building such systems. The Urban Mass Transportation Administration is exhibiting increased criticism of proposals to build similar systems in other cities and has suggested that Los Angeles seek cheaper solutions more appropriate to its population density. Such systems, newly built, generally cost between $30 million and $65 million per mile or as much as $100 million per mile in New York City.

The UMTA is currently showing interest in what it calls light rail technology, which is to say streetcars on private right-of-way or semi-private right-of-way, as in median strips of roads. By 1906 streetcars carried some 90 percent of urban trips. In light of society's subsequent abandonment of the streetcar, recent enthusiasm for this form of transport in the planning process is probably a transitional stage away from enthusiasm for rail transit at all.

The other principal expenditure of program funds has been on bus replacements for transit systems. Such expenditures have provided a politically acceptable alternative for cities of too low population density to warrant investment in rail systems. William B. Tye, III, in a dissertation on this aspect of the program at Harvard University, has demonstrated that by reducing the capital costs (through most of the history of the program) to a third of what they otherwise would have been, the expenditures have caused the substitution of depreciation for maintenance and have reduced the optimal life expectancy of buses in the calculation of transit systems by about one half. The program has also given the incentive to use more capital intensive buses.[8]

Thus, in at least three respects the program aggravates what is already wrong with the industry: it tends to substitute rail systems for the most heavily travelled bus lines; it substitutes more capital intensive buses for less; and in several respects it tends to strengthen industry unions.

In a consideration of planning, it is notable that transit planning has tended mainly to be a reactionary activity, moving from rubber-tired transport to the technology which society used prior to rubber-tired transport. This has meant a return to rapid transit, suburban rail, and streetcar technology. This is not surprising, for although the UMTA participates with the Federal Railroad Administration in the Department of Transportation Experiment Station at Pueblo, Colorado, it is in the main a disbursing agency rather than an innovative body. As a result it tends to choose between existing technologies; and since the program was established out of dissatisfaction with certain aspects of rubber-tired transportation, it is unsurprising that the UMTA has invested primarily in its most conspicuous existing rival, which is rail technology.[9]

MAINTENANCE OF INLAND NAVIGATION

The entire center of the United States is served by a single system of waterways, the Mississippi and its tributaries, known in the 19th century as the Western Rivers, but now more frequently known as the Inland Rivers. This river system was expected to be the principal means of internal communication in the central United States in the 19th century and, in fact, was so until various improvements in railroad technology after the Civil War gave the railroads a small margin of superiority over steamboats. Because of its long-standing importance, development of this river system has been one of the most long-lived planning operations of the United States Government.

The Inland Rivers systems has only one major natural barrier, a limestone outcropping which runs diagonally across the Ohio River at Louisville. Accordingly, the first major improvement in the river system was the bypassing of the falls of the Ohio by the Louisville and Portland canal, built by private capital in 1830. This canal was designed for the steamboats of the time and was initially anticipated to be large enough for the steamboats of the foreseeable future. Beginning about 1845, towboat-and-barge technology was developed for downbound coal movements from Pittsburgh. Subsequently this technology was adapted to more general bulk commodities. Except for the Louisville and Portland canal, use of the rivers was free. Indeed, the Northwest Ordinance provided for toll-free navigation of the Ohio.

The absence of fees for the use of the river, plus the potential for infinite expansion in the size of barge tows, presented a situation in which river operators had an incentive to optimize as between crews, towboats and barges, but not to economize upon the use of the river. In the case of roads and airports, discussed above, fees were so low as to cause the operators to act almost as if the facilities were free to them. In the case of the Inland Rivers the facilities were and are, in fact, free. Thus the situation was perfectly calculated to evoke the political demands for improvement in navigation facilities but to provide no incentive to economize on those facilities, once constructed.

As a further problem, this form of transport was highly dependent on the level of rainfall. The costs of operation of steamboats varied inversely with the level of the water: the higher the water, the deeper the draft of the steamboats which might be used, the larger the number of sloughs or chutes that might be traversed, and thus the faster the navigation. Under extreme drought conditions, the river might cease to be navigable at all, as for example in the summer of 1856. Under low water conditions at the end of a drought, the river was particularly likely to freeze over, so that then when the spring freshet came, an ice gorge formed from the raised ice could do great damage to moored steamboats, bridge pilings and other stationary obstructions. Consequently there were continuing political demands for improvement in river navigation. Beginning in 1875 the federal government inaugurated a program of dam-building to assure navigation of the Ohio River regardless of drought conditions. The program eventually took the form of a series of 53 locks and dams, the first of which was opened at Davis Island below Pittsburgh in 1885. The last was completed in 1929. The Louisville and Portland canal was incorporated into this series of dams as a free facility under government ownership.

The subsidy which these facilities gave to operators, along with snag removal, dredging for removal of bars, and other federal assistance to navigation, encouraged considerable economic activity along the rivers, and also gave a great incentive to further development of towboat-and-barge technology.Diesel towboats were introduced after World War I and by the mid-1950s had superceded steam vessels almost entirely.

Because of changing technology, the original system of dams was thought to be obsolete, and in 1954 the U.S. Army Corp of Engineers was directed to replace the fifty-three dams with nineteen larger dams, to reduce the number of lockages and to permit barge tows of 1,200 feet. This multi-billion dollar project is not yet completed, but as might have been predicted, towboat design has now advanced to the point where the 1,200 foot locks are already thought by some observers to be obsolete. Towboats of 11,000 horsepower are now available. The size of tows they can handle is constricted temporarily by the strength of cables for reversing operations, but stronger cables will assuredly be developed. In absence of pricing of the facility, it is not clear there is any finite limit to the size of tow which could be inaugurated on the rivers.

The Panama Canal, though a facility for which fees are charged, has had an experience parallel to the foregoing. The charges encourage a large number of movements by small vessels, and the absence of fees on navigable water generally encourage the development of successively larger ships. The fees of the Panama Canal are not graduated on the basis of time of use, thus, peak demands evoke a political demand for a second crossing of Central America, the location of which has been in continual controversy throughout the post-World War II era.

The St. Lawrence Seaway is one of the most conspicuous government planning operations of the post-war period. After decades of discussion, the Canadian and American governments undertook to expand existing navigation facilities in the St. Lawrence River to accommodate ordinary deep-sea freighters of 27-foot draft. Since the 19th century, it had been possible for ocean vessels to enter the Great Lakes via the St. Lawrence or the Rideau Canal, though only small ships could do so. After the improvement in the Welland Canal by the Canadian government in 1932 the Great Lakes were accessible by small ocean vessels of the type used for European coastal navigation. The St. Lawrence Seaway was an effort to make the lakes accessible for the ordinary ocean freighters of the time.

As is well known, this effort was not successful, and the Seaway proved incapable of attracting ocean shipping in the volumes anticipated. The inability of a freshwater facility to provide year-around service was a severe handicap, especially given the practice of ocean shipping cartels of providing a deferred rebate to year-around users. Further, the planning effort for the Seaway did not predict the adoption of containerization of most general ocean cargo. The container, a truck body without wheels, is a device for minimizing the cost of intermodal transfer. Accordingly, the container gave an incentive to use year-round salt water ports and to ship the cargo to inland points by rail or truck. The St. Lawrence Seaway has recently not

earned its interest, and its financial future at the present writing
is in doubt. Federal planning efforts of merchant ship design
had a similar experience with respect to containerization.[10]

AMTRAK

The Amtrak program was established in 1970 to inaugurate
operation of a nation-wide federal system of passenger trains,
beginning May 1, 1971. The reasons for establishing Amtrak
were somewhat different from those of the programs considered
previously. Here Congress intervened to prevent market forces
from phasing out of form of passenger transportation on which
the nation at one time had almost entirely depended. In the
mid-1890s about 95 percent of intercity trips had been made by
passenger trains. Thereafter, the passenger train pursued a
rather typical pattern of decline. The rural trolley lines of New
England, built beginning in the early 1890s, caused the first
major diversion of passengers from the railroads. They were
followed by the interurbans, primarily in the Midwest, built
principally between 1899 and 1908. The private automobile
became a common means of intercity transportation in the
1920s, and the intercity bus rose to prominence in the same
period. The absolute volume of passenger-train ridership
peaked in 1921, declined slowly in the 1920s and more abruptly
thereafter. Passenger service of the railroads as a whole became
unprofitable in 1930. As a significant rival to the intercity passenger train, the airlines date from the introduction of the DC-3
in the mid-1930s. The introduction of jet aircraft in 1958 greatly
accelerated the diversion of passengers from rail to air.

At the same time, in the Transportation Act of 1958 powers
over the discontinuance of passenger trains were first vested in
the Interstate Commerce Commission. Before that time authority over termination of passenger trains had been in the hands of
state commissions, which varied greatly in the stringency with
which they handled discontinance applications. While the ICC
was expected to enforce nation-wide standards for passenger
train termination, it did so under conflicting incentives. Pas-

senger service was being operated under a typical regulatory cross-subsidy arrangement, in which railroad freight operations were expected to generate monopoly gains, which would be dissipated in the operation of passenger trains. The demand for railroad passenger service, however, was highly concentrated in the Northeastern United States, where the railroads were the weakest in the nation, and the least able to bear their passenger losses. Even elsewhere the industry was sinking to a point where its ability to bear passenger losses was questionable. The Western Pacific, for example, was dissipating about half of its net revenue from freight on the operation of a single passenger train. The Commission, like regulatory bodies more generally, could not confiscate the property of a railroad by requiring indefinite continuation of losing operations. Following its doctrine on branch line abandonments, the ICC announced it would not indefinitely require the continuance of an unprofitable passenger train merely because the railroad as a whole was profitable.

Almost simultaneously with its acquisition of powers over discontinuance of passenger trains the Commission received a report from one of its examiners on the problem of passenger trains. The Hosmer Report of 1958, which was an excellent piece of applied economics, demonstrated that the decline in demand for railroad passenger service could be extrapolated with confidence and that the passenger train was not cost-competitive with its rivals.[11] Examiner Hosmer concluded that the passenger train was doomed to extinction, but the political pressure for continuance of passenger service was considerable. The Commission was unwilling to accept the Hosmer Report and instead issued a doctrine that the passenger train as a whole was a vital part of the national transportation system, which should be expected to continue indefinitely. Thus, the Commission had enunciated two irreconcilable doctrines, for, given the Hosmer Report's demonstration that currently profitable passenger trains would inevitably become unprofitable, it was impossible in the long run for the Commission to perpetuate the passenger train as a national institution, while refusing to perpetuate unprofitable trains individually simply because the railroads operating them remained profitable.

The ICC throughout the 1960s tried to implement both of these doctrines, invoking one or the other, depending on the political circumstances of the case.[12] As it recognized that the cross-subsidy of the passenger train was becoming increasingly unworkable, the Commission sought to perpetuate a basic network of the most heavily-travelled trains between major cities until a public system could be set up to run them. The Commission, consequently, became a leading advocate of such a system.

The proponents of a national railroad passenger system held exaggerated hopes for the ability of the passenger train to reclaim intercity travellers. As might have been expected, travellers of high valuation of time had deserted the passenger train earliest, so that the demand for Pullman and dining car accommodation declined more rapidly than demand for coach service. The railroads adapted to the decline in demand by reducing their offerings of Pullman, dining, and lounging service, and other luxury aspects of railroading more rapidly than trains were withdrawn. This was interpreted by groups which retained a desire for high quality of service, who nevertheless had a low evaluation of time—notably the affluent elderly—as a conscious effort of railroads to discourage use of trains by lowering the standards of accommodations. Those who held this view, who were numerous, believed that massive revival of passenger traffic could be brought about through increasing the quality of service. The National Association of Railroad Passengers, the principal lobbying group for the federal system, expressed the hope that intercity passenger volume could be restored to about the 1950s level.

Accordingly, the National Railroad Passenger Corporation (Amtrak) developed a plan embodying two major elements: first, the determination of the geographical passenger service; and second, an effort to upgrade the quality of service. Although Amtrak was set up as a public corporation seeking a profit, it did not develop its national network to maximize net receipts, but rather attempted to provide a nation-wide rail system with service on the major transcontinental routes. Thus, for example, Amtrak established routes between New Orleans to Los Angeles, Chicago and Los Angeles, Chicago and San Francisco, Chicago and Seattle, and in particular a route up and down the west coast from San Diego to Seattle. Initially, it was thought that this arrangement required Amtrak to squander its resources on long-distance trains of limited traffic potential through the arid west. At the time, it was argued by proponents of the system that the passenger train had a comparative advantage for service in corridors of up to 400 miles, as for example, Chicago to St. Louis, Detroit, and Cleveland. There was a further bias in the system's network resulting from the fortuitous location of political strength in the formulation of policy. Because the chairman of the House Commerce Committee and a prominent member of the ICC come from West Virginia, at various times three passenger trains have been run east and west through the state, which has limited demand for passenger service. Similarly, Amtrak has had to provide two routes through Montana on the former Great Northern and Northern Pacific main lines because of the political strength of senators from Montana. Because members of Congress from Ohio have shown no especial interest in transportation, that populous state receives a relatively small coverage of passenger trains: Cleveland was not served by Amtrak at all in the initial plan and only recently has a train been instituted through Cleveland on the former New York Central main line.

The upgrading of the quality of service has been implemented in part through extensive restoration of dining car and lounge car service, and by institution of Pullman cars on all long distance trains. Such equipment is extremely labor-intensive, but Congress secured no quid-pro-quo for establishment of the system in the form of relaxed work rules from the unions. As a result, the labor intensiveness of passenger service, which was a principal force driving passenger trains to extinction, has not only failed to be ameliorated, but has actually been aggravated by establishment of Amtrak.

In fiscal 1975, Amtrak trains earned a revenue per passenger mile of 6.30 cents. The cost per revenue passenger mile was 13.61 cents, resulting in a loss of 7.31 cents per revenue passenger mile. In other words, the cost of providing the service was somewhat more than double the revenue from it. Yet despite this subsidy, Amtrak's ridership has declined since the petroleum shortage of 1974. Amtrak has thus continued the previous pattern of rail passenger service in its inability to retain passengers attracted by temporary impediments to or increases in the cost of rival services, such as airline strikes. This record suggests that Amtrak has no considerable growth potential in ridership and that all that can be hoped for is some small marginal movement to trains in response to improvement in their service, or movement of the fare differentials between train and bus in favor of the train. Unfortunately, since the cost of moving people by train is somewhat more than double the cost of moving them by bus, this can be accomplished only by considerable subsidy.

In spite of the fact that the passenger train continues to fail a market test, the statutory authority of Amtrak requires the corporation to institute an experimental train service each year. A service between Chicago and Boston, for example, has just been instituted. Thus, the network is expanding in the face of market indications that it should contract. In a recent publication of criteria for expansion and contraction, the corporation indicated its own position on the problem by stating that it looks upon discontinuance of trains as a last resort.

The principal consequence of the federal government's operation of the Amtrak system is interference with the comparative advantage of buses for short to medium range movement. Proponents of the Amtrak program had anticipated that trains would show a comparative advantage for trips up to 400 miles, but outside of the northeast corridor services these have proved the most unprofitable of Amtrak's operations. Amtrak's short-haul trains other than its Boston-New York-Washington trains, have grossed 6.12 cents per revenue passenger mile and cost 19.69 cents per revenue passenger mile to operate, for a loss of

13.57 cents per passenger mile. In contrast, the Washington-New York-Boston trains have lost only 4.89 cents per mile, and Amtrak's long haul trains have lost only 7.06 cents per passenger mile. This situation interferes with the cross-subsidy of lightly travelled bus routes by major bus routes, for Amtrak competes almost exclusively with the bus companies' mainline operations. Similarly, the Washington-New York-Boston trains of Amtrak interfere with the cross-subsidy of Eastern Airlines' services to minor points from its earnings on its New York-Washington, and New York-Boston shuttle services.

The planning which went into the Amtrak system has been essentially conservative: to preserve from extinction a form of transportation which has failed the market test. The planning for novelty in the system has been limited to the introduction of some articulated turbine trains of French manufacture, but these have not been able to overcome the intrinsic disadvantages of rail transportation. The net consequence of the program, as stated, has been interference with the realization of comparative advantage of bus and air carriers and interference in the cross-subsidy in their operations.

CONRAIL

The ConRail system for merger and operation of the bankrupt Northeastern Railroads is up to now entirely a planning operation. At the present writing, the ConRail system is in the process of formation but has not yet begun operations. Accordingly, the nature of the planning process is clear, but the experience is yet in doubt.

The weakness of the northeastern railroads is a manifestation of the decline of the railroad industry relative to its rivals over approximately the past sixty years. The forces for the railroads' decline may be classified under three headings: an inappropriate economic organization; an undesirable geographical pattern; and an archaic technology of coupling and braking.

The economic organization of the railroads is a mixed private and public cartel. The private portion is a set of regional cartels, the descendents of the railroad pools of the late 19th century, no longer engaging in pooling, and currently known as rate bureaus. The public portion of the cartel is the Interstate Commerce Commission, a body established in 1887 for the stabilization of the private cartels, but converted in 1920 to an outright cartelizing body with rights of minimum rate regulation and the other usual accoutrements of a cartelizing organization. The cartel was extended to common carriers and contract carriers by road in 1935 and by water in 1940, though both of these classes of carrier have abundant exemptions. This is, in fact, a cartel of 100 percent of railroading, about 39 percent of trucking and somewhat under 10 percent of inland barge operation. It is essentially a non-pooling cartel, which is to say that the ICC has no powers to issue quotas to the carriers.

Rather, the Commission uses its rate regulation powers to allocate traffic among carriers. As Professor Ernest W. Williams has demonstrated, when confronted by a controversy for traffic between railroad and truck lines, the commission habitually sets the rates at levels at which some shippers will prefer the higher quality of service at higher rates by trucks and some the lower quality of service at the rail rate.[13] This practice prevents the price system from allocating traffic among the modes of transport in accordance with the comparative advantage of each on the basis of distance, damage proneness and other characteristics. Worse, the cartel produces the predictable cartel consequence of extensive idleness of resources, which manifests itself in this instance in underutilized railroad main lines, survival of branch lines on which traffic has largely disappeared, empty truck movements, and underutilized towboats.

The policy pursued toward this industry has perpetuated the 19th century geographical pattern of the railroads, in which the companies which parallel one another between major points are organized into individual cartels, as for example Chicago-Omaha, Chicago-Twin Cities, Chicago-Kansas City, and Chicago to the east coast ports. The consequence is a geographical balkanization of the railroads and an organization of the industry in which the firms are continually both rivals and joint venturers. This situation produces a thoroughly undesirable set of incentives for the firms. A railroad receiving a shipment from a connecting railroad has an incentive only to get it to its destination as cheaply as possible. The receiving railroad receives no reward for speed and has no penalty for damage to cargo, the claims for which, in general, are borne by the originating railroad. This results in highly irregular arrival times, relatively low rate of utilization of cars, and high incidence of damage claims relative to rival forms of transport.

This economic organization and geographical pattern of the industry tends to perpetuate the technology of the Janney coupler and the Westinghouse air brake, which were developed in the immediate post-Civil War periods. This technology, which was automatic by the standards of 1870, entails a longitudinal movement of couplers which is damaging to cargo, and a pneumatic transmission of the brake impulse which is necessarily not instanteneous. This technology adds to the adverse damage experience of the railroads through the slack action, especially in high speed braking operations. It also presents dangers to on-line communities from derailments of trains through track-train dynamic interactions. In addition, this technology tends to produce strong unions by providing many groups an opportunity to tie up railroading by interfering with coupling, braking, classification and operation. The coupling impacts with which cars are brought together in the coupling braking system is the principal source of the damage claims which constitute one of the industry's principal handicaps.

The Eastern railroads have recently suffered somewhat more than the rest of the industry from the forces acting against the railroads. The country has shifted from a pattern in which manufactured products were produced mainly in the northeast and shipped out in box cars which brought agricultural products back to the northeast. American industry is now concentrated in three major strip developments: from Portland, Maine to Norfolk, centering on New York; from Green Bay to Utica, centering on Chicago; and from the Mexican border to the north suburbs of San Francisco, centering on Los Angeles. Raw materials tend to move toward these strip developments for manufacture, but the manufactured products tend to move toward destinations within the strip developments by truck.

Because the eastern railroads have older and poorer physical plants, they are more expensive to operate. Much of their mileage was built to serve coalfields (especially in the anthracite area of eastern Pennsylvania), which are no longer economic. Recently as they have declined, these railroads have become more dependent on the steel industry at a time when the country appears to be losing its comparative advantage for steel production. The eastern railroads over time have become mainly inbound terminating facilities for industries whose products move by truck. The area they serve increasingly produces services such as medicine, higher education, insurance and financial services of all sorts, the products of which are not shipped at all.

Among the inappropriate incentives which the present organization of railroads gives to member firms is the incentive to merge parallel lines. A pattern of end-to-end mergers could create nation-wide railroads which, with a containerized technology reaching off-line points by truck or water carrier, would allow the industry to be competitively organized. The railroads have no incentive to merge in end-to-end fashion; rather, they have the incentive to merge parallel lines to consolidate terminal facilities and to use the better of the parallel rights of way for long distance traffic. Similarly, the Interstate Commerce Commission has no incentive to produce end-to-end mergers, but rather is to merge weak railroads with strong so as to cross-subsidize the weak railroads and to perpetuate mileage for the gratification of the political interests which exert pressure on the Commission.

The merger of the Pennsylvania Railroad and the New York Central Railroad and New York, New Haven and Hartford into the Penn Central system in 1968 had aspects of both motivations. The Pennsylvania and New York Central wanted to merge to consolidate facilities and route long distance freight over the New York Central's superior physical plant. The ICC exerted strong pressure to accept the New Haven which had ceased to be viable as an independent railroad. The merger proved to be a disaster. The combined railroad proved to be more expensive to operate than the predecessor companies and the Penn Central went bankrupt in 1970. It proved to have no prospect of reorganization as a profitable carrier under Section 77 of the Bankruptcy Act. Seven other eastern railroads were also bankrupt by 1973, only one of which, the Boston and Maine, was thought to be capable of reorganization as a profitable corporation. The aggregate mileage of the eight carriers was 26,790, of which 72.6 percent was the Penn Central. The trustees of the Penn Central estimated that as a railroad of about 11,000 miles, some 57 percent of the company's 19,480 miles, the Penn Central could have been economic. The ICC's abandonment control prevented paring of the railroad down in this fashion. Similarly, the railroad was unable to relieve itself of its passenger obligations, which remained a source of losses even though virtually all its passenger trains were operated under subsidy.

By 1973 the trustees of the Penn Central concluded that the company could not be reorganized profitably and proposed to sell it off in pieces. The organization of the company in leased lines would have facilitated this controlled dissolution. Such a resolution of the problem would have made possible a movement toward a geographical pattern that would make industry competitive. That is, if the leased lines of Penn Central had been sold off to western and southern railroads, the industry would have moved away from its present geographical balkanization toward a pattern of nation-wide railroads.

This was not done, however. Rather, in the Regional Rail Reorganization Act of 1973, Congress authorized an elaborate process of planning the ConRail system as a northeast regional carrier based mainly on a reduced mileage of the Penn Central. According to the Final System Plan of ConRail, presented to Congress on July 26, 1975, the federal government will establish a single ConRail system of about 15,000 miles which means only about 5,700 miles of the bankrupt carriers will be abandoned. The east end of the Erie Lackawanna will be sold to the Chesapeake & Ohio and the west end abandoned. The C & O system will sell its Washington-New York line to ConRail, and the New York-Washington line of the Penn Central will be transferred to Amtrak. Small portions of the bankrupts will be transferred to the Norfolk & Western and the Grand Trunk Western.

Apart from perpetuating the present regional pattern of the railroads, the act of 1973 will invest about $1 billion to $1.5 billion in rights-of-way and some larger amount, possibly as much as $7 billion, will be put into locomotives and rolling stock, plus some incidental betterments. Thus by investing in present technology, the planning operation will tend to perpetuate the Janney coupler and the Westinghouse airbrake.

The planning operation also preserves the present economic organization of the railroads, for ConRail is explicitly to be a railroad within the present framework of public policy, which is to say within the sponsored cartel and subject to existing common carrier obligations.

Consequently, the planning operation involved in formation of ConRail is a conservative one in the most rigorous meaning of conservative: perpetuating what currently exists, rather than being innovative in any sense. The plan tends to perpetuate essentially all of what is wrong in railroads and to make ultimate resolutions of the problem more difficult. Like most such policies, the ConRail program will have the effect of making people dependent for income on the resource misallocations produced by the policy, and therefore, like other such policies, it will tend to generate its own political support for continuance.[14]

CONCLUSIONS

While American transportation planning has ranged over a wide area of institutional problems, it is a highly consistent activity. The policies considered here have revealed six common characteristics: (1) There is no effort to achieve an optimum allocation of resources in the economic sense. Although cost-benefit analysis is conducted in road building and investment in public facilities of some other sorts (though not in transit planning), no effort is made to achieve optimality in the economist's sense of equating marginal cost and marginal benefit, and assuring that resources have gone to their highest valued use. None of the statutory authorities of the programs considered here specify an effort to optimize the use of resources in this sense, and program administrators do not seek such optimality.

(2) The principal implementation of the planning is investment. In all cases no effort has been made to secure economical use of the facility through appropriate pricing-devices. This situation follows from the nature of the incentives upon Congress and upon the administrators of the program. No one can secure an entrepreneurial gain or other private benefit from economization of the facilities through prices, which would maximize net receipts. Rather, pricing devices which encourage chronic excess demands under peak demand conditions consequently create political demands for additional investment, which is consistent with monument-building by the authorities in charge.

The experience with automobile emission and safety requirements is a variation of this. The implementation requires investment in anti-pollution and safety devices rather than imposing variable user charges on roads and taxes on noxious emissions. Such pricing would, among other benefits, yield a considerable improvement in highway accident experience by increasing the vehicle loads, reducing the number of peak-hour trips, and reducing home-to-work distances. It was noted in connection with highways and rail transit that the implementation of policy by investment is so extreme as not even to provide adequately for maintenance and operating expenses. Analogous to this in auto emission controls, no incentive is given to maintain the control devices. Indeed, there is an incentive either to neglect or to disconnect them. Similarly there is an incentive, for those whose preference is not to have safety control devices on the vehicles, to disconnect them or otherwise to circumvent their use. In general, no charge for such circumvention is made except the rather remote threat of police action if circumvention is detected.

(3) The planning in each case accepts any inappropriate economic organization which may exist: the cartelization of airlines, the monopolization of transit systems, the geographical pattern of railroading created by the late 19th century railroad cartels, and the strength of unions throughout the transportation industry.

(4) The planning tends to solidify and perpetuate existing technologies, as for example, the 40-to-50-passenger Diesel bus, the streetcar, the multiple-unit subway car, the technology of the passenger train, and the present system of railroading with independent locomotives, the Janney coupler and the Westinghouse airbrake. Similarly, both safety and pollution regulations have tended to freeze the design of front-engined, water-cooled automobiles of the present American type.

(5) Transportation planning has been a poor innovative device. It failed to anticipate containerization in merchant ship design. The only two major efforts to move forward into new technologies which the market would not bring forth were unsuccessful: personal rapid transit[15] and the supersonic transport.[16] Judgment must be reserved on the air bag until it has been tried or been subjected to greater experimentation.

(6) Planning has interfered with the market mechanism's function of phasing out activities. It has perpetuated the intercity passenger train in the face of superior alternatives that would have extinguished it. It has perpetuated monopolized linear transit systems in the face of a preferable alternative, jitney systems.

The principal lesson to be drawn from American transportation planning with respect to the prospects for more general public planning in the economy is that planning tends to be counter-productive relative to its advocates' intentions. It tends to be inherently conservative or even outrightly reactionary with respect to innovation, and also to the economic function of phasing out activities. Interference with these functions in the economy more broadly promises to be exceedingly costly.

HOUSING AND LAND USE

RICHARD MUTH
Professor of Economics, Stanford University

This paper will consider the problem of government housing and land use planning in three parts. The first will consider urban housing problems and the performance of the private market in the post-World War II period. The second will examine shortcomings in prior government intervention into lower-income housing markets, as well as outline several better approaches for improving lower-income housing. And the final section will consider the underlying rationale for public land use planning and suggest several important reforms for government actions affecting urban land uses.

THE NATURE OF URBAN HOUSING PROBLEMS

At the present time, many people believe that our urban housing problems result from institutional shortcomings which have caused deterioration of inner-city housing. The same people often attribute deterioration rather vaguely to a lack of planning and collective control.[1] But they also cite many specific sources of deterioration as well. Among these are external diseconomies imposed by hostile land-uses, the failure of municipal governments to establish and enforce proper zoning or other restrictions, and the failure of local governments to supply various sections of the city with adequate schools, parks, and garbage disposal. Whatever reason given for it, deterioration is almost always said to explain why previous residents moved out and were replaced by lower-income families who cannot afford better housing. What is needed, therefore—this analysis concludes—is better planning, more zoning restrictions, and stricter building and occupancy code requirements, to prevent further deterioration of our central cities.

This theory in my judgment is almost totally incorrect. First, it attributes neighborhood deterioration to reduced demand for housing in these neighborhoods by groups previously living there. If this were true, housing in these neighborhoods should be very cheap. Yet it is also widely believed, with little empirical support, that poor-quality housing is especially expensive for its inhabitants. Furthermore, when areas are redeveloped under programs like the Federal Urban Renewal Program, which supposedly exist to encourage more valuable uses of land, the sales value of the cleared, redeveloped land should exceed the cost of acquisition and redevelopment.[2] Yet precisely the reverse has been true for virtually all urban renewal projects. Finally, if past deterioration has resulted from lack of appropriate government intervention into urban housing markets, the quality of central city housing should have grown continually worse during the post-war period. This is widely believed to be the case, but as I will argue presently, precisely the opposite is the case.

In the post-war period, changes in central city housing have resulted primarily from increased market demand for lower-income housing. During and after World War II, most central cities in the United States experienced increased immigration of lower-income families (especially black families) from the rural South. This immigration is explained by earnings differences: in 1949, average annual non-white, rural farm incomes were only $486, whereas in the Great Lakes states, for non-white urban and (non-farm rural) incomes, the figure was $1,753.[3] Following the first waves of migrants to this country arriving here in the middle of the last century, recent urban migrants tended to live primarily in older, more centrally-located urban housing. As their numbers grew, the rental values of lower-income housing tended to rise relative to the rentals paid by higher-income residents living near them. It therefore became profitable for owners in better areas adjacent to the lower-income areas to sell to lower-income families. The lower-income neighborhoods of the city thus tended to grow outward from the center, though more rapidly in certain directions than others.

Since the lower-income families unsurprisingly spend less for housing than higher-income families, the outward expansion of the former caused conversion of dwellings, accomplished in part by physical alterations to accommodate a greater number of persons per structure. But conversion was also accomplished by reducing current expenditures for maintenance and operation, therefore allowing newly acquired lower-income housing to deteriorate in quality. Thus, deterioration did not cause succession to lower-income occupancy, but, rather, resulted from it.

There is strong empirical evidence that the quality of a housing stock adapts to the income level of its occupants. In examining the relation of housing quality to income and a variety of other factors, I have found a strong and consistent relation between housing quality and income.[4] Thus, for example, a 10 percent increase in income will tend to reduce by about one-third the fraction of dwellings substandard—that is, dilapidated or lacking certain plumbing facilities.

Now it might be argued that such a relation results (as among different parts of a given city) because of the effect housing quality has on income. However, I found the latter effect to be small.[5] In addition, the same relationship can be found in comparing different central cities, where the effect of quality on income is presumably smaller than it is in comparing different parts of the same city. Furthermore, the relations found at a given time are quantitatively consistent with changes occurring for the nation as a whole during the decade of the 1950s. Another study which examined changes taking place during the 1960s found substantially the same relationship: the primary cause of the change in the number of low-quality dwellings in different cities was the change in the number of lower-income families.[6]

It is widely believed that the quality of central-city housing has deteriorated throughout the post-war period. Nothing could be further from the truth. According to a study comparing data on housing quality from 1950 to 1956—except in New York City, where rent controls existed during the period—the fraction of dwellings substandard declined during that period by about one-third.[7] Furthermore, 90 percent of the decline resulted from improvement in the quality of given units, with only 10 percent resulting from demolitions, mergers, or other changes. Moreover, a comparison of data on dwelling condition between 1950 and 1960 revealed that the fraction of dwellings substandard in forty or so central cities declined during the 1950s from roughly 20 percent to 11 percent, or by about one-half.[8]

The 1970 Census of Housing collected no data on structural condition, which makes it impossible to calculate strictly comparable totals of units lacking plumbing facilities from the 1960 and 1970 Census tabulations. Estimates have been made, however, that the stock of central-city housing units lacking plumbing facilities declined by at least 55 percent, and perhaps by as much as 60 percent during the most recent decade.[9] If these trends continue—and there is every reason to believe they will—housing equivalent to the worst fifth of the stock in 1950 will all but disappear from our central cities by 1980.

It is not difficult to understand the striking improvement in central-city housing once it is realized that occupant income is the strongest factor determining housing quality. To be sure, as the absolute size of, say, the lowest fifth of the population by income grew, the area they inhabited grew as well. In the process, some dwelling units deteriorated in quality and, no doubt, passed from standard to substandard quality level. At the same time, average income levels, including those of the lowest fifth of the income distribution, increased dramatically during the post-war period.[10] With higher incomes, lower-income families were willing to spend more for housing, and the quality of housing demands therefore rose. The owners of existing units thus found it profitable to improve them. The evidence discussed earlier reveals the extent to which the private market has responded to effective demand for improved housing.

THE EFFECTS OF GOVERNMENTAL HOUSING PROGRAMS

Advocates of governmental housing programs argue that the programs are needed because the private market has failed to provide suitable housing for lower-income families. The argument is deficient in two respects. In the first place, it is not clear that the private market has failed in providing housing for lower-income families. While the increased numbers of low-income families in our central cities have increased the number of lower-income occupied units, at the same time the evidence just discussed clearly indicates that rising income levels have improved average housing quality. Lower-income families are certainly less well housed than most of us who are better off, but they are also more poorly fed, clothed, and provided with medical and legal services. The problem is not housing, but poverty, and poor quality housing is merely the most visible manifestation of poverty.

Even granted that the private market has failed to provide lower-income families with the quality of housing many of us would like them to have, it by no means follows that government should therefore provide lower-income housing. Since the problem of the poor is poverty and not housing, government provision of housing will almost certainly result in wasted resources—that is, it will improve the well-being of the poor less than their well-being could be improved by an equal cost of resources used in other ways.

Moreover, government intervention into lower-income housing markets may actually make lower-income families worse off than they would have been without the intervention. If this sounds fanciful, in 1968 the Douglas Commission estimated that governmental programs have caused the demolition of at least one million dwellings, most of them inhabited by lower-income families.[11] Roughly one-third of these occurred under the public housing program, one-third under urban renewal, and one-third under the federal highway program. The Commission was unable to estimate demolitions under local code-enforcement programs, although these have almost certainly removed many additional dwellings from the lower-income stock. On the other hand, as of 1968, the public housing program, which was the principal construction program up to that time, had provided only about two-thirds of a million units. Thus, in contrast to the private market, which has substantially improved the quality of central-city lower-income housing, on balance, government programs have probably reduced housing opportunities for the lower-income population as a whole.

In view of their quantitative importance, it is useful to analyze more carefully the impact of demolitions on the lower-income population. The initial result of tearing down units previously inhabited by lower-income families is an excess demand for lower-income housing at current rentals. This leads, in turn, to increased market rentals for lower-income dwellings. Increased rentals may well induce some lower-income families to spend still more on housing to maintain the quality of their housing. But many others will remain in poorer-quality dwellings, either by doubling up and/or inhabiting dwellings of still lower quality than they otherwise would have. It is by no means true that making housing more expensive for lower-income families will improve their average housing quality.

Increasing lower-income rentals will encourage the private market to respond and undo the initial effects of demolition. The rise in rentals will make it profitable for some private owners to convert once better-quality housing to lower-income occupancy. The rise in lower-income rentals will also induce owners of structures to spend more on them, thereby improving already-existing lower-income housing. This increased private output of lower-income housing moderates the rise of rentals paid for lower-income housing. In the long-run, therefore, the private market will repair at least part of the damage caused lower-income families by government demolitions.

While many people now realize that demolishing private lower-income dwellings hurts the poor, few realize that strict enforcement of building and occupancy codes has similar effects. By limiting the ways in which existing dwellings may be modified for lower-income occupancy, code-enforcement increases the expense of converting better housing to lower-income occupancy. In the short-run, it is true, stricter code-enforcement may permit some lower-income families to inhabit better-quality housing than they would otherwise. But in the long run, as the lower-income population grows, strict code enforcement will reduce conversion to low-income housing, and therefore by reducing the total stock of low-income dwellings, will increase lower-income rentals. While code-enforcement can improve low income housing, it can only do so by increasing the rentals paid for it.

When government directly provides low-income housing, housing opportunities will improve for the lower-income population as a whole. Since fewer low-income families must now seek housing in the private market, the effects on that market are essentially the reverse of the effects caused by demolitions. At the same time, the long-term effect on private rentals is probably small.[12]

There is no question that families given the chance to live in government housing are thereby made better off. In the public housing program, for example, waiting lists for admission are often as long as the lists of occupied units, a fact which strongly indicates its superiority to private housing, at the same rental.

Although housing programs for the poor do improve their well being, for the same cost those who benefit from these programs could be made still better off. There are two reasons for this. Except for the Rent Supplement Program and Section 8 (neither of which have yet had much impact), government housing programs reduce the rents paid by lower-income families by subsidizing the capital costs of housing. Under the public housing program, local housing authorities finance the acquisition of structures by the sale of bonds, whose interest income is exempt from federal income taxation. Historically, the federal government has paid 90 percent of the interest and amortization costs of these bonds, and local housing authorities pay no property taxes. Under a variety of other programs, low-income dwellings are financed by mortgages at rates substantially below market rates. Rarely, however, does the government subsidize current expenditure for maintenance and operation.

As a result, local housing authorities and other providers of low-income housing under governmental programs can reduce rentals (and increase subsidies) by increasing capital outlays and reducing current expenditures. There are many ways they can do this. Among them, they can use more expensive and durable construction materials, more insulation to reduce heating costs. If, as under the Public Housing Program, a dollar's worth of capital costs the local housing authority five cents and the authority pushes the substitution of capital for current expenditure to the limit, the economy will have sacrificed—which means wasted—ninety-five cents worth of output on the marginal unit of capital used. This means, of course, that if less capital were used per public housing unit, a greater number of units could be built for the same resource cost to the economy as a whole. I have estimated that five public housing units could have been built for every four actually built if rental payments had been subsidized directly, rather than indirectly through capital subsidies.[13]

It is possible, of course, to correct the mistakes of past governmental programs and a start has been made in that direction. Among other reforms, demolitions of private lower-income units have been reduced in recent years. Furthermore, the Housing and Community Development Act of 1974 now directly subsidizes rental payments, rather than capital costs of low-income housing.[14] All subsidy programs, however, suffer a similar, fundamental defect: the value of additional housing is worth less to a low-income family than an income subsidy of the same cost to the government.

In allocating limited incomes to maximize their value all families divide their expenditures on food, housing and other items, so that the added value they derive per dollar spent on each item is the same. Thus, when a family's income rises, it will generally spend more on every kind of consumption. The reason is that the added value or satisfaction received from a dollar spent on housing depends on how much furniture the family has, the amount of fuel for heating and lighting it uses, and so on. It is widely believed that as incomes rise, expenditures on housing rise but at a smaller proportional rate. Properly interpreted, however, the evidence suggests that housing expenditures rise at least in proportion to income.[15] Regardless, it is safe to assume families adopt patterns of expenditure which they find best for themselves. If left free to spend its additional income as it wishes, each family can maximize the value of additional income and preserve the equality of the additional satisfaction it gets from each dollar spent. And no realignment of its consumption expenditure can make the family better-off.

The situation is quite different, however, under a housing subsidy program. Under these programs a family is typically given the opportunity to live in a larger, better-quality dwelling unit than it would (or could) have purchased for the same expenditure on the private market.[16] The program does nothing, however, to permit the family to increase expenditures on other kinds of consumption. The extra housing is worth less to the family than the cost of providing it; the family would feel better off if it were permitted to increase its housing consumption less, but its other consumption as well. To pick an extreme case, an additional bedroom may be worth relatively little if a family does not have furniture for it. As a result, the family could have been made as well off by giving it a lesser amount of income to spend as it wished than the cost of producing the additional housing provided under the housing program.

Not only is the extra housing worth less to the family receiving it than the resource cost of providing it, the discrepancy grows relatively larger, the greater the amount of housing provided. As a matter of fact, relatively few low-income families, perhaps one in ten, have benefited from federal housing programs. Those who do benefit, however, receive relatively big increases in their housing consumption.[17] Seen in these terms, the value of the public housing program to the average lower income family is about $5 per month in 1965 prices. But if the additional housing produced by the public housing program had been equally divided among the lower-income population, it would have been worth about $8.30 per month. Moreover, if the subsidy had been given equally and in cash, it would have been worth $9.10.[18] Thus, although a general income subsidy is superior, in principle the benefits of federal housing programs have been diluted primarily by concentrating them on a small fraction of the lower-income population.

What justification is there for having a housing program rather than an income subsidy program for lower income families? In part, housing and other such programs might be justified if they produced what economists call external benefits—that is, beyond those received directly by the individual recipient but received indirectly by the public as a whole. Many sources of indirect benefit have been suggested. Limitation of space make it impossible to analyze them here. In my judgment however, the external benefits of housing programs are likely to be small.[19] On the other hand, some people argue for housing programs on the grounds that Congress will enact housing programs, but not income subsidy programs. This is a complicated issue and one I do not feel competent to appraise. But accepting it as valid for sake of argument, what kind of housing program would produce the greatest benefit at a given cost?

First of all, the program should avoid demolitions and stricter code enforcements, both of which may improve average housing quality somewhat, but will do so only by making housing more expensive to low-income families. Second, the program should avoid capital subsidies to producers of housing because they increase the cost of providing additional housing for lower-income families. Finally, housing subsidies should be divided equally among the whole low-income population rather than concentrated (as now) on a fraction of those families. Thus, the dilution of program benefits in relation to cost is kept to a minimum.

Housing allowances or rental voucher programs are ideal

vehicles for accomplishing these objectives. Under these programs each low-income family is given a voucher which it can use to supplement its own resources in purchasing housing in the private market. Landlords, in turn, can redeem these certificates for cash. Under a voucher program, the total subsidy could readily be divided among the whole of the low-income population, with allowances perhaps being made for income and family size in determining the voucher size for individual families. Since rental payments would be subsidized, producers of housing could use the additional rental receipts for maintenance and operation as well as for capital improvements. Finally, instead of demolition, private producers would have an incentive to rehabilitate existing structures.

In addition, the program would be simple to administer. The principal task would be to determine eligibility, and this could be done the same way that income tax withholding rates are determined. Families would be less readily identified as subsidy recipients than they are under current programs, and they would almost certainly be less concentrated spatially. The principal objection to such a program is that rents would simply rise without any quality improvement. The post-war improvement in central-city housing quality that resulted from rising incomes and housing expenditures, however, suggest a different result. At any rate, a ''yardstick of competition'' could easily be provided by allowing local housing authorities and limited dividend corporations to participate in the program.

LAND USE PLANNING

Since World War II, as our urban areas have grown in population and land area, arguments have increased for government intervention in the urban growth process. The purposes of intervention address a number of perceived problems—but the primary purposes are to limit population of urban centers and the land area they occupy, and to utilize urban land more efficiently. As in discussions of central-city housing quality, proponents of urban land use planning blame the problems they see on shortcomings in the market allocation of resources. However, even more than with central-city housing, problems of urban land use result from past government mistakes; and increasing the government's role in land use planning would be rather like assigning the fox to guard the hen-house.

Post-war urban growth is the result of two primary causes: population increases, and migration from rural areas. A long-term decline in demand for farm labor relative to non-farm occupations, combined with a long-standing over-allocation of labor to Southern agriculture, were the major causes of farm-to-city migration. But migration was also encouraged by government agriculture programs which reduced the land input into farming, and together with fixed prices for farm products, thereby reduced the demand for farm labor. Apart from eliminating the effects of misguided government intervention in agriculture, there is little rationale for limiting farm-to-city migration. For such limitations only limit the opportunities of part of the population to earn an income, and thereby reduce the nation's income.

Besides population increases, our urban land area has grown because of the tendency for greater urban population growth in peripheral areas than in the older, central cities. This "flight to the suburbs" is widely attributed to deterioration in the physical condition of the central city. Actually, physical deterioration has had little to do with post-war urban decentralization.[20] Decentralization has, rather, continued a process that has been going on for at least a century. Post-war suburbanization, like that which preceded it, is the result principally of two factors—rising income and improvements in commuter transportation.

Increasing incomes have increased the amount of housing the average family wishes to consume. In the short run, demand for suburban housing rises because suburban housing is typically larger and of better quality than older, central-city housing. However, the fact that at a given moment those cities where incomes are higher are also more decentralized, suggests that long-run forces are also at work.[21] Housing demand at different distances from the center of an urban area depends upon the relation of housing expenditures to the costs of commuting an extra mile to a downtown job. The greater housing expenditures are relative to commuting costs, the farther from the center the average family will live. As income rises, expenditures for housing tend to rise more rapidly than expenditures for commuting. As income rises, then, the demand for housing in the outer part of the urban area rises relative to demand close to the center, and population grows more rapidly in the area's outer parts. I have recently calculated that higher income accounts for roughly two-thirds of the decentralization occurring from 1950 to 1970.[22]

The other important cause of decentralization has been a reduction in the cost of commuting. Perhaps two-thirds of commuting costs are the cost of time spent in commuting. Though time costs have risen because of commuters' increased earnings, this rise has been more than offset by increases in the speed of commuter travel. The construction of urban freeways, largely with federal funds, has substantially increased—perhaps doubled—the speed of automobiles used in commuting, from something like twenty to forty miles per hour. As with an increase in income, reducing the cost of commuting increases demand for housing in the outer parts of urban areas and leads to greater rates of population growth there. Quantitatively, post-war reductions in commuting costs have had about the same impact upon urban population distribution as rising incomes. These two factors together have reduced by one-half the degree of urban population centralization.[23]

By reducing the time spent in commuting, commuters' time and other resources are saved. However, it is not clear that the benefit of that saving is worth the cost of increasing commuter travel speed. My own tentative calculations suggest that land used in housing is far more valuable than land used for urban streets.[24] This means, of course, that we have spent too much on urban transportation and produced too much decentralization. My calculations suggest that our urban centers occupy perhaps 50 percent more land area than they would if land were allocated to equalize the value of uses for transportation and other uses.

The federal government has also encouraged too much decentralization by reducing the cost of owner-occupied as compared with rental housing. It has done so in two important ways: by income-tax treatment of income from owner-occupied housing, and by federal mortgage interest subsidy programs. Under the federal and by most state personal income taxes, homeowners need not report the imputed rental value of their homes as income, as they would if they rented it to others; and they can deduct mortgage interest and property taxes paid. The dollar cost for a homeowner occupying his house is thus substantially below the cost of his renting the same house from someone else. Moreover, the reduction in interest cost of homeownership provided by FHA mortgage insurance and VA mortgage guarantees is another important factor in reducing the cost of ownership, as compared to renting. I have estimated that the two factors together may reduce the price of housing by as much as one-third.[25] Reducing the cost of homeownership as compared with renting, in turn, encourages more urban decentralization than would otherwise occur. My calculations suggest that the land area occupied by cities is perhaps 15 percent larger because of the federal income tax advantage to homeownership alone.[26]

To recapitulate this discussion of forces producing urban growth, there is little reason to suppose that urban decentralization has resulted from undesirable central city conditions which better planning might prevent. Government itself has encouraged the growth in land area occupied by cities in several ways through undesirable policies and bad planning. Federal farm programs, in reducing land used in agriculture, have reduced farm labor demand and contributed to urban population growth. Through government we may have over-invested in urban roads, reducing the cost of commuting greater distances, thereby substantially increasing urban decentralization. Tax treatment of income from homeownership and federal mortgage programs, by reducing the cost of homeownership vs. renting, have also encouraged decentralization to an important degree. Since government policies themselves have contributed considerably to urban decentralization it is far from clear that increased government intervention in urban land markets is a means for limiting future urban decentralization.

There are a variety of evils which are said to result from unregulated urban growth. Some of these, however, are not evils at all and are quite adequately handled by the market mechanism. It is often argued, for instance, that urban growth uses land needed for agriculture. At the same time, this country has long been a net explorer of farm products, and until quite recently federal farm programs even sought to remove "excess" farm land from agricultural production. The coastal areas of California are among the few places where conversions of orchards and vineyards to urban land have had a significant, practical impact on the amount of land used for particular farm crops.

But even here the market has an appropriate corrective mechanism. If the conversion of land has a significant impact on agricultural land, the price of the affected farm product, and of other land suitable for raising it, tends to rise. The rise in price of the final product tends to reduce its consumption. At the same time, the rise in rental value of suitable farm land encourages more intensive cultivation of the product on land not yet converted. It also encourages additional land being devoted to the product's cultivation, and to a rise in the cost of land used for urban purposes. The latter serves to limit urban expansion.

Moreover, many of the genuine evils that are exacerbated by urban population growth and decentralization are easily and more appropriately eliminated by means other than direct controls on urban land use. Rush-hour congestion on urban freeways is a good example of this. It is true, of course, that with given facilities, an increase in an area's population will make congestion worse. But freeways are already over-utilized during rush-hours, principally because the charge imposed for using them is too low. If forced to pay a toll or congestion charge for using a freeway which is equal to the additional costs his using it imposes on all other drivers, each driver would incur the whole social costs of his own action. Freeway use would then be appropriately limited to the point where marginal private benefits are equal to marginal social costs, and additional controls or governmental regulation would be unnecessary.*

Problems of air and water pollution in urban areas are similar to the problem of rush-hour freeway congestion. Like the use of highways, the use of air masses and bodies of water for waste disposal has value to so-called polluters as well as to society as a whole. Waste disposers, however, impose costs on others in the form of cleaning and medical costs which the polluter does not have to bear. As with the case of freeway congestion, the appropriate remedy would be for government to impose charges for waste disposal equal to the social cost of that activity. So-called effluent charges are one way of doing this, although the difficulty in determining the correct level of such charges might recommend auctioning permits for the use of air and water for waste disposal as a superior system. Regardless of the control method, however, problems of pollution result principally from the failure of governments properly to regulate resources not privately owned.

As a final example of problems possibly aggravated by urban expansion, consider so-called open space. It is frequently argued that as open areas surrounding metropolitan regions are converted to urban uses, the enjoyment derived from the environment is reduced. As a purely practical matter, because of the rising incomes and improved transportation which have contributed to urban decentralization, the typical American almost certainly enjoys open space and other beauties of the environment far more today than, say, a half century ago. It may be, however, that we should conserve more areas in their natural form than we do now. Private owners of open space, it is true, have little incentive to conserve it; while the farmer can sell his produce for a fee on the market, there is no way he can charge those who enjoy the view as they drive past his farm. At the same time, by levying additional taxes and buying up the right to sell his farm for urban development, government would not

*For a more complete discussion of government planning of roads, see George Hilton's chapter in this volume.

only preserve open space but also impose a charge for its enjoyment. However, in the absence of a charge reflecting the social cost of the open space, people will undoubtedly want more open space than that space is worth in relation to other uses.

These examples demonstrate that although problems do arise from urban growth, past experience indicates that increased government regulation of private land-use may only aggravate these problems. As in the case of lower-income problems, the problems resulting from urban growth arise not nearly so much from private market failure as from misguided and short-sighted government intervention into the market mechanism and from the failure of government to perform those economic functions required of it by a free society. Increased governmental regulation of the market mechanism, whether at the national or at the local level, would only move us farther from the proper role of government, not closer to it. By exercising its legitimate function to transfer income to less fortunate members of society, government will at the same time solve the problem of poor-quality urban housing. For the evidence strongly indicates the private market's ability to provide better housing to those with the means to pay for it. In similar fashion, by exercising government's proper role in regulating collective consumption—the use of urban roads, air masses, and open space—society can mitigate the major problems associated with urban growth.

ENERGY: THE RECORD OF THE FEDERAL ENERGY ADMINISTRATION 1974–75*

RICHARD MANCKE

Professor of Economics, Fletcher School of Law and Diplomacy, Tufts University

The search for an improved U.S. energy policy brings into conflict two fundamentally different approaches. On the one hand, opponents of central planning point to the costly failures of past U.S. energy policies such as oil import quotas, natural gas wellhead price regulation, and too-ambitious mandatory motor-vehicle emission standards, and argue that less government planning and greater reliance on market forces and private expertise are the master keys to improving U.S. energy policymaking. Conversely, planning proponents, although also recognizing the energy problems caused or aggravated by poorly-conceived planning, argue for designing and implementing far more detailed and comprehensive plans aimed at coordinating decisions made in all phases and sectors of the energy business.

The Federal Energy Office (FEO) and its successor, the Federal Energy Administration (FEA), were the first formal organizations explicitly charged with developing and coordinating a more comprehensive U.S. energy policy. A review of their performance casts considerable doubt upon the thesis that more

*This paper has benefitted from the perceptive comments of a referee.

detailed and comprehensive governmental planning offers the way out of the energy problems now facing the United States.

During the early months of the 1973–74 OAPEC embargo, the United States faced the very real danger of running short of oil.* Reacting both to this crude-oil shortage and to an earlier shortage of refined petroleum products, Congress passed legislation instructing the President

> to assure the equitable distribution of crude oil, residual fuel oil, and refined petroleum products at equitable prices among all regions and areas of the United States and sectors of the petroleum industry including independent refiners, small refiners, non-branded independent marketers and among all users.[1]

The President assigned responsibility for implementing this directive to the newly-created Federal Energy Office.

The FEO responded by promulgating numerous allocation regulations, which—though well-intentioned—nevertheless, on balance, actually complicated the nation's immediate oil supply problems. In December 1973, for example, the FEO issued regulations allocating gasoline supplies to service stations on a monthly basis, and allowing refiners and dealers to raise gasoline and number 2 heating-oil prices to offset higher costs only once per month. Hence, many service stations closed before the end of the month because they had sold their entire allotment. And since gasoline prices could be raised at the start of a new month, a few dealers found it profitable to lock their pumps before the end of the month even though they still had some gasoline. As a result, severe end-of-the-month gasoline shortages often "miraculously" evaporated at the beginning of the new month once higher prices could be charged and new allotments were received.

Other FEO regulations were designed to force refiners with crude oil supplies greater than the industry average to sell some of their "surplus" to crude-poor competitors at a subsidized

*OAPEC—the Organization for Arab Petroleum Exporting Countries—must be distinguished from OPEC, which includes Iran, Indonesia, Venezuela, Equador, and Nigeria.

below-replacement cost price. These regulations had the perverse effect of discouraging both crude-short and crude-rich
companies from importing oil in the midst of the OAPEC embargo. Specifically, these regulations penalized crude-short
companies because each barrel of imported oil reduced the
amount of "cheap" domestic crude that they were allowed to
buy; crude-rich companies were penalized because each barrel
of imported crude raised the amount of domestic oil that they
were obliged to sell at a below-replacement-cost price. As a
result, for each barrel of oil imported, inter-refinery crude-oil
allocation regulations meant reduced oil company profits.
Nevertheless, despite strong financial incentives to reduce their
oil imports, both crude-short and crude-rich refiners continued
to import substantial quantities and thereby helped to alleviate
U.S. oil shortages. This was not behavior one would have expected from greedy, socially-irresponsible companies.

The petroleum shortages ended by May 1974. And at that
time, Congress authorized the Federal Energy Administration
to take over the duties of the Federal Energy Office. The FEA
had two principal assignments: First, to implement policies
aimed at reducing the United States' vulnerability to future
petroleum embargoes by stimulating faster development of secure energy supplies and by discouraging growth in energy
demands; and second, to enforce petroleum price controls (established by the Cost of Living Council) and associated allocation regulations. Unfortunately, because they have discouraged
companies from making some of the investments necessary to
expand oil supplies, oil price controls have had the undesirable
effect of increasing U.S. vulnerability to future embargoes.

Domestic crude oil prices began rising in early 1973. As part
of its program to combat inflation, and to prevent owners and
producers of previously-developed supplies from reaping
windfall profits, the Cost of Living Council set ceiling prices on
all crude oil classified as "old"—which the Council defined as
oil from leaseholds producing prior to 1973. The CLC believed
that this action would not for the most part lead to reduced
production of old oil because the out-of-pocket cost of produc-

ing oil from most already-developed sources was far lower than the ceiling price. However, to assuage the tens of thousands of politically-powerful independent oil producers, Congress explicitly exempted from all price controls any oil produced from low-productivity stripper wells (i.e., wells producing less than 10 barrels per day). Stripper oil production costs were already near the ceiling price and rising sharply because of rapid price inflation of drilling equipment and supplies. Therefore, Congress reasoned in justifying the exemption, imposing price ceilings on these marginal fields would make it unprofitable to continue producing from them, and would also make it unprofitable to rework closed fields, and to make the investments necessary to boost output from stripper wells already in operation. Unless these marginal fields were exempted, therefore, effective price ceilings would discourage crude oil output, precisely at a time of tight supply, when an increase in output was most needed.

The Cost of Living Council also recognized that higher crude oil prices would encourage oil companies to expand greatly their investments for exploring, developing, and producing oil from new sources. Hence, the Council also exempted from the price ceilings "new" crude oil—defined as production from a leasehold above the level achieved in 1972. To provide additional incentives to develop new oil, producers were allowed to release a matching barrel of old oil from the price ceilings for every barrel of new oil they produced. The result of these exceptions for the stripper, new, and released oil was that 35–40 percent of all U.S.-produced crude oil was exempt from price controls during 1974–75.

Before the imposition of price controls, oil refiners paid prices for specified barrels of crude oil corresponding directly with their economic value. Thus, they typically paid premiums for higher-gravity crudes, which yield proportionately more gasoline; for low-sulphur crudes, which are cheaper to refine and whose products contain fewer pollutants; and for crudes located relatively close to major refining and consuming centers. After the imposition of price controls, the price paid for a barrel of crude oil also depended on its classification as old, exempt, or foreign. Old oil was the cheapest—its average well-head price having been fixed at $5.25 per barrel since late 1973. In sharp contrast, from October 1973 to October 1975 the cost of exempt domestic oil of similar quality has risen from about $6 to more than $13 per barrel.

Well before the start of the 1973–74 OAPEC oil embargo, it was evident that the price ceilings on old oil had been set far below market clearing levels. As shortages developed, crude-short refiners, desperate for refinery feed-stocks, began to bid up the price of exempt crude oil. And desiring even more oil, they sought ways to circumvent the old oil price controls. According to reports appearing in the trade press prior to the OAPEC embargo, some succeeded by agreeing to tie together purchases of old and new oil from a given supplier: they bought old oil at the controlled price, but bought new oil at a price so high that the weighted average price for the total purchase rose to near the market clearing level.

Not surprisingly, U.S. petroleum supplies became even scarcer during the OAPEC embargo. Realizing that producers of old oil would almost certainly require tie-in purchases in order to circumvent the price controls, the Federal Energy Office issued regulations freezing all old oil buyer-seller arrangements as of December 1, 1973. This ruling eliminated tie-in sales and thereby saved the controls on crude oil prices from total emasculation.

Some refiners process much greater proportions of "cheap" price-controlled old crude than others. To prevent these fortunate refiners from reaping vast windfall profits, the Federal Energy Office enforced differential ceilings on the prices charged for refined petroleum products. Specifically, each refiner could charge a maximum price determined by adding a cent-for-cent pass-through of all increased costs to the price it charged during a pre-embargo base period.

These pricing rules resulted in intercompany differences of as much as 12 cents per gallon in retail gasoline prices in the midst of the OAPEC embargo.

During the OAPEC embargo the shortages of all petroleum products permitted even high-cost refiners who processed relatively small amounts of the price-controlled old oil, to charge higher prices for their products without losing sales. However, once the embargo ended and the shortages eased, these high-cost companies confronted the dilemma of either maintaining higher prices and watching their sales plummet, or cutting prices and incurring huge losses. To prevent this, the Federal Energy Administration established inter-refinery allocation regulations requiring refiners with above industry-average old oil supplies to pay competitors with below industry-average old oil supplies $6–$8 per barrel for entitlements to refine their own old oil. As a result of this entitlements program, refiners with above industry-average old oil supplies have had to make payments totalling well over $1 billion in 1975 to their competitors. Requiring those firms that were prudent enough to develop domestic oil supplies to subsidize their less prudent competitors is a poor way of encouraging the needed development of additional domestic oil supplies. These subsidies would be unnecessary if crude oil price controls were abolished.

The Congressional mandate forcing the Federal Energy Administration to continue to enforce old oil price controls has caused two classes of problems. First, as long as prices for some domestically-produced petroleum are fixed at levels so low that demands far exceed supplies, the FEA must continue to enforce a variety of highly detailed regulations aimed at allocating available supplies "fairly." These allocation rules have cost the FEA millions of dollars to promulgate and enforce and the oil companies additional millions to implement. Far worse, since each group of consumers and refiners has a different definition of what constitutes a fair allocation of low-cost petroleum, all of the FEA's allocation regulations have precipitated rancorous public debates. Such a politically-charged atmosphere has not been conducive to passage of good energy policy legislation.

The second type of problem with old-oil price controls is that, as implemented, they subsidize OPEC oil to the extent of $2 to $3 per barrel. The ultimate result of such a policy is an increased level of oil imports and, hence, an increase in the United States' vulnerability to future oil embargo threats. If below-market-clearing prices are temporary, the resulting supply-demand distortions may not lead to costly additional domestic oil shortages. Unfortunately, petroleum price controls have not been temporary—they have been enforced almost continuously since 1971. The United States' rapidly-worsening shortage of natural gas, which has been effectively price-controlled since the Federal Power Commission adopted area-wide price controls in 1960, offers graphic evidence of the disastrous consequences of using controls to enforce persistent below-market-clearing prices for an important type of energy. Natural gas shortages have grown progressively worse since 1970, which has forced a sharp growth in U.S. oil imports—the only immediately available natural gas substitute—and therefore has greatly increased the United States' vulnerability to oil embargoes. Likewise, the continuation of existing crude-oil price controls will make it exceedingly difficult for the U.S. to reduce its oil-import dependence, which also increases American vulnerability to future oil-embargo threats.

The chief benefit claimed for oil-price controls is that they are necessary to prevent oil companies from reaping windfall profits as a result of quintupled foreign oil prices. In view of the need for voluntary public support of energy conservation measures during the OAPEC embargo and the enormous public distrust of the oil industry, both Congress and the President concurred on the desirability of this goal. This was probably a proper policy goal as long as oil was in short supply because of the embargo, although even then objections could be raised to controls on oil profits. Most important, it placed the government in the difficult position of defining acceptable profit levels. Judged by the most common measure—the after-tax rate of return on equity investments—profits of most American oil companies were below the average for all U.S. industrial firms for the ten years prior to 1973. But even after oil company profits rose sharply in 1973 and 1974, they were only slightly higher than the average earned by all U.S. manufacturing.

Moreover, oil profits began to fall off in the last quarter of 1974, and this trend accelerated during 1975. The fact that unusually high profits were earned for a period of less than two years is not sufficient to establish that the industry's profits are excessive and therefore must continue to be controlled.

Besides entailing complicated allocation regulations and giving rise to costly distortions in U.S. oil supplies and demands, the oil price controls failed to achieve their main goal of preventing temporary windfall profits resulting from the OAPEC and quintupled foreign oil prices. Price controls failed to check the rise in the oil companies' immediate post-embargo profits for two principal reasons. First, large inventory profits were realized when foreign crude bought at pre-embargo world prices was sold at sharply high post-embargo world prices. Price controls on domestically produced crude oil could not limit this one-time source of approximately half the higher oil industry profits attributable to the embargo. Second, because they did not wish to weaken the incentives to find and develop new domestic oil sources, the designers of the price controls wisely exempted 35 to 40 percent of all domestic crude oil. The embargo-caused oil shortage promptly pushed prices of exempt domestic crude oil from less than $6 per barrel on the eve of the embargo to nearly $10 by late December 1973.

There have been no shortages in petroleum supplies, from both domestic and foreign sources, in the United States since the end of the OAPEC embargo in late spring of 1974. Hence, there remains little justification for the Federal Energy Administration to continue the nearly impossible (and extremely expensive) task of assuring equitable distribution of petroleum supplies at equitable costs. The FEA should instead concern itself with reducing the United States' vulnerability to future petroleum embargoes. Unfortunately, because the FEA-enforced price controls have promoted increased petroleum demands while discouraging additions to domestic supplies, FEA policies have thereby actually increased American vulnerability to future embargoes.

An examination of the emergency allocation regulations and

petroleum price controls enforced by the Federal Energy Office and the Federal Energy Administration offers little support for the contention that more detailed and comprehensive governmental planning will alleviate American energy problems. The experience of recent U.S. energy policy initiatives suggests, instead, that to be effective, future energy policy planning must take into account five lessons relating to recent energy problems:

1. First, we must determine the objectives of U.S. energy policy precisely, and—to prevent policymakers from being overwhelmed by too many conflicting considerations—ruthlessly exclude all extraneous issues. For this purpose, four primary energy-related objectives deserve consideration.

a) *Guaranteeing access to secure energy supplies.* The principal threat to the United States' energy security is the demonstrated power of a group of large oil exporters to embargo oil sales. This danger will persist as long as any coalition of large oil exporters has sufficient cohesion to maintain monopoly power and the U.S. remains a substantial oil importer. Hence, the oil security threat can only be reduced by policies designed either to foster disintegration of the economic and political ties presently binding the large oil exporters, or—and this would have the same effect—to encourage substantial increases to domestic energy production and substantial reductions in U.S. oil demands.

b) *Reducing high energy resource costs.* By reducing the productive resources that its citizens consume in obtaining energy, the United States can have more resources available for producing other socially-desirable goods and services. Policies should therefore be designed to facilitate increased production of the relatively cheaper (in resource costs) domestic fossil fuels—Alaskan and Outer Continental Shelf crude oil, natural gas, and coal—rather than increased commercial production of much more expensive fuels like oil shale, tar sands, and coal synthetics.

c) *Limiting environmental degradation.* Some degradation of the environment or of public health and safety is a by-product of the production, transmission, and consumption of all types of energy. However, different fuels produce large differences in environmental degradation. At present, increased production and consumption of natural gas and crude oil places the fewest demands on the environment and public health, and their production and consumption should therefore be encouraged.

d) *Limiting undesirable changes in the distribution of income.* Prices of all fuels soared in the aftermath of the OAPEC embargo. This resulted in a large transfer of income and wealth from energy consumers to the owners (both domestic and foreign) of low-cost energy supplies. The largest single portion of this income and wealth transfer goes to the governments of the oil-exporting countries. Except for adopting measures that may ultimately lead to either the dissolution of the oil-exporting countries' cartel or to reduced consumption of imported oil, the United States is powerless to reduce this part of the energy-related income and wealth transfer.

Because of higher corporate profit taxes, lease bonus payments, and royalties, a sizeable portion of the higher prices paid for domestic energy already goes into federal and state treasuries. Nevertheless, post-embargo high energy prices have led and will continue to lead to income and wealth transfers totalling several billion dollars annually to the owners of low-cost energy reserves. To reduce the size of this income and wealth transfer, Congress might consider introducing higher taxes on energy producers and rebating the proceeds to consumers via income-tax cuts. However, considerable study should precede any such action and care taken to insure that these tax hikes do not discourage new domestic production.

All energy policy proposals ought to be judged according to how much they are likely to advance or hinder achieving each of these goals. Unfortunately, most policies will almost certainly yield mixed results. For example, eliminating all price controls on crude oil and natural gas will encourage higher production of both fuels, and in turn, should enhance U.S. energy security, reduce the resource cost (but not the price paid by consumers), assure the United States' energy supply, and, since these are the cleanest-burning fossil fuels, reduce environmental damage. However, abolishing price controls will increase wealth and income transfers to petroleum owners and producers. Energy policymakers must weigh these offsetting benefits and costs. It is my view at present, that obtaining secure and lower resource-cost energy supplies deserves more weight than the problems associated with environmental degradation and the alleged "worsening" domestic income distribution.

2. Energy policies must be flexible in the sense that they either adjust automatically or with modest administrative input to substantial changes in underlying economic, political, and technological facts and circumstances. Such flexibility requires that policies must, of necessity, rely on market forces and private enterprise.

Policy flexibility is important, because at all times knowledge of changing circumstances is uncertain and ambiguous. If specific energy policies cannot adjust to these underlying changes, great inefficiencies will inevitably result. Furthermore, the combination of factual uncertainty with uncertainty about the actual consequences of policy changes, makes it unlikely that policymakers can successfully fine-tune energy policy.

The importance of flexible policies whose success does not depend on specific events is readily deduced from the United States' unfortunate experience with natural gas price controls. The controls were imposed primarily to prevent an income transfer from consumers to natural gas owners and producers. There was no immediate harm, because natural gas supplies were relatively abundant. However, as time passed, the demand for low-priced, clean-burning natural gas increased, but, as it was becoming less profitable, new exploration and development began to diminish. The result has been ever-worsening shortages, combined with rapidly-climbing prices of natural gas. The cost of the shortages to the American economy, in terms of both reduced oil security and unnecessarily high energy-resource costs, soared in the aftermath of the OAPEC embargo. Recent U.S. experience with natural-gas and crude-oil price controls prompts me to suggest that all such controls be avoided in the future.

3. The long time lags and massive investments necessary to develop new energy supplies greatly complicate the policy-maker's job and increase the likelihood of costly planning failures. Important examples of the large investments and long time lags include the following:

a) It takes ten years and more than $1 billion to plan and install a single new nuclear-powered electricity generating plant; construction of a new uranium enriching plant will take as long and, depending on its design, could cost more than $6 billion.

b) Oil companies have spent more than $12 billion since 1970 to acquire leases to Outer Continental Shelf (OCS) lands. Exploration and development of newly leased OCS lands takes three to six years; the exploration-development time lag has been more then ten years on the Alaskan North Slope.

c) The investments necessary to develop oil shale or to gasify coal commercially are well over $1 billion per plant and will take at least ten years to complete.

In sum, investment decisions made today will determine the magnitude of the United States' domestic energy supplies in 1985 and whether those supplies will be obtained at wastefully high costs. The prospect that future domestic energy supplies will be inadequate and/or unnecessarily costly becomes more likely if highly-detailed energy planning is done by public officials who are either ignorant about these economic and technical constraints or are forced to downplay their importance because of the need to accommodate political pressures.

4. Unnecessary indecision or ambiguity by policymakers creates costly uncertainty for energy consumers and producers, and frequent changes in established energy policies can lead to obsolescence of some large capital investments.

The long delay in receiving commercial quantities of oil from Prudhoe Bay and the unnecessary costs borne by automakers and electric utilities—because unfeasible time tables for meeting air emission standards were relaxed only at the last minute—illustrate the costly consequences of energy policymakers' indecision and ambiguity. In 1975 the Federal Energy Administration promulgated regulations designed to force owners of 32 oil-burning electricity-generating plants to spend an estimated $260 million to convert to coal. Earlier, owners of many of these plants had spent millions switching from coal to oil in order to satisfy federal clean-air standards. The switch from coal to oil and back to coal graphically illustrates how policy changes can create unnecessary obsolescence and waste.

While unnecessary policy changes should be avoided, that is not an argument for maintaining the status quo at any and all costs. Once available evidence suggests that an existing energy policy has failed, it should be eliminated quickly, and promising new policies and modifications should be introduced. On the other hand, because new policies frequently have unintended deleterious consequences, some preliminary testing is desirable whenever feasible.

5. The fifth lesson is that strong Presidential leadership is essential if the United States is to develop a set of flexible policies designed to achieve the four energy goals. Presidential leadership is necessary because regional differences have hopelessly fragmented Congress on most energy-policy issues: most important, citizens from oil-producing states tend to endorse policies that promote higher domestic oil prices and lower federal oil taxes, while citizens from consumer states (especially energy-short New England) argue vociferously for the opposite. Few Congressmen can be expected to possess sufficient statesmanship to oppose these regional political realities. Thus, it is fatuous to expect that any Congress—even one heavily dominated by one political party—will take the lead in developing and passing a tough energy program that does not pander to popular political interests.

The Congress' recent flirtation with politically-popular proposals to establish a federal oil and gas company illustrates this problem.

Senator Adlai Stevenson summarized the principal rationale behind most proposals to establish a federal company which would participate in one or more phases of the petroleum business when he stated that Americans could no longer "afford to turn sole responsibility for [the] price and supply of natural gas and oil over to the very same companies which have already used the gasoline shortage they helped to create to drive their competition out of business."[2] In the first place, the oil companies did not create the gasoline shortage (indeed, there has been no such shortage since May 1974 when the OAPEC embargo was over). Secondly, no evidence exists that any substantial number of competitors have left any segment of the oil business. This casts serious doubt upon the wisdom of any policies based on these arguments.[3] Nevertheless, since the proposals to establish a federal oil and gas company are becoming increasingly popular, they merit a more detailed criticism.

Senator Stevenson's legislation to create a Federal Oil and Gas Company (FOGCO) proposed granting it extensive powers:

> The Corporation would have access to publicly owned gas and oil rights on Federal lands, as well as the power to acquire similar rights on private lands. It could enter into the full range of activities necessary for the exploration, development, refining, transportation and marketing of petroleum and gas products. . . .
>
> The Corporation would have the authority to issue bonds to cover its indebtedness, and Federal appropriations in the amount of $50 million per year would be authorized for the first ten years.[4]

And he defined the purpose of this legislation as being

> not . . . to provide a forerunner for nationalizing the American petroleum industry. The purpose is to develop public resources —and preserve the free enterprise system in the petroleum industry. But private oil companies need a spur, a yardstick, an incentive for competition. This Corporation would provide that yardstick.[5]

FOGCO proponents maintain that it is not a precursor to nationalization of the petroleum industry, but rather an attempt to stimulate competition. Whatever the announced intention, there can be no doubt that creation of a FOGCO-type public energy company would represent a fundamental change in government-corporate relations. Before legislating such a dramatic change it would be prudent for Congress to make a serious effort to assess the likely consequences. Two examples suffice to illustrate potential problems. First, when the FOGCO advocates argue that it "would give the Nation a 'yardstick' against which to judge the performance of the private oil companies" are they correct?[6] The Chairman of the Board of Standard Oil of Indiana gives a persuasive answer:

> . . . the major fallacy in the use of the "yardstick" concept is that a yardstick is employed to measure similar entities. With no taxes to pay, no leases to purchase, no stockholders to reward, and the choice of government acreage on which to operate, customary business measurements would be completely lacking in the case of a Federal Oil and Gas Corporation. Any so-called "yardstick" thus established would be totally artificial and without meaning.[7]

Second, could a government-owned and managed oil company hope to be as efficient as its private counterparts? Most FOGCO critics answer no and point to the present problems of two widely-criticized public enterprises: Amtrak and the U.S. Postal Service. This analogy is probably inappropriate—at their creation both of these public concerns were saddled with an obsolete physical plant and the responsibility for providing numerous money-losing services. Presumably FOGCO would not be so encumbered.

Much more serious is the prospect that FOGCO's management is likely to discover that it must consider the political ramifications of what should be merely business decisions. This is likely to create severe administrative problems in a business that is already risky and requires high levels of technical expertise. For example, will FOGCO's management feel free to risk hundreds of millions of dollars on necessary wildcat exploration when its performance is being monitored continuously by Congress? Also, will Congress and the President allow FOGCO to operate without considering certain political realities; e.g., the necessity of making investments in several states, not just in those few where oil investments are likely to prove most promising? No doubt a federal energy company could be designed so that it would not be subject to these and similar pressures. However, in light of the fact that recent U.S. energy policymaking has been highly politicized, I have serious doubts that FOGCO would be so designed.

In conclusion, Congress cannot be expected to ignore political realities and draft a comprehensive, well-designed, and flexible energy policy. Fortunately, President Ford has displayed some inclination to do so. Moreover, he apparently realizes, correctly, that decontrolling prices of domestic crude oil and natural gas is necessary to the success of any successful program. Unfortunately, the President lacks the power to force such a program through a reluctant Congress. In addition, some Ford proposals—most notably the recently suggested $100-billion Energy Independence Authority to subsidize the development of high-cost and frequently high-polluting energy supplies such as oil shale and geothermal power—indicate that the President has also failed to fully grasp the five energy policy lessons. This suspicion is buttressed by the President's failure to recommend strong measures aimed at attacking directly the source of the United States' oil-security problem, the oil-exporting countries' monopoly power.[8] At this writing a well-designed U.S. energy policy, responsive to economic and technological realities, remains a pipe dream.

REGIONAL VERSUS LOCAL GOVERNMENT: THE LESSONS FOR NATIONAL PLANNING

ROBERT B. HAWKINS, JR.
Fellow, Woodrow Wilson International Center for Scholars

According to its advocates, national economic planning is necessary because the regulated market system is chaotic, unplanned, and inefficient. Planning advocates argue that rational, comprehensive planning can solve such problems as inflation and unemployment, which they see as a consequence of the present system.[1]

Similar arguments are made about the present structure of local government. From adjectives such as fragmented, unplanned, and uncoordinated and inefficient, reformers propose remedies that favor consolidation of authority and responsibility to areawide or regional organizations.

While the movement to reorganize local government may seem far removed from proposals for centralized economic planning, there are important similarities. Both assume that centralized and rational intervention can produce a more efficient and responsive system. And both assume that centralized organizations led by experts are superior to decentralized systems based on competition.

This paper will examine the arguments made for what we have called local government "reform" to anticipate the consequences of consolidating and centralizing local government functions. The discussion has important implications for the public debate on national economic planning, because there is good reason to believe that the consequences of central planning for local government will be similar to the consequences of a centrally-planned economy.

The paper is divided into two sections. The first deals with existing empirical evidence on the claims made against the present local government structure. Particular attention will be paid to claims made for increases in efficiency, effectiveness, and responsiveness through consolidation of local government into large, centralized (planned) units. Second, we will analyze the arguments for comprehensive regional planning. In this, we will be concerned with three primary issues: the ability of regional agencies to remain voluntary and to limit their activities to making recommendations; the relationship of regional agencies to other political units; and the effect of regional agencies on local government. Many of the examples herein will be based on the experience in California.

FRAGMENTATION AND CHAOS

Critics of the present fragmented local-government system maintain that consolidation and "planning" will significantly improve both the efficiency and responsiveness of local government.[2] To pick an example, the governmental structure of the San Francisco Bay area has eight counties, seventy-three cities, and two-hundred-one special districts, and this is taken as *prima facie* evidence that something must be done. In the area of planning, with over eighty-one planning commissions, common sense would tend to indicate that consolidation into an integrated system would produce a more efficient and responsive system.

Despite appearances to the contrary, the fragmented structure of local government, especially in California, has not evolved at random. Several key factors explain its development. In the early stages of statehood, with relatively weak state government, local government was the only feasible way to produce many public goods and services. From mining camps to irrigation districts, citizens were encouraged by state law to undertake public activities through local instrumentalities. As the state grew, diversity reinforced this policy of local option. Citizen choice, effective local government, and home rule also helped solidify a political culture that supports diverse and multiple choices in designing local institutions.

Critics contend that this diversity is pathological, because of the complexity of modern society and of the inability of many local governments to utilize space-age technologies and modern management techniques.[3] The Advisory Council on Intergovernmental Relations echoes the sentiments of these critics:

> At the close of the 1960s academicians and practitioners alike were questioning whether power had been too dispersed, whether responsibility had been too diffused, and whether the overall operation of the federal system had become simply too chaotic. The common point of reference for many of these people was the fragmented metropolitan areas of the nation.[4]

In short, at least to its critics, the present structure of local government presents an excellent example of institutional failure. The traditional criteria used in determining institutional failure have been efficiency, effectiveness, adequate intergovernmental relations, equity, and responsiveness. The key policy question hinges on whether citizens have been rational in creating and maintaining this system of local government. We thus turn our attention to the evidence to evaluate the effects of fragmentation and to see if local government, in its present fragmented form, has failed according to the standards set forth above.

THE EVIDENCE

Arguments for consolidation of local government units into larger centralized organizations are based on appeals to the public interest. Consolidation is in the "public interest" if it results in clear gains in efficiency, effectiveness, and responsiveness to the *preferences of citizens*. Existing empirical evidence indicates that the arguments for consolidation are unwarranted. These findings fall into three categories:

Efficiency

A number of studies have found that few economies of scale can be realized in local government functions.[5] Local government units serving populations of 17,000 to 375,000 are capable of realizing most economies of scale. From limited studies, special districts are also like other units of government in realizing such economies.[6] The primary reason for these findings is that most local government services are labor-intensive while economies of scale generally occur in capital-intensive services. But one does find that local governments have used a variety of different institutional devices—to realize economies from private provision to the creation of special organizations.[7] Thus, a number of different organizational arrangements of varying size are capable of efficient operation.

Effectiveness

Effectiveness is a difficult concept to define and test, because it attempts to measure the quality of service rendered. This task is complicated by the fact that to a large extent quality is determined by the subjective preferences of citizens. Thus, there are few reliable studies on the effectiveness of local government services. However, several studies have looked at the relationship between size and output. Size is a critical factor in consolidation because of the predicted benefits of increased administrative capacity and competence. A number of studies have been undertaken in the area of school size and output, and a recent review of them came to the following conclusion:

> all of the studies that have tried to relate school or school district size to educational outcomes have found either no relationship or a negative one between school enrollments and the level of educational output. . . . Yet what cannot be dismissed is the consistency of the conclusions—that while diseconomies of scale ap-

pear, economies of scale do not—despite differences in the techniques of analysis, samples of schools, measures of educational outcomes, and so on.[8]

Other studies tend to reinforce this finding. A 1974 State of California study found it would cost fifty-four percent more to have the State Division of Forestry provide service to rural areas presently receiving fire services from special districts.[9] The California Local Government Reform Task found that special district sewage treatment facilities were just as efficient, at comparable levels of quality, as city and county operations.[10] A study conducted by the Environmental Protection Agency found that private garbage collection was only fifty-seven percent as costly as equivalent services provided by the public sector.[11] And a private fire company in Scottsdale, Arizona, not only reduced local fire insurance rates but also reduced per capita fire costs by forty-seven percent.[12]

According to the evidence, large size does not appear to be a critical factor. In fact, size is often positively associated with decreasing levels of effectiveness. As with efficiency, there appear to be a number of organizational options open to local communities in designing effective institutions.

Responsiveness

Since effectiveness of governmental services is largely determined by the subjective citizen evaluations, satisfaction with services becomes a critical ingredient in the design of political institutions. Reform movements have assumed that increasing the size of governmental organization will increase responsiveness to citizen preferences. If this were so, one would expect citizens to approve consolidation proposals at the polls and to experience increased satisfaction as the size of a city increases. However, in the last twenty years consolidation proposals have been rejected at a rate of three to one, and these results reveal some things about citizens' attitudes toward local government. Two recent government studies have documented some of the probable reasons for citizens rejecting consolidation proposals.

The California Local Government Task Force surveyed 1,500 citizens and reached the following conclusions:[13]

1. Citizen satisfaction with government increases as the size of the governmental unit decreases.
2. Citizen satisfaction is, in part, negatively associated with the degree of state and federal intervention in the particular service.
3. A strong desire exists to decentralize authority and responsibility to local government.
4. Local citizens also share a strong desire for state and federal governments to pay an increased share of government costs, particularly in the social program areas.
5. In large central cities significant demands exist for neighborhood organizations to deliver public goods and services to individual communities.
6. Citizens feel a strong preference to maintain the autonomy of local governments, instead of elevating authority to higher levels of government.
7. Citizens are very clear in their desire to determine the structure of local government through the ballot box rather than through the State Legislature or appointed local officials.

This evidence contradicts "reform" notions that citizen satisfaction will increase with the size of a governmental unit. A Harris poll of over 16,000 citizens found similar results:[14]

1. Citizens found larger cities to be more disorganized than did their counterparts living in smaller cities, which are serviced by more units of government.
2. Citizens living in smaller units of local government tended to use their local governments more than those in large cities.
3. Citizens in smaller jurisdictions tended to have higher levels of satisfaction than those in large cities.

Only one systematic study has attempted to assess the effects of consolidation on citizens. Twenty years ago the Swedish government implemented a policy of reducing the number of local government units by eighty percent—a policy very similar to that recommended by the Committee for Economic Development (CED).[15] While the study is of Sweden's implementation of such a policy, weakening to some degree its applicability to the United States, the results are nevertheless provocative and interesting. The study found the following:

1. Voter participation in local elections declined appreciably as the local units increased in size;
2. Citizen participation in joining voluntary civic and service organizations declined appreciably as the local units increased in size;
3. As local units got larger, local elected officials differed more markedly from their constituents in such characteristics as income level, social status, and level of education;
4. The resistance of local elected officials to spending programs decreased as the size of the local unit increased; and
5. Local elected officials in larger units of local government tended to follow the "dictates of their conscience" rather than the demands of their constituents, probably because of lack of contact with and concern for constituent preferences.

A group of American scholars who surveyed existing empirical evidence on the question of local government reform in metropolitan areas reached very similar conclusions.[16] They found:

1. An almost universal effect of metropolitan reform has been the increasing impact of professionals upon policymaking.
2. In general, few economies of scale have been associated with reform, except for the metropolitan special districts.
3. The access of minorities is guaranteed, in the short run, but may be diluted in the long run.
4. Performance levels tend to rise, but so do the fiscal burdens accompanying increased expenditures.
5. The functional emphasis upon tangible goods, rather than upon amelioration of social problems remains unchanged.
6. There is no immediate, short-term impact upon the distribution of power and wealth.
7. By and large, restructuring reduces citizen participation in the local electoral process.

The empirical evidence that we have suggests that there are very poor odds on realizing increased levels of efficiency, effectiveness or responsiveness through organizational consolidation.

CHANGING DIRECTIONS

Increasing evidence on the inefficiency and unresponsiveness of consolidation, as well as citizen opposition to it has forced reformers to shift grounds. For example, the Advisory Council on Intergovernmental Relations has weakened its recommendation for organizational consolidation in favor of sub-state regionalism.[17] This approach has the advantage of leaving existing units of government in place and creating a regional coordinating agency. The primary function of such an agency is to regulate the activities of local government, primarily to achieve comprehensive planning, to coordinate the activities of local government, and reduce the negative effects of the present structure. While equity considerations and regional provision of services are also stated as goals, we will concentrate on the first three.

Sub-state regionalism shares with national economic planning a rejection of competition and bargaining within a system of property rights as capable of effectively realizing goals of public policy. Since the questions regarding the effects of a competitive local government structure are separable from the probable outcomes of regionalization, a few comments will be made about the former.

Competitive Local Government Systems

Opponents of local government see it as chaotic.[18] To the untrained eye this analysis seems confirmed as one surveys metropolitan areas and sees multiple and diverse, often overlapping decision-making structures. On the other hand, as one travels through these same areas, one finds that roads do connect, households have water, and in general, order prevails. This order is primarily the result of two factors. First there is what amounts to an invisible hand operating at the local government level.[19] Local governments receive from state constitutions and governments decision-making rights which provide the necessary liberty to produce public goods and services. These rights, however, are not absolute, because local actions are also constrained by state and Federal law. Public producers of water, for example, must meet certain health standards; sewage treatment facilities must meet minimum effluent standards; and police departments operate within the parameters set down by state and Federal criminal justice system.

The second factor is self-interest. Local officials, like state and federal officials, are interested in maximizing multiple and often conflicting sets of values. Since they operate with scarce resources, they have incentives for economic behavior. When there is an opportunity for joint benefit, local officials will have an incentive to cooperate. Thus, it is not surprising that local governments in the Los Angeles and San Diego basins joined together to form the Metropolitan Water District of Southern California to transport water from the Colorado River.[20] For each community to undertake such an activity individually would make no economic sense. But local governments will undertake such cooperative ventures when clear gains in efficiency and responsiveness can be realized.[21] Self-interest is thus another important regulatory principle at work in the metropolitan area.

At present, very little information exists on the degree and regularity of intergovernmental cooperation. But as several studies indicate, where the self-interest of local officials is maximized, it is safe to assume that cooperative activities will occur on a regular basis. A study of police departments in the St. Louis Metropolitan area indicates that smaller police departments regularly engage in cooperative activity to increase the capacities of their departments.[22] A study in California found that special district fire departments increase emergency assistance to other departments as they served more urbanized areas. Likewise, water districts were more likely to have emergency interties with adjoining systems as they become more urbanized.[23] If fire and water districts were to prepare for every possible emergency, the cost would be prohibitively high. Sharing facilities is one way of meeting emergencies and reducing costs. In each of these examples, advantage could be gained by mutual aid agreements.

In situations where local units of government produce negative effects on each other, one of two forms of governmental action tend to deal with the problem. The first of these occurs through state legal and regulatory control. The second occurs when local governments form institutional arrangements with sufficient authority to solve conflict problems. In California, the Orange County Municipal Water District was formed to reduce salt water intrusion into the Santa Ana Water Basin. The problem was created by public and private producers of water who did not see it in their short-run interest to reduce consumption. Salt water intrusion therefore resulted from a lowering of the water table. In this case local governments obtained enabling legislation from the state to solve the problem.

Claims that there is no order to the existing structure of local governments in metropolitan areas will not withstand serious analysis. Much of this order is created through state legal systems and the exercise of self-interest on the part of local officials. Cooperative ventures are also instruments for creating ordered relationships between units of government. Such ventures do not come from coercive legislation imposed from state or federal governments, but rather from competition, conflict, and bargaining by interested parties at the local level.

THE ARGUMENT FOR REGIONALISM PERSISTS

From the preceding analysis it is reasonable to assume, as with any other organization, that constant, marginal adjustments are necessary to ensure the effective and responsive operation of local governments. According to critics, the setting of priorities, developing regional plans, and coordinating local governmental activities are problems that justify the regionalization of local government authority.

Advisory Status is Not Enough?

The movement towards regional governance is in many ways analogous to what will surely occur with national economic planning. During the late 1950s and early 1960s regional organization was sold on the notion that the creation of voluntary associations would help local governments to solve pressing areawide problems. The sharing of information, joint planning, and the interaction of local officials in regional forums were thought to be adequate tools.

After ten years of experience and the formation of numerous regional councils of government, these organizations have been found to be unsatisfactory. Not surprisingly, this finding comes from regional organizations themselves. Proponents of regionalism, supported by professional administrators, now contend that effective regional organization will only be realized when local government membership is made mandatory, when regional decisions become binding on the membership, and when an independent revenue base is established.[24] The move from voluntary-advisory association to governmental agency with coercive and revenue power is now said to be needed to provide the necessary tools to realize regional goals.

The reasons for the change in position is no mystery. As regional organizations have grown in membership, staff pressures have played a more significant role. Regional plans can be ignored by member agencies. With mandatory organizations, this problem would be significantly reduced and planners would have increased leeway to impose their plans.

Can such an organization plan comprehensively? As Vincent Ostrom has noted elsewhere in this volume, man does not have the necessary mental capabilities to plan comprehensively. The practical effect of this limitation is illustrated by the experience of one of the most successful ports in the United States.

The Port of Oakland, a leader in containerized cargoes, presented its view on comprehensive planning at a legislative hearing on the subject. Of particular interest is the experience the port has had in basing its expansion policies on planning data. In 1957 the Army Corps of Engineers forecast that the Oakland Harbor could expect a rate of growth of 40,000 tons annually and in fifty years would be handling 1.9 million tons. In early 1966, the port hired a professional maritime consulting firm to estimate the tonnage that would be passing through the port in 1980. The consultants estimated that one million tons would be a reasonable figure. In late 1967, the port updated its long-range plan with another independent estimate that gross tonnage across the port in 1980 would be 2.9 million. In 1969, the port handled over 3 million tons and in 1972 over 4.5 million tons. After noting the fluidity of international trade, currency fluctuations and uncertainties of international relations, the executive director of the port somewhat understated the point when he commented: "It is [also] difficult for any long range planning exercise to accurately predict the implications of technological advances."[25]

Planning in a Federal System

Comprehensive planning is not only hampered by informational problems, but also by politics. Advocates of comprehensive regional planning make several assumptions about the planning ability of regional organizations. Many local officials advocate regionalism because they believe that, more than anything else, the fragmentation of local government is responsible for federal and state intervention into local affairs. They believe that a unitary organization at the regional level will be able to plan comprehensively and thus reduce federal and state intervention.[26]

This line of argument fails for a number of reasons. First is the paradox between comprehensive planning and politics in a federal system. Comprehensive planning not only presumes adequate information, but also the ability to manipulate and hold constant those factors necessary to realize the objectives of a plan. This necessarily implies the ability to control individuals and organizations relative to the plan. On the other hand, it is unreasonable, in practice, to expect that any planning organization will be given such power in a federal system, where authority is shared and decisions are made through the concurrent action of diverse authorities.

To further draw out this problem, it is obvious that in order for a regional organization to plan comprehensively, adequate authority is necessary to control all significant federal and state actions which affect the realization of the plan. One must ask why self-interested congressmen or state legislators are going to give any regional organization the kind of authority necessary to undertake comprehensive regional planning? Or why would administrators at the state or national level favor such moves? The answer is, they won't; they will not give up power on a scale necessary for comprehensive regional planning. In practice, the proposals for planning are very different and far removed from the planning process itself.

The principles of political design incorporated into draft legislation for comprehensive land use planning in California demonstrate these incentives. Assembly Bill #2242, after setting forth the need for comprehensive land use planning, develops an organizational structure based on a commitment to planning from the bottom up. Local governments have the initial authority to plan the uses of land, using state standards. Local land use plans are then forwarded to a regional land use commission that has the authority to resolve conflicts between local plans, again in accordance with state standards. Finally, a State Land Use Commission has the authority to resolve conflicts between regional plans and also between local plans. The legislation also holds that,

> In the event that reconciliation is not possible, the goals, policies, and objectives set forth in . . . the State Land Use and Resources Management Goals and Plan, shall prevail and any conflicting plan, program, or action of any regional or local agency shall be made consistent with the state goals and plan.[27]

This legislation, besides giving the State Commission adequate authority to enforce compliance to its plans, also carries the seeds for state dominance and preemption over local and regional affairs. Some of the effects of this bill on the organization of planning at the regional level are:

1) Regional planning organizations will not have the authority to plan comprehensively. They will have partial authority at best.

2) Performance and reward incentives for planners will not rest with local government but will in large part be set by the State Lands Commission. Thus, as Buchanan and Tullock have outlined elsewhere in this volume, planning activities will be affected if not controlled by politics.

3) Nor will the State Land Use Commission plan comprehensively. It will be part of a political system where compromise through bargaining among relevant clientele groups will be the order of the day.

Local Government and Regional Planning

Bureaucratic planning within a centralized political framework will also affect the efficiency and coordination of local government affairs. Coordination of local government affairs (one of the key reasons for regional planning) will be conducted on different turf. No longer will coordination take place between semi-autonomous entities through cooperation, negotiation, and compromise. Coordination will instead occur within a complex hierarchical bureaucratic system. The effect of this coordination process is not hard to imagine. The East Bay Municipal Utilities District, for example, planned an improvement on its sewage treatment facilities which was expected to cost $35 million. After consulting the nine state and federal agencies which had to review the project (each with the power to veto) and after the three years which this review process took, the district was tentatively allowed to implement its plan—at an estimated cost of $62 million.[28] Three years and a $27-million increase are high costs to pay for more "efficient" coordination. Promises again diverge from performance.

The East Bay Municipal Utilities District example is not an isolated one. The Port of Oakland has faced the same problems and reached the following conclusions. They state:

> From past experience, we can state with confidence that government-sponsored plans have a tendency to be long in development and fairly rigid when established. They are usually slow to react to the economic realities of a constantly changing trade pattern.[29]

The creation of regional comprehensive planning agencies is unlikely to produce either comprehensive planning or an overall improvement in the system. A more likely result will be the creation of one more governmental entity, which will increase by one the number of agencies that regulate the activities of local government. The likely effects of this new agency on local government are several.

1) It will increase the costs of any activity requiring regional-state-federal approval.

2) It will decrease the ability of local governments to respond to the preferences of its citizens. Citizens will be asked to bear the costs of foregone options, in order to maximize the "social welfare."

3) The intergovernmental process will become more cumbersome and slow to respond as authority centralizes in state and federal bureaucracies.

4) As regional-state-federal planning agencies constrain the decision-making authority of local officials, one can expect these officials to undertake fewer experimental and creative programs.

WHAT CAN BE DONE

Advocates of regionalization cannot make a convincing case that local government system as a whole is failing institutionally. What empirical evidence we have suggests that except for its relationships with federal and state governments, in general local government is enjoying considerable vitality. While local governments are not without their problems, at the same time a proper balance between different levels of government requires an understanding and appreciation of local government which at present is lacking. Both the theory and evidence we have strongly suggest that comprehensive regional planning will not be comprehensive, nor will it increase the capacity of the present system to perform. If we are correct in assuming that centralized public organizations generally operate under similar incentives, we have little reason to suppose that a National Economic Planning Board will operate differently at the national level.

THE CONTRAST BETWEEN GOVERNMENT AND BUSINESS PLANNING: MARKET ORIENTATION VERSUS CENTRALIZED CONTROL

MURRAY L. WEIDENBAUM
Center for the Study of American Business, Washington University, St. Louis

The widespread use of planning techniques in private business has led many observers to draw parallels to government planning.* Senator Jacob K. Javits, the co-sponsor of legislation to establish national economic planning,[1] has stated in support of his bill: "If corporations are to take a look at where their companies are heading, it seems appropriate for the government to do the same."[2]

In the same article, Senator Javits refers to a school of thought which finds planning "perfectly acceptable" for corporations but unacceptable for government. Those of us who actually have been involved in planning for both the public and the private sectors may also be aware of the important differences as well as the similarities between public and private planning. As a former planner in the aerospace industry, voluntarily retired, I cannot help but note that for a number of years the industry

*The author gratefully acknowledges the contribution of Linda Rockwood to the research for this paper.

looked up to Lockheed for the most structured, sophisticated, and widely emulated long-range planning in the defense industry. Is business planning more a case of the closer you get, the worse it looks?

Clearly some examination of the development and workings of the planning process in the private sector should be useful in the current debate over the desirability of setting up a formal long-range planning mechanism for the Federal Government.

DEVELOPMENT OF LONG-RANGE BUSINESS PLANNING

Long-range planning in American business is primarily a post-World War II phenomenon.[3] It has undergone two distinct phases, although many corporations still have not made the full transition to the second phase. The first phase was essentially an extension of long-range budgeting and sales forecasting. Past and present performance was simply extrapolated into the future on the basis of rather rudimentary techniques. The implicit but underlying assumption was essentially passive—that business would primarily respond to current market forces rather than attempt to influence future developments.

The second phase is more activist in outlook. It seeks to identify the major issues and options which will face the corporation in the future and to indicate possible new courses of action.[4] It is often predicated on the belief that the pace of technological and environmental change is more rapid now than it was in the past and that the new trend will continue into the foreseeable future.

With the widespread establishment of corporate planning staffs in most of the large corporations and in many medium-size companies, a business planning fraternity has developed. A variety of professional associations and journals has been established. The Budget Executives Institute was renamed the Planning Executives Institute. And, inevitably, business planners frequently meet to exchange experiences, if not to provide mutual moral support.

With the rapid growth of planning staffs, planning documents, and planning personnel, what has been the impact on the companies themselves? How successful have the planning efforts turned out in practice? Frankly, there are few objective measurements of this essentially subjective activity. We do have the evaluations provided by observers of the process.

David Ewing reports in his classic study of long-range business planning, "The paradox is that the planning movement, despite such strong motives to make it succeed, has not generally been blessed with success. The triumphs have been stunning—but few."[5]

Planning consultant Malcolm W. Pennington rates 99 percent of all corporate plans as failures because planning (a) has changed the way companies operate in only a very few cases and (b) has rarely satisfied the needs and desires of top management. "Certainly no other function has survived so much futile work, or such frequency of failure."[6]

Patrick H. Irwin reports that, to his knowledge, fewer than one company in twenty has succeeded in instituting a well-developed system of long-range strategic and operational planning.[7]

E. Kirby Warren, in a major study of business planning, concluded that few executives were satisfied with their company's ability to translate long-range planning into meaningful practice. It is intriguing to consider Warren's observation that each company management took solace in the fact that, while their company was not doing a very good job in this area, neither was any of its competitors. "Frankly, this was quite accurate in 1958, and, unfortunately, there are relatively few exceptions today," according to Warren.[8]

In his summary of the state-of-the-art of business planning, Robert J. Mockler presents the following evaluation: "In spite of the advances made during the 1960s, relatively few companies have developed effective planning operations—although many have tried."[9]

These essentially negative evaluations tend to be in accord with the detailed survey a decade ago of planning in the government-oriented defense industry in which the author participated.

> . . . inquiries were made into the role that formal planning plays in the corporate strategy decisions that determine the future posture of the firm. The responses suggest the limited role that planning does play in corporate decision-making. Corporate executives tend to rely more on their intuitive judgment as to the significance of current trends and future activities . . .
>
> The executives frequently stated that their decisions are not made from within a detailed planned structure. As one officer put it, they must rely on "taking advantage of opportunities rather than having a deep plot" to achieve successful results in their business.[10]

Even an enthusiastic exponent of business planning such as George Steiner acknowledges the shortcomings that occur:

> In the development of profitable and healthy organizations there is no substitute for long-range planning. For many it has afforded the margin needed to achieve outstanding growth and profitability. Too few companies, however, actually achieve effective long-range planning.[11]

Some of the reasons for the shortcomings in the practice of business planning may be limited to the private sector. Others may be more universal, and their correction in the public sector even more difficult. Mockler, for example, points out that the business planner "works in a vacuum, acting as a sounding board for corporate management's futuristic thinking but isolated from the operating realities of the organization."[12]

Consider how much more serious the consequence would be of the government planner working in a vacuum, isolated from reality. He nevertheless would be involved in what could be critical decisions affecting the future of individual private sector organizations and individuals.

Irwin lists as one of the four reasons for the lack of success of business planning, the failure to provide a system that integrates the goals of the company with those of individual managers.[13]

The problems of integrating the goals of 200 million citizens, including tens of thousands of private sector managers and decision-makers, are surely staggering.

Despite the various shortcomings, many American business firms do continue to engage in formal long-range planning efforts and apparently believe that the benefits exceed the costs. A variety of reasons is given, not all of which may be applicable to or desirable in the public sector. Many company managements state that planning is a powerful instrument for tightening organizational discipline and control of the business. Others contend that planning can be used to lend authenticity and plausibility to the corporate leader. In this latter view, a chief executive officer of a corporation with a formal plan, neatly printed and indexed and properly illustrated, preferably with detailed statistical appendices, provides the image of having the management task well in hand. His counterpart who still relies on intuition and the proverbial back of the envelope may be at a psychological disadvantage.

According to David Ewing, one of the most important and recurring motives for planning has been the desire for controlling what people do.[14] In the words of the manager of planning of Stauffer Chemical, ''The only time the planning department is doing a useful purpose is when it is doing something that the chief executive wants done. . . . The planner is at his most powerful when he has the unequivocal support of a strong chief executive.''[15]

Many individual business planners and planning organizations survive and prosper because of the importance of the ancillary functions they may perform. These range from diversification studies and merger negotiations to economic forecasting and market research to providing a corporate focal point for social responsibility concerns and governmental relations. Moreover, the chief planner may essentially serve as an internal management advisor. He or she may be a useful individual to be included in corporate management groups, particularly where the other participants are committed to representing specific company divisions or large functional areas.

BUSINESS VERSUS GOVERNMENT PLANNING

Even if the shortcomings of the state-of-the-art of business planning are not as universal as indicated above and can be reduced or eliminated with additional time an effort, there are important differences between business and government planning. These differences should influence our views toward the desirability of adopting a stronger and more influential national planning system. Boiled down to fundamentals, we are dealing with the difference between forecasting and reacting to the future and trying to regulate it. Corporate planning of necessity is based on the principle of trade—attempting to produce the types of goods and services that the rest of society may wish to purchase; the controls that may accompany the plan are internally-oriented. In striking contrast, the government is sovereign and its planning ultimately involves coercion, the use of its sovereign powers to achieve the results that it desires. Its controls are thus externally-oriented, extending their sway over the entire society.

At the onset, the proponents of a formal national economic planning system say that they would not set specific goals for General Motors, General Electric, General Foods, or any other individual firm. But what would they do if these companies would not conduct themselves in the aggregate in accordance with the national plan? Would they leave the actual results to chance or the free market? Hardly. They state that the planning office "would try to induce the relevant industries to act accordingly."[16]

And the inducements of course are not trivial. The totality of the government's powers to tax, to purchase, to subsidize, to "assist" and to regulate are awesome. The most powerful and sophisticated planning system in the private sector lacks the ability to levy taxes and to funnel the revenues from those taxes away from one potential sector of the society and to another.

Although much of the rhetoric favoring a national economic planning system is in terms of merely developing and providing better information, improved fact gathering appears to be a means to another end. Daniel Patrick Moynihan referred, in a somewhat different connection, to that increment to central control that seems to accompany enlarged information gathering.[17]

Even a cursory examination of the literature on American business planning demonstrates that planning is intended to be far more than improved information accumulation and analysis. Malcolm Sherwood offers one of the more comprehensive statements in this regard, based on work of the American Management Association:

> Planning is an analytical process which encompasses an assessment of the future, the determination of desired objectives in the context of that future, the development of alternative courses of action to achieve such objectives, and the selection of a course or courses of action from among these alternatives.[18]

Robert G. Murdick offers a variation on that theme: "A plan is a predetermined course of action over a specified period of time which represents a projected response to an anticipated environment in order to accomplish a specific set of adaptive objectives."[19] Ewing offers what is perhaps the most terse rendition of the objective of business planning (although, as noted, the objective may not often be achieved): "Planning is to a large extent the job of making things happen that would not otherwise occur."[20]

The proponents of centralized government planning do not leave the matter in any doubt. They clearly state, "The heart of planning is to go from information to action."[21] They go on to point out, "In order to be effective and useful, an Office of National Economic Planning must be set up at the center of our most influential institutions . . . The Director of the Office of National Economic Planning should be designated as the chief adviser to the President for economic affairs."[22]

The essential difference between public and private planning is the locus of decision-making. If Ford or General Motors or Chrysler are not selling as many automobiles as they had planned, there are a limited number of things they can do about the matter. They can—within their available resources—lower the price or change the nature of the product. But—as evidenced by the demise of the Edsel, the LaSalle, and the DeSoto—they may at times simply be forced to abandon the project. The consumer remains the ultimate decision-maker.

The situation is quite different in the public sector. Compared to the largest private corporation, there are more options available to the government. If the government does not think that the American public is buying enough cars it can lower the price to the consumer as much as it likes via tax reductions, down to zero if it so determines. Alternatively, the government can subsidize the private manufacture of automobiles, or it may purchase outright the output of the automobile industry, or simply take over the ownership and control of the industry. The government certainly has demonstrated the willingness to involve itself in the production of motor vehicles to the extent of deciding by fiat many aspects of their design and operation, under its safety and environmental powers.

Senator Hubert Humphrey has made the same point much more vividly:

> What can government do about it? Government can do a lot about it. For example, the size of automobiles, and consequently energy consumption, can be influenced a great deal by taxing cubic displacement, horsepower, or weight. A tax will slow down purchasers of large cars and give a premium to small-car buyers and buyers of cars with high fuel efficiency. Government can also influence industry by giving an investment tax credit to companies that produce fuel-efficient automobiles. These are just two ways in which government policy can influence the private economy.[23]

The Senator also reminds us that the government is a large purchaser of goods and services: "Everybody else fades into insignificance in comparison. From the viewpoint of purchasing power, General Motors is a peanut stand compared to the United States Government."

Mr. T. A. Murphy, Chairman of the Board of General Motors, has provided a clear distinction between business and national planning:

> If all we were talking about were government plans that are comparable to business plans, there would indeed be nothing to debate. Government units, of course, should try to anticipate future demands on their resources and plan to meet them, just like any private business. We wish them well at it and would like to see them do an even better job. But that isn't the issue.
>
> Unlike a business, a government may not plan—it may also command. A business can set goals only for itself; a government body can set goals for other people as well.[24]

The point here is not that private planning does not involve control, but that those subject to its control powers are quite different. Once a private corporation adopts its long-range plan, it may push hard on the various units of the corporation to meet their goals and objectives. But the controls are essentially internal—incentives and sanctions focusing exclusively on the officers and employees of the corporation; if things go wrong, the onus falls on the officers, employees, and shareholders. Government planning, in contrast, focuses on "guiding" or "influencing"—and thus ultimately controlling—the activities of the entire nation. If things go wrong in public sector planning, it will be the taxpayer and consumer who bear the main burden. Note the close connection between selecting planning objectives and the programs to carry them out in the statement of the proponents of centralized planning: "It goes without saying that the final choice among all feasible alternative planning objectives and programs belongs to Congress."[25]

Consider carefully the comment of Senator Hubert Humphrey, co-sponsor of the Balanced Growth and Economic Planning Act of 1975, "I don't think we ought to compel, but we surely can influence."[26] As Herbert Stein has noted, if the government can make a private citizen an offer he cannot refuse, it can exercise coercion.[27]

In a sense, there may be two types of government planning that need to be distinguished. The external planning—which has been discussed here—involves all sorts of extensions of government powers over the private sectors of the economy. A second type of government planning is more internally-oriented, and may be more comparable to private sector planning. This second type of planning really relates to the management of government's own activities. The advocates of more powerful government planning tend to merge the two, using shortcomings in government's management of its affairs as a reason for extending government power and influence over consumers and business.

In his far-ranging statement advocating national economic planning, Senator Humphrey deals in passing with this second aspect of government planning:

> . . . we don't have any economic impact statement for governmental decisions. The government goes around willy-nilly making decisions of consequence. There was no estimate of the economic impact of the Occupational Safety Act, for example. I happen to be for the occupational safety program, but what were its economic implications? Did anyone think that through? No.
>
> . . . the manner in which we are presently utilizing government resources and government agencies is a haphazard, helter-skelter enterprise . . . we can show that with some planning in our government, just a modest amount, a little more than we're doing, we can reduce governmental costs and get better governmental services.[28]

It would appear, however, that a government which is being conducted on such a haphazard, helter-skelter basis would be reluctant to take on the extremely ambitious task of managing the entire economy prior to getting its own house in order. Moreover, attempts in the recent past to apply business planning techniques to the management of the government's own affairs do not inspire confidence. Certainly, they do not form a satisfactory basis for an expansion of government planning efforts.

THE PLANNING-PROGRAMMING-BUDGETING SYSTEM AND OTHER PLANNING EXPERIMENTS

There is little need to guess at the impact of a government-wide planning system at the federal level. We need only examine the planning system that was instituted by President Lyndon B. Johnson. On August 25, 1965, he announced with great fanfare the introduction of "a very new and very revolutionary system of planning and budgeting throughout the vast federal government, so that through the tools of modern management the full promise of a finer life can be brought to every American at the lowest possible cost."[29] President Johnson went on to describe his view of what was given the acronym PPBS in some detail:

> Under this new system each Cabinet and agency head will set up a very special staff of experts who, using the most modern methods of program analysis, will define the goals of their department for the coming year. And once these goals are established this system will permit us to find the most effective and the least costly alternative to achieving American goals. . . . So this new system will identify our national goals with precision.[30]

PPBS initially was greeted with great enthusiasm. For a while it created a land-office business for the services of economists, statisticians, and program analysts. Professors Bertram Gross and Michael Spring enthusiastically described PPBS as "potentially the most significant management improvement in the history of American government."[31] The August 1965 announcement did have a substantial history behind it. Since January 1961, Secretary of Defense Robert S. McNamara and Assistant Secretary Charles J. Hitch had been attempting to apply the principles of program budgeting to Pentagon decision-making. And a substantial portion of the McNamara-Hitch reforms have endured in the Pentagon, notably the five-year projections of force structures and budgets, as well as the review of budget submissions along program rather than merely service lines.

Some of the enthusiastic overreactions in the implementation of PPBS perhaps were inevitable and not fundamentally different from private sector experiences. When one divisional manager of a large electronics company was asked to state his division's basic goals as an input to the corporate planning process, he listed 400 different "basic goals." Another division manager's plan consisted entirely of 100 pages of statistics, with not a single word except for column headings. Also, it takes many years, not the mere months in President Johnson's timetable, to establish a planning system. As pointed out by Harold Henry, formal planning systems do not materialize in "a period of a few weeks." Such a system is developed gradually over "a period years."[32] R. Hal Mason estimated a 60–108-month time sequence for the establishment of a full-fledged planning organization.[33]

In retrospect, it is quite clear that PPBS—at either the Pentagon or White House levels—did not help the Federal Government avoid fundamental overcommitments either at home or abroad or to avoid an unusual array of "crises." Those who blithely assume that the "successes" of business planning can readily be replicated at the national level may well ponder over both the failure of the Edsel in the private sector and the nature of the major federal decisions which were made at the peak of the PPBS enthusiasm—a deeper American involvement in the Vietnam War and the overpromising of the Great Society domestic programs.

The point being made here is not that the attempt to introduce organized planning led to these failures but rather that it clearly did not prevent them. David Ewing offers a stronger conclusion, "For sheer magnitude of fiasco, however, business cannot compete with planners in the military and government."[34]

Since 1969, the PPBS apparatus has largely been dismantled in the Federal Government. What remains is performed in a more modest manner and as part of the annual budget preparation. One of the more sympathetic but balanced appraisals of the PPBS effort was prepared by Jack W. Carlson, a professional economist who was involved in the program in a major way at the Office of Management and Budget:

> The U.S. experience was clearly short of the ideal.
>
> Initially, PPBS became a different, somewhat competitive channel for decision-making . . . the intent was to provide more useful information for the development both of budgets and legisla-

tion, but that was not the initial result. . . . The government, not to mention the private sector, already turns out thousands of analyses, evaluations, and studies every year. Their influence on policy is usually negligible.[35]

In view of the impact of a more formidable planning system, such as that utilized in Great Britain, perhaps we should be pleased that the results of PPBS were mainly paper-shuffling, wheel-spinning exercises. In his analysis of Britain's experiences with centralized planning, John Jewkes painted a rather dismal picture: "I believe that the recent melancholy decline of Great Britain is largely of our own making . . . At the root of our troubles lies the fallacy that the best way of ordering economic affairs is to place the responsibility for all crucial decisions in the hands of the State."[36]

In his analysis of the French planning experience, John Sheahan cites a different type of problem, the possibility of large private corporations coming to dominate the government planning process. This would be an extension of the widely-held "capture" theory of federal regulatory agencies, whereby the industries being regulated may come to dominate the decisions of the government agencies set up to regulate them. Sheahan contends that planning by consultation and negotiation in France tends to drive the government planners into such close alliance with business interests that the planning board becomes a champion of the firms which it finds it easiest to deal with. Since these are usually the largest businesses, government planning thus has weakened competition and may have resulted in neglecting social concerns.[37]

Under none of these alternatives does a comprehensive scheme of national economic planning appear to improve the overall performance of the national economy. If anything, it would tend to shift even further the focus of private enterprise away from dealing with market forces and meeting consumer demands and toward reaching an accommodation with an ever more powerful governmental bureaucracy. A company might find it desirable to shift resources from conventional marketing activities toward convincing the government to adopt more generous production targets for its industry. Thus, the payoff from traditional consumer market research might be less than from new efforts to persuade the government to treat the industry more generously.

We could readily conjure up visions of civilian companies following some of the practices of that branch of American industry, defense production, which is now most closely tied to governmental decision-making. Business-financed hunting lodges and fishing trips for civilian government planners might seem to merely follow an older defense industry tradition. But, legal or not, such public sector "marketing" activities would seem to be a low-priority usage of business resources. Yet, given the incentive of any organization to grow and prosper in the environment it faces, this result would not be surprising under a system of strong national economic planning and decision-making.

CONCLUSION

The advocates of national economic planning who base their case on an extension of business planning activities overestimate the state-of-the-art in the private sector. In a study of thirteen large, technically-oriented manufacturing companies, the author and his colleagues reported that most of the output of long-range planning groups was found to be more in the nature of scheduling current programs with long lead times, rather than in the development of the long-range business plans.[38]

The study concluded that typical long-range plans contained excessive amounts of trivia, such as monthly delivery schedules, the recruiting budget, square footage of storage space by type, and so forth. "This may—in a small way—help to explain why business plans are so infrequently used as real decision-making tools."[39]

The rapid turnover of planning staffs and business planners is striking testimony to the basic dissatisfaction with the results. On the basis of many years of attending meetings with business planners, the author developed the following rule of thumb: anytime you hear a business planner explain how planning is done in his or her company, remember that the odds are better than one out of two that in two years that planning staff will no longer exist, that person will no longer head the planning operation, or both.

It is apparent that no amount of formalized planning has eliminated any company's uncertainty concerning future technological change, the vagaries of weather, discoveries of energy or other natural resources, outbreaks of war, assassinations of national leaders, or even shifts in the desires of the fickle consumer. As Gerald Sirkin has stated, "Planners have no crystal ball," or as James Matheson, Director of the Decision Analysis Group of the Stanford Research Institute, put the matter, "In this age you can't plan on your plans." [40]

Yet, of course, business planning continues, and for a variety of reasons, including the sheer momentum of past activity as well as the useful by-products of the information provided to the management. There is an important "opportunity cost" involved that should be recognized. The manpower and other resources that are devoted to the planning effort are unavailable for other purposes.

Both the high cost and the often modest results have led many companies to scale back the originally overly ambitious planning efforts on which they had embarked. In good measure this may have been the natural pattern of reaction and accommodation to the overselling of a new management activity, but one avowedly with more durability than the short-term fad. Yet, at least in the case of one major corporation (General Motors), apparently the word planning no longer is used in any corporate title or to describe any corporate activity. [41]

As pointed out earlier, the possibilities for building on business planning experiences to mold a national planning system are not attractive. Even discounting the very serious shortcomings of existing business planning techniques, the differences between business and government decision-making are fundamental.

Despite all of the sophisticated apparatus, business planning is based on the traditionally implicit—and increasingly explicit—assumption that the ultimate decisions on the allocation of resources in the society are to be made by individual consumers. An important corollary of that is if a company guesses wrong on what consumers buy it will suffer the consequences.

Government planning, implicitly or explicitly, is based on a fundamentally different set of assumptions. Government determines what it considers to be in the society's overall interests. If the public does not respond accordingly, it is not the planners who are considered to be at fault. Rather, new and more effective devices must be developed to get the public to accommodate to the planners' view of the good (or great) society.

Boiled down to its essence, business planning is part of a decentralized decision-making process where the individual consumer makes the ultimate choices. National planning is a centralized process in which the key economic decisions are made in the form of governmental edicts. The greater danger of adopting a form of centralized economic planning is that it will, perhaps unintentionally at first but inevitably as its initial results prove disappointing, propel the society away from market freedoms and toward greater governmental controls over individual behavior.

PART IV
THE DYNAMICS OF
CENTRALIZED PLANNING

SOME PARADOXES FOR PLANNERS: HUMAN KNOWLEDGE AND ITS LIMITATIONS

VINCENT OSTROM
Professor of Political Science, Indiana University

The unique element in the human condition is the relationship of knowledge to future developments. Knowledge is composed of two ingredients: learning and language. Learning is characteristic of all organisms that have nervous systems, and it depends on a capacity to discover patterns of variety and constraint in an environment which can be used to advantage either in avoiding dangers or securing benefits. In learning organisms memory develops by storing images so that each organism, during its lifetime, can accumulate learning and act to improve its adaptive potential. The accumulated learning for species other than homo sapiens is largely lost when life expires: very little information is transferred from one generation to another.

Language introduces a radical new dimension to human experience. Sounds of speech and markings are used to symbolize or stand for objects, events and relationships. These sounds are the basis of language, which can be used to communicate learning to contemporary or succeeding generations. The use of language to organize and communicate learning has greatly amplified the human capacity for accumulating and using large bodies of knowledge.

Knowing patterns of regularities permits people to anticipate and predict events, and to manipulate elements and relationships and thereby to control various factors in their environment. Knowledge is thus the most critical element in man's ability to plan.

The growth of human knowledge is cumulative. Prior or existing knowledge is transmitted from one generation to the next through education. New learning contributes new increments to this process, and the search for new learning and knowledge has been greatly increased by the development of new methodologies associated with modern scientific inquiry. Scientific experimentation has yielded new knowledge about learning how to learn. As a result, new knowledge has grown and is growing at an exponential rate producing a virtual explosion in the generation of new knowledge and new technologies during the last century.

KNOWLEDGE AS AN INSTRUMENT FOR PLANNING

Learning and knowledge are essential to all purposive action. By drawing on knowledge about patterns of variety and constraint, human beings can anticipate or predict the consequences that will follow from various conditions. Wherever knowledge serves to anticipate and predict, it can also be used to plan and control. Realizing a material objective or a planned consequence requires that appropriate means (causal conditions) be arrayed to produce the desired consequences or end. Different methods may be used to produce any given result, but the method selected will depend on the criteria of choice—which means on the values of the person choosing. For example, if the criterion of efficiency is used, means will be chosen to provide the desired result at least cost.

Whoever uses knowledge to select conditions to produce an intended effect is engaged in planning. In the sense that human conduct is purposive behavior, all human conduct is organized by reference to plans and expectations.

However, all knowledge and therefore all planning is subject to serious limitations. To understand these limitations, we will examine three key problems: 1) the problem of language; 2) new knowledge and the problem of change; and 3) the problem of increasing relative ignorance. We will then pursue the implications of these considerations for planning.

THE PROBLEM OF LANGUAGE

All languages use words to categorize and classify phenomena according to specifiable attributes or relationships. This is an essential characteristic of all languages: using words implies classification and generalization. The process of translating reference to events into words necessarily implies that some information is lost in communication, for the use of words always implies simplification. The generalizations necessary for human reason are gross simplifications devoid of time and place information.[1] Despite our propensity to talk about "reality," human thought as mediated through language can only comprehend *simplifications* of "reality."

Formal knowledge states generalized relationships. Using formal knowledge for practical application requires specific information about unique events in specific space and time conditions. The costs of procuring such specific information is considerable, and even then the fallible planner will fail to consider all information relevent to a planned effort. Errors will therefore result.

Even if a planner knows the appropriate variables to be considered, a substantial problem will remain to procure appropriate information about those variables. Any effort to plan for human welfare, for example, must consider incredibly complicated and diverse factors relating to "needs," "tastes," "preferences," or "demands." All of these refer to internal or subjective states—which modern science and technology is notably unable to "read."

Given the inability of people to read each other's minds, we must rely on language and explicitly-structured opportunities for individuals to reveal their preferences to one another. One such opportunity is the economic market. Price can be used to measure preferences or demands to the extent that money can be used as a medium of exchange to measure the value of goods and services. But not all valued events are exchanged for money. Changing preferences and conditions of scarcity may lead to radical shifts in the values assigned to human efforts. Political mechanisms also play an important part in allowing for the formation and articulation of public opinion. Among these mechanisms are elections, forms of political representation, election campaign debates, and public policy debates on legislative decisions. The margin of error for politicians who are skilled in "reading" the changing currents of public opinion is large enough. But the margin of error among others, less skilled than politicians, will be even greater.

Even where reliable knowledge exists for calculating general relationships between conditions and consequences or means and ends, that knowledge will be inadequate to deal with discrete time and place contingencies. Some information about time and place variables can be acquired at a cost. But even then the practical artisan confronts substantial difficulties in working with those time and place constraints. Some information such as that reflecting "values," "preferences," or "demands" can never be directly and reliably observed.

Milovan Djilas was correct when he observed: "History does not abound with instances of thinkers' predictions having come true, least of all those relating to social patterns and people's attitudes and ways of life."[2] This generalization holds for the future as well as the past; for planners as well as "thinkers" and scholars.

THE PLANNERS' PARADOX: THE GROWTH OF NEW KNOWLEDGE AND THE PROBLEM OF CHANGE

The growth of new knowledge creates disturbing problems as it alters and disrupts established conditions. New knowledge gives rise to new possibilities, which manifest themselves as new events, relationships or occurrences.

New knowledge and new possibilities place severe limitations on the ability of planners to anticipate future events and contingencies. *Under conditions of rapidly expanding knowledge and technological development, long-term, comprehensive planning becomes impossible.* So long as human beings can learn and generate new knowledge, planners face an uncertain future, which they cannot take into account in formulating their plans.

The creation of new knowledge and therefore new possibilities necessarily subjects human efforts to anticipate future events to limited time horizons. Thus, all planning and developmental efforts will become obsolete as old knowledge and techniques give way to new. *Under conditions of rapidly expanding knowledge and technological development, planning is subject to an increasing magnitude of error, the further projections are extended into the future.*

Long-term, comprehensive plans designed to be "master plans" providing a "blueprint" to predetermine the future course of events will be futile endeavors. Failure in long-term planning is documented well enough by many other contributors to this volume. Planning can be a useful strategy for organizing information to assess alternative possibilities only within limited, specified time horizons, and only by acknowledging uncertainties caused by the obsolescence of old knowledge and the generation of new knowledge.

So long as human beings continue to learn and acquire new knowledge, each new generation confronts the future with uncertainty. Without perfect knowledge, it is impossible to anticipate all courses of action. On the other hand, if perfect knowledge existed, there would be no need for continued learning. The opportunities inherent in continued learning imply that human beings must necessarily bear the burden of living in an uncertain world.

If long-term, comprehensive planning is impossible, then decision-makers must move to second-order solutions by relying upon decision rules to order and change social relationships. Relying on decision rules to order social relationships implies using the political process to deal with uncertain futures. In these terms, legislation is an appropriate form of contingency planning where harmful possibilities can be foreclosed as unlawful, leaving other possibilities open to choice. The task of legislation is to change decision rules to reflect new developments in knowledge, technologies, and the material condition of human societies. Thus, societies can adjust and respond in an orderly way to the growth of new knowledge.

THE PARADOX OF THE LEARNED IGNORAMUS: THE PROBLEM OF INCREASING RELATIVE IGNORANCE

Rapid growth in the aggregate pool of human knowledge and in the generation of new knowledge causes increasing difficulties for decision-makers and planners in an increasingly complex society. The Spanish philosopher José Ortega y Gassett, in *The Revolt of the Masses,* advanced the thesis that specialization of knowledge produces a "new barbarian" whom he characterized as a "learned ignoramus."[3] *As the aggregate pool of human knowledge increases, the relative ignorance of each individual increases in relation to that pool.* This is the problem of increasing relative ignorance or the paradox of the learned ignoramus.

The condition of increasing relative ignorance is recognized in the whimsical observation that: "A specialist is one who knows more and more about less and less." Or its corollary: A generalist is one who knows less and less about more and more. Each observation implies limits to the knowledge available to individual persons. Everyone risks being a learned ignoramus unless he is aware of his own relative ignorance.

No one can "see" or "know" the "whole picture." All decision-makers are fallible, and all decision-making occurs under conditions of uncertainty. No decision-maker knows all of the consequences that will flow from his choices or his actions. And all decision-making is therefore subject to error.

Where it is understood that decision-makers are fallible, the decision-making process can develop mechanisms to correct mistakes. Successful corrective mechanisms require ongoing and diverse forms of assessment to estimate the probable consequences of alternative courses of action. Since an objective understanding of citizen preferences or utilities is impossible, mechanisms permitting diverse elements of the population to express preferences are also important for decision-makers concerned with advancing people's welfare. Efforts to understand those preferences require substantial time and effort in the course of decision-making. Unfortunately, the increasing complexity of modern societies will require increasing expenditures of time and effort in decision-making without any "guarantee" that errors will be avoided.

The paradox of the learned ignoramus does not, of course, foreclose the possibility that planners or decision-makers will assume that they are omniscient. On the contrary. An analyst who assumes his own omniscience will assume he can "see" the "whole picture," "know" what is "good" for people, and plan or predetermine the future course of events. Although such a presumption will likely increase his proneness to error, the increased probability of error will not, obviously, eliminate recourse to the presumption: as we know all too well, the myth of omniscience is extremely persistent.

In *The Myth of the State,* Ernst Cassirer discusses how those who presume to be omniscient observers can substitute a technique of modern political mythology for critical inquiry and analysis.[4] Decision-makers and political analysts, who assume they can "see" the "whole picture," develop a rhetoric which substitutes slogans for reasoned analysis. Where they are considered social imperatives, these slogans receive mythical status and take on the attributes of magical words.

In the modern political mythology, decision-making processes are transformed into rites, in which the frequent repetition of slogans reaffirms through magical words the faith of the devout. In such decision-making rites, evil forces are exorcised as impediments to the ideal state while the faithful reaffirm their devotion to the struggle for social imperatives, and the new medicine men promise cures for all social evils.

The rhetoric associated with the "war on poverty," the "urban crisis," the "environmental crisis," and "comprehensive planning" is acquiring the status of political mythology. Decision-making processes associated with this mythology are also taking on ritual characteristics. Comprehensive, all-inclusive solutions are called for. Sources of evil are identified as having "special interest" opposed to the "public good" of the greater community. Those who resist the solutions proposed by "omniscient observers" are accused of being exploiters and obstructionists unwilling to assume the burdens of poverty, congestion and erosion in the environmental quality of urban life.

IMPLICATIONS

The growth of new knowledge implies that the potentials for human development are subject to unforeseeable changes. The price of progress is an uncertain future. Since long-term plans are therefore destined to fail, how can man cope with the limitations that are inherent in the organization and use of human knowledge?

The critical question involves how institutional arrangements can improve the quality of information and thereby encourage more intelligent decisions in a given time and place. Market institutions, for example, generate information about the relative value of marketable goods and services by prices in competitive markets. Buyers give potential vendors information about demand by the price they are willing to pay. Preferences are revealed and vendors can adjust supply conditions to meet demand in light of cost calculations at going prices.

Economic transactions in market economies generate a broad spectrum of information. By aggregating data revealed in individual transactions, all participants in an economy can secure information about aggregate economic productivity and changing patterns of demand. Each individual can do his planning in light of his own estimate of future expectations based upon existing information and trends. Markets, as generators of information, enable all members of a society to plan their own endeavours so as to take advantage of the opportunities they perceive to be available. If they err, they bear the costs of their own mistakes in light of the information available to them and to everyone else.

By contrast, a highly-centralized decision-making system operating through hierarchically-organized command structures creates serious distortions of information and a high propensity for errors. In his *Politics of Bureaucracy,* Gordon Tullock has demonstrated how a hierarchically-ordered structure functions as a transmitter of information and develops selective biases at each link in the communication chain.[5] This process results from two assumptions Tullock makes about centralized structures: that superiors have a controlling influence over the career advancement of subordinates and that subordinates as self-interested individuals will act so as to advance their career potentials. Thus, Tullock argues, at each link in the hierarchical chain of command subordinates will advance information reflecting favorably, and repress information reflecting adversely, upon their career potentials—thus causing a selective biasing or distortion of information.

In large-scale bureaucracies, subordinates will amplify information pleasing to superiors and repress contrary information. Expectations will diverge from events; and promises from performance. Credibility gaps will occur as information conveyed by leaders diverges from the experience people have with subordinates at operating levels of the bureaucracy. This is anything but surprising: credibility gaps, goal displacement and error-proneness are inevitable in any structure where information is systematically biased or distorted.

These conditions are exacerbated where central decision-making authorities make basic economic decisions in a society. The greater the discretion of central authorities to allocate economic goods and services, the greater the incentives to make such decisions in secrecy. For advanced information will enable some to act so as to discount the effects of the expected decision. Those who correctly anticipate a decision to impose price controls and rationing, for example, will have incentives to stockpile reserves to meet expected shortages. Advanced information will thus tend to frustrate the objectives of a price-control and rationing policy.

However, secrecy in central decision-making may induce errors for want of due deliberation. Central authorities rarely surround themselves with their critics; they tend to make decisions without critically considering and debating alternatives. Without critical assessment, the probability of error increases.

In addition, preemptive decisions, made secretly and without advanced public information, increase the probability of error and failure for those who did not anticipate the new turn of events. The failure of those affected by preemptive decisions is not accountable to error for which they must assume responsibility but to the preemptive actions of central authorities. Citizens are no better in reading the minds of bureaucrats than bureaucrats are in reading the minds of citizens. Centralized decision-making encourages distortion of information, secrecy, and proneness to error. These tendencies go a long way toward explaining the consistent record of failures produced by efforts everywhere to plan even limited sectors in an economy. By the same token, the same tendencies that are endemic in centralized systems can be reduced by constitutionally distributing authority among diverse decision structures.

Perhaps the most pervasive self-governing structure is the economic market, which we have already referred to, and which is discussed by various other contributers to this volume. But beyond the economic market, the founding fathers appreciated the importance of distributing authority in the American political system. Thus, the separation of powers, with its checks and balances, encourages a due process of inquiry, which serves as a self-correcting mechanism that minimizes the chances for error.[6]

Constitutional and legislative decision-making are organized to consider public policies in open public deliberation. In such a system, anyone who wants to communicate about matters of public concern with his fellow citizens or with public officials can assert constitutional rights to freedom of speech, press, petition, and to due process of law. He need not be the member of an inner circle to attempt to influence the course of decisions in relation either to his fellow citizens or his elected representatives.

Furthermore, legislative bodies are organized to secure the representation of diverse interests in the community at large. Legislatures serve as forums which institutionalize public discussions and deliberation on matters of public policy. Decisions are thus made after due deliberation, rather than in secret consultation. Justifications must be made before decisions are made—not after. When legislatures act within proper limits, they formulate general rules of action designed to serve some common purpose or public benefit. The rules are formulated in advance to guide future actions.

The executive branch has responsibility for implementing legislative enactments. Legislative rules stipulate the proper measures for holding executive agents to account for their actions.

Anyone adversely affected can independently scrutinize and challenge executive acts through the judicial process, to hold executive officials accountable to standards of public law. In the courts, litigants present alternative claims and arguments, with supporting evidence to lay the basis for judgment. Thus, the judicial process again provides opportunities to aggregate and array information so that an informed decision can be rendered in light of conflicting interests. And judgment is made in light of prior legislation.

Thus, the diverse structures and processes of government decision-making contribute to a due process of inquiry, and can correct for the distortion of information and proneness to error that inhere in highly integrated, large-scale bureaucracies. This is only possible when the diverse structures can function independently of the central executive authority.

The information-generating capabilities of diverse structures operating in any single unit of government can be greatly amplified in a federal system in which all problems do not have to be processed through a single unit of government.*

Different problems impinging different communities of interest can be resolved at an appropriate level of government where all essential parties of interest are contained within a given jurisdiction. A federal system of government, thus, gives multiple problem-solving capabilities among the many units of local, state and national government.[7]

CONCLUSION

The human potential for learning means that all decisions must be made under conditions of uncertainty about the future. The best human beings can do is draw upon existing knowledge to array alternative possibilities and choose those possibilities that will enhance expected well-being within limited time horizons. Those who presume to be omniscient observers and who wish to ordain the future, do not understand the fundamental creativity of the human species. This very creativity places a correlative burden upon every member of the species to face an uncertain future. All of life is an effort to take best advantage of changing opportunities and possibilities. Everyone plans as best he can in light of the information he can mobilize in relation to the choices he must make. The best planning will occur in societies that generate the best flow of information, provide mechanisms to articulate conflicts of interests, and search out mutually-agreeable solutions that increase potential well-being. Self-governing societies depend upon the planning capabilities exercised by everyone—not by a select few.

*Robert Hawkins discussed another aspect of this problem in his contribution to this volume.

THE POLITICS AND
BUREAUCRACY OF PLANNING

JAMES BUCHANAN
Professor of Economics, Center for Public Choice,
Virginia Polytechnic Institute

GORDON TULLOCK
Professor of Economics, Center for Public Choice,
Virginia Polytechnic Institute

The great body of the (discontented) party . . . are commonly
intoxicated with the imaginary beauty of this ideal system, of which
they have no experience, but which has been represented to them in all
the most dazzling colors in which the eloquence of their leaders could
paint it. Those leaders themselves, though they originally may have
meant nothing but their own aggrandizement, become, many of them,
in time the dupes of their own sophistry, and are as eager for this great
reformation as the weakest and foolishest of their followers. . . .

The man of system . . . seems to imagine that he can arrange the
different members of a great society with as much ease as the hand
arranges the different pieces upon a chess-board; he does not consider
that the pieces upon the chess-board have no other principle of motion
besides that which the hand impresses upon them; but that, in the great
chess-board of human society, every single piece has a principle of
motion of its own, altogether different from that which the legislature
might choose to impress upon it.

Adam Smith, *The Theory of Moral Sentiments*

255

INTRODUCTION

In order to stick to our last, we must resist several temptations. We forego the enticing prospect of reviewing the enthusiasm for national planning that surfaced in the 1930s and 1940s, along with a discussion of the deflation of those planners' dreams. We reluctantly hold back our proclivities to teach lessons (allegedly a Scottish trait) to those who refuse to understand the age-old economic verities. Finally, and most importantly, we must force ourselves to take seriously proposals which are all too easy to ridicule.

Our purpose is to concentrate on the politics and bureaucracy of planning. By this we mean the political and administrative structure within which institutions for national economic planning will operate, including the incentives that will affect the behavior of persons who act in those institutions. In other words, we shall concentrate on the politics of planning, with politics understood in its public-choice meaning. We shall develop our discussion in two separate settings. In the first we assume that the proposed agencies for national economic planning are to operate within a democratic framework, with "democratic" here being defined as roughly descriptive of modern American politics. In the second setting, we shall assume that the proposed agencies for national economic planning are to be "divorced" from democratic politics.

DEMOCRATIC PLANNING

We should, at the outset, indicate some agreement with those who advance proposals for planning. We agree that much is amiss with the national economy, much that seems to require fixing. "Stagflation," high unemployment along with continuing inflation, suggests political, institutional, and/or policy failure. Disagreement arises only when we come to examine alternative remedies. The first question to be asked is whether or not national planning will make things better or worse. Those who are tempted to respond that things could scarcely be made worse tend to forget the excessive costs imposed on all taxpayers from yet more bureaucratic units in Washington.

Let us first look at what planning agencies might be able to accomplish that is not being accomplished now. What specific reforms might they be able to implement? Rather than seek an exhaustive listing of potential reforms, let us concentrate attention on a single one that would, if accomplished, do much toward getting unemployment within tolerable bounds.

Consider what is perhaps the most obvious example of an economic policy reform that has long been acknowledged to be needed by any economist worth his salt. This involves removal of the labor market structural distortions created by minimum wage laws. Widespread and double-digit unemployment exists among teen-aged potential members of the labor force, especially among minority group teen-agers. This particular concentration of joblessness is substantially the result of minimum wage restrictions that prohibit low-productivity workers and potential employers from reaching voluntary contractual agreements on terms that are mutually beneficial to all parties. Any meaningful reform in the structure of national labor markets would surely have to include either an outright repeal of the law or at least the introduction of differential minima allowing young workers to work at lower wage levels.

This reform does not require new knowledge, either in the form of ivory-tower analytics or in new accumulations or processing of data. The effects of this reform are known to all economists, both within and without the current bureaucracy, and also to the elected representatives in Congress, many of whom are highly sophisticated on economic matters. It is sheer folly to presume that ignorance lies at the heart of at least this economic-policy failure. Neither ignorance nor evil intent prevents these politicians from enacting the required reform. They retain the minimum wage because it is in their rational political interest to do so.

This much may be acknowledged. The question then becomes whether or not the proposed agencies for national economic planning could produce differing results. Would an

"Office of National Economic Planning," an "Economic Planning Board," or a "Council on Economic Planning" be likely to produce significant change in minimum-wage restrictions? The answer seems clear; these agencies would be no more likely to produce effective action than those political institutions now in existence, including the Department of Labor, the Council of Economic Advisors, or the United States Congress. And for precisely the same reasons.

The senior office holders in the proposed planning agencies would, of necessity, be responsible to elected politicians in the Executive Branch and in Congress. Would we expect them to be nonresponsive? Would we want them to be? Consider the position of a single top-level planning agency official who might have secured his appointment by the President and who might have been approved by the Senate. He is not likely to have been appointed and approved at all if his political supporters predicted that he would behave like a maverick, and that, on assuming office, he would begin to act counter to the political interests of these same supporters.

The fact is, that the change in bureaucratic structure will not change one whit the political interests that insure the survival of minimum-wage restrictions, even in the face of widespread unemployment. It will remain organized labor's interest to oppose, and strongly so, any effort to weaken the discriminatory protection provided by minimum wage laws to both union wage workers and nonunion workers at higher levels. Very few politicians, regardless of party or ideological persuasion, have been observed to oppose minimum wage restrictions, and the illusion of national economic planning is not likely to change this behavior pattern.

The top-level agency official who refuses to consider the "planning" reform to eliminate minimum wage laws proposed by his more isolated junior-level bureaucrats would not be acting either "irresponsibly" or "irrationally." He will not knowingly place himself, and his agency, in the position of advocating or recommending structural reforms that are predicted to run afoul of the interests of strong and concentrated groups. To do so will insure either the demise of the agency or, more likely, his own removal from office.

The behavior of the top-level agency bureaucrat is not difficult to predict, and indeed his behavior is no different from the behavior commonly observed within the bureaucratic units that already exist in abundance. His behavior is relatively simple to understand and explain once we so much as glance sideways at the incentive structure in a democratic political setting. The top-level bureaucrat wants to retain his office along with its perquisites while elected politicians seek to remain in power. How will mere addition to the number of agencies modify this result? How will the creation of agencies charged with national planning insure that overall economic efficiency will be given more weight, and that those not represented by labor organizations, including the teen-aged unemployed, will be paid more attention? Without reforming the incentive structure itself, there seems little chance that major changes can be effected.

An advocate of national economic planning may accept the argument made above. He may acknowledge that any newly-created agency, regardless of its general charge, may be ineffective in securing any institutional reform that is strongly opposed by concentrated pressure groups in the society. But he may continue to support such agencies to enact numerous reforms for which there would be no concentrated opposition. The assumption is that ignorance is, indeed, the barrier preventing the reforms from being enacted now.

This assumption seems open to serious question. Consider another example, and one without concentrated pressure group interests of the normal variety. It can surely be argued persuasively that real rates of income tax paid to government by individuals and by corporations should not depend on inflation rates. Congress should explicitly legislate tax rates and they should not be determined indirectly by the monetary authorities. Nevertheless, despite the widespread expectation that inflation will continue, there is little serious interest in the reform which could have isolated real rates of tax from inflation. We observe relatively little pressure to introduce indexing of tax brackets, exemption and deduction levels, and bases for depreciation and for capital gains. Would a national economic planning agency be more likely to call attention to this general reform which does not attract concentrated group interests from the private sector?

We must first try to explain and to understand why tax indexing has not been more widely discussed. Is this due to ignorance? Hardly. The indexing of taxes has not proven a popular reform measure because of the opposed interests of the governmental bureaucracy itself. The continued increases in real rates of income tax that inflation generates allow government to grow disproportionately. This offers a built-in engine for the relative growth of the public sector in the economy. We should not, therefore, be at all surprised when we observe that the Treasury Department bureaucracy has consistently opposed this reform. Why should we expect a national economic planning board to behave differently?

A national planning agency, supposedly being more comprehensive in its view than the Treasury, might pay less heed to the strict revenue potential of the inflation-induced increases in real rates of income tax. But the built-in bias toward the support of any institution that insures the relative growth of government could not be absent. Individual bureaucrats, especially at the middle levels of office, are highly mobile as among separate governmental agencies. Hence, they will clearly be motivated to support measures which increase the size and number of their bureaucratic alternatives.

We may consider a related example of policy reform in which roughly similar conclusions will follow. Economists now widely agree that one of the most urgently required reforms would involve a reduction in the number and size of government regulatory agencies. But would anyone seriously predict that a national planning board or agency would take the lead in recommending and advocating that several of the long-established, old-line regulatory bureaus be eliminated? As in all of the examples discussed, ignorance is not the primary causal influence that prevents structural reform. As economists, we need only to look at the direction which individual self-interest will lead, whether this be the interest of those in the private or the public sector.

We may consider in somewhat more detail the specific motives of a member of a National Planning Board or, indeed, any other high-level government agency. Many of the advocates of planning appear to believe that if legislation instructs a high-level government official to promote the public good or to increase economic growth or to prevent unemployment, he will devotedly and intelligently work toward the objective so specified. High-ranking officials, however, are not machines. They do not necessarily carry out the duties defined in the first paragraph of the enabling legislation. They are far more likely to attempt to maximize their own goals than those which have been specified for them.

If we want government officials to perform some task, we must establish a system in which their own personal incentives lead them in the direction in which we wish them to go. The simple and traditional way used by all private employers to get individuals to do as their employer wants is to have their terms of employment related to their success in carrying out the employer's wishes. This works in private employment and it would also work very well in government employment. But the problem with government is that very commonly the activity that will get a bureaucrat fired or have his powers reduced is not a violation of the theoretical specifications in the enabling act but the activity of carrying out such specifications.

Consider the member of a hypothetical planning board who has been instructed in the act of Congress that he should attempt to increase the rate of growth, raise general prosperity, reduce unemployment, and eliminate inflation. All of these goals are desirable (although to some extent mutually conflicting), but unfortunately, it is unlikely, given the way democratic government works, that the bureaucrat will be subject to dismissal if he does not achieve them. On the other hand, unfortunately he may be subject to removal, or at least to having his powers reduced, if he *does* attempt to maximize these goals at the cost of injuring various pressure groups.

Probably the largest single conflict of interest between any employee, whether private or public, and the desires of his employer, whether that employer is the national government or a local store, is the desire of the employee not to work as hard as the employer would like. Once again, in private business the employer threatens the employee with firing if he does not work. As we move up the pyramid of command in private businesses, however, it becomes harder and harder to monitor the employee's efforts. At the top level, where policy decisions are made, it may be almost impossible to tell whether a decision-making employee is thinking as hard about the policy alternatives as the employer would like him to think. In private business this may make little difference, since the employer can consult the balance sheet. If the organization is not making a profit, the president can be fired. There is no similar procedure in government; and higher-level government officials will surely take advantage of the absence of an effective monitoring structure.

This is not to suggest, and especially with high-ranking government officials, that "nonwork" involves idleness; "nonwork" is likely to involve pursuing personal hobbies, frequently very vigorously. Usually the people who rise to high rank are vigorous types and interested in both physical and mental activity. However, they are not generally motivated to undertake the kind of intellectual effort which would make it necessary for them to change their minds on various subjects or to adopt the value patterns of their employer rather than their own. Thus, one would anticipate that high-ranking bureaucrats would turn out to be less well informed about their subject matter than we would hope and to promote various personal interests rather than those of the nation as a whole. So far, no one has even remotely succeeded in working out an institutional means of dealing with this problem, for a planning administration, or for any other part of the bureaucracy.

Leaving aside the tendency to "shirk," the individual bureaucrat or high official of a planning board would have two general motives, one of which is essentially protective, i.e., the desire to avoid or deflect attacks upon himself and his commission and, in particular, not do anything which might lead the legislature to reduce the power of the agency. Second, he would like to seek positive gains, to do things which are likely to expand the power and influence of his commission. And in this vein, he will seek in a somewhat less direct way to increase the power of the government as a whole, for a general enhancement of government power will have the effect of enhancing the power of his commission. This last consideration is somewhat modified by the fact that severe squabbles are very common among agencies of the government. These are essentially power struggles in which each agency tries to add to its power by taking from its neighboring agency; it is only an accident that the outcome accords with what we might call the "public interest."

The protective function is the one perhaps most emphasized by students of the regulatory commission, and it should be noted that the National Planning Board will function much like a regulatory commission. The careful studies, for example, of the Canadian National Bank, which has responsibilities for the Canadian economy rather like those of the Federal Reserve Board, indicate that its actions are very hard to explain if one assumes that it is attempting to deal with inflation and unemployment in a rational way.[1] Indeed, those people who try to explain it on these grounds invariably come to the conclusion that the National Bank is simply stupid. On the other hand, if you consider the Bank's behavior as an effort to minimize the pressures on it by groups of people who have influence with the Parliament, it turns out that the policy is rather well explained. By act of Parliament, the Bank of Canada is supposed to maximize the well-being of the country. It persistently sacrifices the well-being of the country, however, to the well-being of the Bank of Canada and, in particular, to the well-being of the president of the Bank of Canada and its board.

No such careful study has been made of the Federal Reserve Board. Indeed, most students of the Federal Reserve Board follow the view that the Federal Reserve Board is attempting to keep unemployment and inflation in hand and just doing a very bad job. It seems likely, however, that a similar study would turn up evidence that the Federal Reserve Board, for essentially protective reasons, also is maximizing, quite reasonably, variables other than those which are specified. It does not want its wings shorn by contests with other government agencies who have support in Congress.

As a brief digression, those interested in national planning and a national planning board should consider carefully the history of the Federal Reserve Board. Over the last 50 years, it has had many of the duties which it is thought should be carried out by a national planning board, and it clearly has done a very bad job of carrying them out. It is extremely dubious that a national planning board would be composed of higher quality personnel or be more carefully insulated from political pressures than is the Federal Reserve Board; hence, it seems very dubious that a national planning board would do better.

It is because we predict such protective activity on the part of a national planning board that we predict that such an agency would not decide to abrogate the Minimum Wage Act. A strong stand against minimum wages would immediately create political enemies for the agency and would not generate any offsetting political support.

As another example, consider the grain export problems in the United States. A national planning board presumably would be brought into the policy discussion. Given the varying interests involved in grain export problems, it is not easy to predict exactly what policy such a board might recommend. However, we can predict that members of the board would select their policy stance in response to political pressures. If they did not choose to make policy in that way, it is surely predictable that Congress would gradually reduce the powers of the agency.

In addition to this sort of defensive activity, we can expect a planning agency or bureau able to engage in offensive activity, in attempting to expand its own power and influence. In general, if it wants to be effective in this expansion, it must seek out areas where it can find political allies. Thus, if a national planning bureau had been in existence during the 1973–74 period, we might predict it would have taken a strong stand of some sort on energy. It is highly likely, however, that this strong stand would not have been aimed at maximizing the well-being of the United States, but simply at whatever happened to be politically feasible. Such an agency might, for example, have followed much the same line as Senator Jackson has followed in his campaign to become President.

This analysis of the incentive structure governing any planning agency does not prove that ''planning'' is not desired and that such an agency should not be established. It may be that the alternatives are worse. Still, until the proponents of planning frankly acknowledge that any planning board or agency will have the characteristics we describe above, and until they present arguments indicating that such an agency would, nonetheless, improve the workings of the economic system, we are obligated to remain skeptical. The positive arguments for the establishment of planning boards universally assume that those boards will carry out the instructions of Congress as presented in the first paragraph of the enabling act. Only if the advocates take a more realistic view can we even begin to compare a planning board with other institutional alternatives.

Of course, we should note that the advocates of a national planning board may not really propose that it do anything in particular. The French planning method, which its proponents refer to as ''indicative planning,'' is frequently referred to as ''decorative planning'' by more realistic observers. Norway is another country which has a planning administration and an annual plan with no effect on anything except the employment of a few civil servants. It may be that proponents of planning in the United States have the same idea in mind. If so, however, they should explain why the expenditure of several million dollars on a planning board for decorative purposes is superior to putting the same amount of money into providing more flower gardens in Washington.

PLANNING BY ADMINISTRATIVE LAW

If effective economic policy reforms are to be implemented, the "constitution" must be modified. The pressure of democratic politics must, somehow, be eliminated over many areas of the political economy. There are two quite distinct ways of proceeding to accomplish such "constitutional" changes. We might look to a genuine contractual rearrangement, a literal restructuring of the effective "economic constitution," in which the interests of all groups, as reflected in the political *status quo,* are taken into account, and from which a new structural framework might emerge. Such a contractual rearrangement would prohibit direct political interference with the workings of ordinary markets on a piecemeal basis, and would provide an appropriate setting for private sector growth and development, including protections against the uncertainties of governmental policy shifts. This pathway toward overall structural reform is constitutional democracy.

The second, and alternative, way of rewriting our effective "economic constitution" is *not* consistent with constitutional democracy. Unfortunately, however, something of this second sort may well be part of the motivation behind the current drive for national economic planning. We may choose, deliberately, to create economic planning agencies which are *not responsible* to political pressures of democratic process, agencies which possess power to implement policy changes by administrative "law," and which are explicitly immunized from the feedbacks of constituencies. The ardent advocate of national economic planning may have in mind something like an "Economic Supreme Court," empowered to modify the whole workings of the national economy.

Such a body could, of course, abolish minimum wage restrictions, to return to our first example. It could, quite simply, issue a directive to the effect that such restrictions are contrary to the "economic constitution," as interpreted (or to some "national plan"). But here lies the rub. With the Supreme Court, at least before the Warren years, law was made by reinterpretation of an existing written document, one that was broadly understood by the citizenry, and one that was understood in fine detail by practicing professionals. Even in the Warren Court's extremities, the majority tried to "explain" its decisions in terms of some ongoing constitutional doctrine. But where could an "Economic Supreme Court" find its comparable basis?

Could we expect professional economists to agree on an "ideal economic constitution"? Clearly, we could not, because conflict among objectives must be resolved before agreement could be reached, and such conflict cannot be removed by scientific inquiry or by professional expertise. What is the "optimal" rate of growth for the national economy? What is the "optimal" mix between the private sector and the public sector? What weights are to be assigned to effort and to need in determining patterns of income distribution? What is the "optimal" spatial structure of the economy? We need do little more than to relate such questions to indicate that scientifically-definitive answers are not possible.

There are two ways in which outcomes representing answers to such questions may be generated. We may allow those outcomes to emerge from the complex process of decentralized decision-making in the private sector, combined with some democratic decision-making in the public sector. Or, we may impose outcomes by the arbitrary dictates of someone, some person or some selected body, in this case the Economic Supreme Court in the guise of a national planning agency.

At this point, we must once again resist the temptation to discuss the philosophical implications of such a delegation of power to a planning agency, as well as the relationship between such a power concentration and the prospects for human freedom, generally considered. Our purpose, however, is the much narrower one of analyzing the incentives that will bear on the behavior of those who might be chosen to wield such extraordinary power over their fellow human beings.

In the American setting, it seems useful once again to refer to the Supreme Court analogue. Contrary to the popular view, the Supreme Court does *not* follow the election returns. This belief is perhaps best understood as a myth designed to provide citizens with an illusion of control over the judiciary that they simply do not possess. The control of the citizenry over the judicial process is, indeed, remote, as would be any such control over a genuinely nonpolitical agency for national economic planning. To get some rough idea as to how the planners might behave, we may look at the patterns of behavior exhibited by Supreme Court justices. But with one all-important difference. Justices are trained in law, and, historically and traditionally, law is embedded in history, in precedent. It is not something which is conceived to emerge whole cloth from the value premises of the judicial decision-makers. The Warren Court did modify this traditional conception of law, and of the Court's role in making law. The personal, private preferences of judges have come to be increasingly important in determining their behavior on the benches.

With the Economic Supreme Court, however, there would be no anchor, no basis from which evaluations independent of strictly personal preferences could commence. An Economic Supreme Court would be analogous to a Warren Court raised to the tenth power, with no legal or constitutional constraints within which to function. The planning decisions that would emerge from such a body could not be predicted to follow any consistent pattern. There would be no citizen feedbacks on planning decisions save for the inclusion of citizen preferences in the planners' own preferences. And it seems highly unlikely that persons who might be both qualified and attracted to seek positions as national planners would behave in the interest of consumers' sovereignty, as envisaged by Abba Lerner.[2] (We shall discuss the personal preferences of planners more fully below.)

National and local planning agencies, empowered to make localized decisions, would have to be set up as subsidiaries to the national units, again more or less on the order of the federal judiciary. And these units could be predicted to function much like the federal judges at the district and appeals court levels. Immune from constituency pressures, individual planners or planning committees and boards could be expected to exercise their powers to promote their own personalized preferences, some of which could be predicted to be quite eccentric and bizarre, again like those observed in the federal judiciary.

An effective national economic planning network, with powers of direction, may, of course, modify the structure of private property rights, and through these, the incentives for individuals and organizations in the private sector of the economy. To the extent that the planners' objectives differ from those outcomes that would more or less freely emerge without planning interference, individuals must be induced or coerced into behaving differently than they would otherwise have voluntarily behaved. The distorting elements which planning would therefore necessarily create would produce new opportunities for extra-plan ("extra-legal"?) profits. To prevent persons and groups from exploiting these newly-created profit opportunities, the planning agencies would therefore be forced to set up enforcement arms and agencies.

The bureaucrats who hold office in these enforcement agencies would necessarily be exposed to strong financial inducements to become partners in "economic crimes." Explicit corruption is relatively minor in the existing American bureaucracy and this is explained, at least in part, by the relative absence of specific opportunities for financial gain. In a national network for economic planning, by contrast, such opportunities would be superabundant.

Consider a single not so hypothetical example. Suppose that the "national economic plan" dictates that gasoline be rationed through coupon issue rather than price, and that the coupons be nontransferable as among recipients. This action would, of course, create widespread opportunities for mutually-advantageous exchanges on terms outside the limits of the planning guidelines. Black markets would quickly develop; ordinary behavior of persons which had previously been fully legal would suddenly become "criminal" once the planning rules had been laid down. (This explicit creation of wholly new categories of "economic crimes" should, in itself, make anyone highly skeptical about any proposal for national economic planning, but this is not our point of emphasis here.)[3] Because of the planners' creation of such widespread opportunities for private profit, some enforcement mechanism would come into being, and the private-profit opportunities would also indirectly create major opportunities for corruption and graft among the enforcers. Black market dealers in gasoline, already beyond legal limits and into "economic crime" under the planning controls, will surely try to take the additional step of attempting to bribe the required regional or local enforcement personnel. For such bureaucrats, the opportunity costs of "honesty" would be dramatically higher than those for their counterparts in the traditional bureaucracies of democracy.

This is not presented as a scary example, designed to clinch an argument against the proposals for national economic planning. We suggest that the example represents precisely the sort of policy change which a national planning agency, empowered with enforceable controls and divorced largely from democratic feedbacks, would be most likely to take. It is surely plausible to suggest that a national agency, charged with formulating an "energy policy" as part of a national plan, would want to restrict gasoline consumption below the levels observed from the ordinary working of the marketplace. But why should we predict that such an agency will opt for coupon rather than price rationing? Why would it not impose a higher tax on gasoline usage?

We can easily predict a preference for direct coupon rationing if we acknowledge that power, prestige, and status will enter the planners' utility functions. Individual members of the planning board, charged with decision-making responsibility at all levels, will tend to choose those instruments of control which offer them the widest opportunities for generating deference among those they controlled. The allocation-distribution of coupons under a direct rationing scheme opens up a whole dimension of planning choices that simply would not exist under any simple scheme of price rationing, even if the overall level of gasoline consumption should be identical under the operation of the two instruments. What criteria can we use in determining what individuals and what groups shall be favored in the allocation-distribution of coupons? The planner secures in this case direct power over the lives of ordinary citizens, and through this insures an enhancement of his own prestige and status in the community, which he will not have under the less direct scheme of price rationing. It would indeed be folly to expect planners to behave otherwise than to choose those control instruments which will increase their own status in the community.

This does not imply that those who become planners will necessarily be different from the rest of us. While arguments might be adduced to suggest that those who seek control over others tend to be most attracted to such positions, these arguments are not required to suggest that anyone, placed suddenly in a position of decision-making authority and faced with a choice among instruments of control, will tend to prefer those options which enhance his own prestige and status in the community. Thus we should be under no illusions that the undesirable consequences of planning controls can be eliminated by careful selection of those who will be the planners. They cannot. With national economic planning independent of democratic political controls, the important men in the nation become the heads of the national planning agencies. The important men in the local community become those who make the local planning decisions. Recognition of this fact alone should make elected politicians wary of proposals for national economic planning. Sponsoring legislation should beware lest they be hoisted on their own petards.

CONCLUSIONS

In fairness, however, to those who support national economic planning, and propose establishment of new planning agencies, in point of fact the agencies to be established will not have the powers of control discussed in the preceding section. The section entitled "Democratic Planning" is applicable here, since the agencies would have powers only to formulate proposals and to make recommendations. At least in the text of the proposed legislation, there is no implied intent of supplanting the ordinary democratic processes.

As our earlier discussion suggests, we predict that, if they are set up, the agencies will not behave differently from those currently in existence. If we need an existing institutional analogue, perhaps we should look to the Council of Economic Advisors, rather than to the Supreme Court. The Council, established during the years of early postwar enthusiasm for macroeconomic policy planning, has come increasingly and predictably to represent a vehicle through which the economic policy positions of the President are presented to the Congress and the public. It is difficult to see how a genuinely responsible, and responsive, national planning board could behave differently.

But let us not be too sanguine in our dismissal of the nondemocratic planning agency, the agency empowered to implement controls by administrative fiat, as discussed in the third section of this article. Suppose that legislation were enacted and an Economic Planning Board established with advisory powers only. Pressures would quickly emerge to grant this board powers to implement its recommendations. These powers might include raising and lowering first-bracket tax rates in response to changing economic conditions, powers to install and remove investment tax credits, powers to raise and lower tariffs and quotas on imports, powers to restrict exports, powers to introduce demand-restricting taxes, powers to introduce coupon rationing for fuels (as noted above). There may be some who think that such a wholesale intrusion of administrative law-making into areas traditionally reserved for explicit legislation by Congress, made up of elected politicians, cannot happen here. But anyone who thinks this way is advised to stop short and look around him. He can observe what the existing bureaucracy *is* doing. There is an ever-lengthening list of administrative law controls over the economy, controls which take the form of *enforceable* directives issued by the Environmental Protection Agency (EPA), the Consumer Product Safety Commission

(CPSC), the Commodities Futures Trading Commission (CFTC), the Agricultural Marketing Boards (AMB), the Securities and Exchange Commission (SEC), the Federal Trade Commission (FTC), the Federal Reserve Board (FRB), the Interstate Commerce Commission (ICC), the Federal Communications Commission (FCC), the Civil Aeronautics Board (CAB), the Federal Power Commission (FPC), the National Labor Relations Board (NCRB), the Food and Drug Administration (FDA), and many, many others. Can there be any doubt that the national economy is currently overburdened with too much governmental regulation, too much regulatory control? That serious proposals for national economic planning should emerge at this time provides the best proof that we neither learn from history nor grow wiser with the progress of science and technology.

PROSPECT OF A PLANNED AMERICA

B. BRUCE-BRIGGS
Resident Consultant, Hudson Institute

I

The question of what America would be like with a centrally-planned economy in a strict sense is unanswerable. Such an America does not now exist, and therefore cannot be studied, analyzed, or evaluated by conventional methods of scholarly research. One can only conjecture about its outlines. We know nothing about the future. We only know something about the past, including that immediate past we call "the present." To consider the implications of a centrally-planned economy in America, we must therefore rely on past knowledge of other planned economies and the history of the American economic and political system. We must necessarily depend on imprecise tools like projection, analogies, and scenarios.[1]

Nevertheless, saying we cannot know the future in any rigorous sense is not to abandon the effort. For all human action is made with the intention of effecting some future outcome. Advocates, for example, of national economic planning expect some future benefits to derive from the effort; similarly, opponents of national economic planning have a less sanguine view of its effects. On all sides of any debate or discussion of any proposed action, including governmental action, is at least an

275

implicit view of the future and how the proposed action will impact upon it.

Making a plausible forecast of a centrally-planned America is an extremely difficult task. Conventional methods of futures studies are of little value. One cannot look at fixed factors, because America has no tradition whatsoever of central planning. Trend extrapolation is useless because there is no trend toward planning or even central planning. Big plans have been made in the past in a piece-meal and spotty fashion for chunks of the economy—banks, canals, railroads, and wars. The present agitation for national economic planning is not the product of a long-term trend in enlightened public opinion, but rather an almost perfect revival of the planning proposals of the New Deal era, which have been dormant for a generation.

Foreign analogy has little relevance to the American experience. An America with national economic planning will still be America. While no serious person would deny the importance of economic organization in the formation of social and political systems, only an orthodox disciple of nineteenth century economists would claim the primacy of economics over other forms of culture. An examination of the industrial societies of the world reveals each of them to be firmly founded upon the type of society which preceded industrialization. The class system of rural England is continued in the factory. German industry carries on the authoritarianism of the baroque military states of Germany. Japan maintains the hierarchy and group cohesion of the days of the samurai. French industry continues the fierce individuality of the *ancien regime*. Russian autocracy is hardly a product of state capitalism, but goes back to the period of the Tartars. So it can be said that the most important aspect of an America with national economic planning is not that it will have such planning, but that it will be America. Presumably, we know a lot about America, its people, its polity, and its economy.

Similarly, historical precedent is of little utility. Given the record of the American people and their institutions, an effective, centrally-planned economy sounds bizarre. American ideology, and more important, American practice, has emphasized "federalism"—that is, the subdivision of sovereignty and power. Since colonial times almost all Americans have held that any form of unitary, centralized, or even concentrated power is evil and dangerous. Americans have gone to a great deal of difficulty to fragment the state through separation and division of powers. The same tendency is evident in the economy. The complexity and fragmentation of the American economic system approaches the limits of human comprehension. Within this country are found examples of almost every conceivable type of economic organization ranging from the individual proprietorship through partnerships, entrepreneurial-owned corporations, shareholder-owned corporations, management-controlled corporations, through all manner of cooperative organizations, socialist enterprises, and even some institutions which, because they distribute services freely on demand, can properly be described as "communist"—all of the previous influenced by myriad local, state, and federal regulations.

Only in America has the ideology that "big is bad" gained such wide acceptance. Only in America are anti-monopoly and anti-trust laws so rigorously enforced. And America is exceeded only by Latin nations in the widespread contempt for government. Moreover, in no country is there as ferocious a Philistine "populist" disdain for and mistrust of educated people, particularly when they attempt to better order the lives of the masses. Governor George Wallace's much quoted attack on "pointy-headed professors" is merely a recent manifestation of a long-term national bias.

The distrust of educated people is by no means limited to the great unwashed; members of the educated classes sneer at one another's particular specialties, and all too frequently at their own colleagues and peers. This is not sufficiently recognized. For example, the advocates of national economic planning in the United States blissfully assume that such planning will be done by economists. There is nothing in any of the existing proposals to suggest that this would be the case. On the contrary, as the experience of the Council of Economic Advisors teaches us, the inclusion of a group of economists in the political process will immediately call into being a fierce opposition of other economists to advise us that the officials are doing exactly the wrong thing and their recommendations, if implemented, will likely be disastrous. Both sides, of course, will buttress their prescriptions and prognoses with impeccable economic reasoning, and superb data. And needless to say, non-economists will chortle over the spectacle. Furthermore, it may even plausibly be argued that if planners have real power, then planning will be too important to be left to planners.

The fact is that no group in America today has the authority to undertake central economic planning. This is one reason why examples of foreign countries are not very relevant to the potential American experience. The French may despise their government and attempt in every way to avoid its machinations, yet they respect the competence of the graduates of the Ecole Nationale d'Administration that man France's chief financial and planning institutions. The British masses may hate their English overlords, yet, until very recently, have conceded their right to rule. What the Russian people think does not matter at all and they know it.

Still, America has had national economic planning, and rather successful planning at that. During the two World Wars the entire economy was directed toward a single goal—victory. Comparisons are difficult, but it seems that the United States mobilized itself much more efficiently than did England or Imperial/Nazi Germany. However, in a very real sense, wartime planning was not *central* so much as *national* planning.

Edicts went forth from Washington and were affectuated, not because they came from the government, but because almost the entire nation was morally mobilized. The national goal was not economic—it was victory, to be achieved in the shortest possible time, with the minimum cost in American blood. It was assumed that the planning system existed solely for the promotion of the war effort, and would be liquidated immediately upon a triumphant peace (thus, of course, giving an incentive for hurrying victory).

After the war, the machinery of central control and direction was dissolved as rapidly as possible. The instruments of central economic planning were of trivial importance compared with the national will to win the war. Economic motives were suppressed and subordinated to national goals, and economic policy was surrounded with an aura of patriotism. Historical experience indicates that such a concentrated effort can only be maintained for short periods. Efforts to turn such a program into permanent policy have rapidly degenerated into cynicism and/or bureaucratic tyranny as exemplified by the U.S.S.R. and its client states.

A very important issue in the planning is how much real power the planners are to be given. The potential effectiveness of central planning depends entirely upon the central institution having real power. And I mean here more-or-less naked power; that is, the means to force people to do what is desired. Without authority, or the ability to be obeyed without threatening sanctions, indicative planning is impossible. Indicative planning could work in Sweden, where the populace, formerly a nation of pirates, were broken to heel by what amounted to four centuries of Stalinism under the Royal House of Vasa. But Americans are still living in the days of medieval liberty. American democracy is fundamentally the liberty of the feudal baron writ large and extended to all adults. Certainly, central planning in America would work if it was organized somewhat like that of the Soviet Union, backed up with control of the entire economy (so that there was no way to escape through economic choice), rigorously-directed media, and of course a loyal, active, and ubiquitous military and internal security apparatus. Of course, such would work. Is anyone willing to recommend such a "solution?" Does anyone think it could be achieved in America in this century? I think not.

II

Another favored method of investigating the future is the "scenario," a hypothetical sequence of events. This is a work of the imagination which seeks to determine plausible routes for getting from the present to some arbitrarily-established condition in the future. But this too is not very helpful to us. Every line of investigation from the present to a hypothetical centrally-planned future runs into a dead end.

Let us recognize that we will not have a complete state socialist system on the Soviet model. Let us grant that we do not have a docile citizenry and/or a humane government like Sweden. Let us then posit a national planning institution. Let us start with the minimum level—that is, a planning agency that can only plan but in no way implement the plan. In the broadest sense, anybody can write a plan, even a national plan. If I or you or Elliot Janeway or Charles Manson or John Kenneth Galbraith wishes to write a national economic plan or plan for anything, it is certainly our right to do so. We can even publish our plans. We can advocate our plans to any part of the citizenry, including the political leadership. Anybody can be a planner. There is at present in Washington, D.C., an organization called the National Planning Association which presumably plans or at least has something to do with planning. Many other people are producing plans of various sorts. I do not know anyone who has been so ambitious (or foolhardy) as to prepare a national economic plan for the United States but someone certainly could if he wanted to. It would probably get a lot of attention. Planning in itself is a harmless exercise. It is harmless because it is innocuous and fruitless. What matters is the ability to carry out the plan.

The next step is a government agency that plans but has no effective ability to carry out the plan. This is what "The Balanced Growth and Economic Planning Act of 1975" proposes.* This is potentially more powerful and/or pernicious than a private plan because its plans would have the *imprimatur* of an official body created by statute reflecting the will of the elected representatives of the American people and the American States and presumably would have whatever prestige such a body would grant. At the same time, the discussion above indicates that at

*Title Humphrey-Javits (S. 1795).

least at present, when all institutions, particularly government institutions, are discredited and when the national media seem intent upon denigrating all official bodies, the prestige and authority of those bodies are very low. But a residue of authority remains. And thus, an economic plan as envisioned by the authors of the Humphrey-Javits Bill would almost by definition be a much more significant document than any private plan.

Let us suppose that the Humphrey-Javits Bill passes into law and the proposed Economic Planning Board is established. What happens, if anything? First of all, some money is spent. A staff must be gathered. Data must be collected. A plan must be prepared, submitted to the President, other members of the Executive Branch, the Congress, the Governors of the States, etc. This can be done fairly cheaply, by federal budget standards, or at enormous expense.* It is likely that the cost will be relatively trivial—a tiny fraction of the error in estimating future federal revenues or expenditures.

Establishing a new agency with new powers always creates the problem of how it will relate to the existing structure of government. The authors of the Humphrey-Javits Bill have attempted to work this out in some detail. Although the system they propose is not the only possible one, no system can more than marginally affect the fundamental problems that are involved in creating a body with so many interests and constituencies. The most recent example of the conflicts and confusion inevitable in the start-up phase of such an agency is the Federal Energy Office. Based upon what is publicly known of the FEO's history, we may reasonably expect that the staffing of a general planning office will be done rapidly and with little thought. The original staff members will jockey among themselves for power

*The Balanced Growth and Economic Planning Act of 1975 does not specify the scale of the planning effort. However, in his editorial endorsement of the bill (which is reprinted in this volume), Myron Sharpe suggests the Planning Board might have a staff of 500, supported by an annual budget of $50 million. As Professor Stein indicates, this would make it about the size of the Office of Management and Budget, and would give it ten times as many people and thirty times the budget of the Council of Economic Advisors.

and position. (This will be made all the more severe because the Humphrey-Javits Bill exempts economic planning board employees from civil service regulations—but civil service would only slightly mitigate the problem.)

Far worse conflicts can be expected between the Economic Planning Board (EPB) and the existing agencies whose work it necessarily preempts. The Council of Economic Advisors cannot but feel, rightly, that the EPB is cutting into their area of expertise. The recently-established Congressional Budget Office is another obvious rival. But the toughest conceivable competitor for the EPB is OMB—the Bureau of the Budget has long been the agency for doing what little planning the national government attempted to do. OMB is manned by very competent and knowledgeable people. And although we may presume that the EPB will be largely staffed from the OMB, difficulties wrought from inter-agency rivalry will only be mitigated for a few weeks, until the old loyalties are broken.

Other dangerous enemies of the EPB are the existing line agencies of the U.S. Government. All of these are now answerable to specific constituencies—the Treasury to the banks, HUD to the housing industry, Agriculture to the farmers, Labor to the unions, Commerce to business, Interior to the resource industry, Defense to the military-industrial complex. The Humphrey-Javits Bill ingeniously tries to deal with this problem by putting representatives of all of these agencies on the Council on Economic Planning. But this means nothing at all. Such a Council would likely meet once a year only to have its picture taken. Organization theory tells us that committees of sixteen people can do nothing. The collapse of the President's cabinet as an effective instrument of government in the twentieth century gives us a lead on what to expect from this council. What will matter is the members of the proposed Economic Planning Board, particularly its chairman.

But the economic planning board proposed by the Humphrey-Javits Bill must prepare a national economic plan. The plan must seek "long-term balanced economic growth" which will pay particular attention to the attainments of the goals of full employment, price stability, balanced economic growth, an equitable distribution of income, the efficient utilization of both private and public resources, balanced regional and urban development, stable international relations, and meeting essential national needs of transportation, energy, agriculture, raw materials, housing, education, public services, and research and development. Such is not an unreasonable list of concerns for a national economic planning agency. As other contributors have pointed out, problems arise in dealing with all of those matters at once. To take a trivial example, most contemporary economists believe in something called the "Phillips Curve," which says that "full employment" must be traded off for "price stability;" the less unemployment the more inflation and *vice versa*. But this is a rather narrow intellectual problem. I think anybody could sit down and write up a list of what they thought should be the economic objectives on all of the above. Whether those are obtainable or not is somehow irrelevant.

The real problem appears if it is thought that something actually will be done to achieve some of those objectives. If the plan is merely written up by a bunch of economists somewhere in Washington and submitted for a lot of Congressional hand-waving and it is filed away, then the plan does not matter much. Such a plan could forward some useful political ends that the assorted national and presidential commissions of the 1960s were intended to achieve. It was never believed that they would do anything about anything, but the establishment of the commissions and the publishing of their results gave symbolic benefits to some interest or another. They showed the government was "concerned." If we had a national government devoted to breakneck economic growth, it would be most appropriate to produce an economic plan which made all the proper curtsies to environmentalists and limits-to-growth agitators. The opposite could conceivably be true: a ferocious stop-growth-now administration could write a plan that would make the hearts of the Chamber of Commerce glow.

Now, there might be a problem with the section of the Humphrey-Javits Bill which specifies that "the President, shall take appropriate actions to ensure that the departments and agencies of the executive branch will carry out their programs and activities in such a manner as to further the objectives of the plan, and to encourage state and local governments and the private sector to carry out their programs and activities in such a manner as to further the objectives of the plan.'' It sounds very hopeful, or ominous, depending upon your point of view. In fact, of course, any public law, especially any law passed after the Balanced Growth and Economic Planning Act of 1975 would have priority over that rather fuzzy statement. Even the most imaginative judicial activists on the court would have grave difficulty trying to use that Act to make the President or any other agency do anything at all that they did not wish to do anyway. Certainly, the Congress is not about to let that paragraph or any paragraph like it override their immediate short-term political goals. The Congress and the President and their agents are going to do what they feel is necessary to get themselves re-elected. Long-range plans do not get anybody re-elected.

Several years ago the *New Yorker* published a cartoon of two executives with the caption, ''Did they push you or put you in long-range planning?'' The low esteem that the nation has for long-range planning is illustrated by the way that Nelson Rockefeller's ambitions were thwarted after he was named Vice President. He was given control of the Domestic Council, which was then mandated to consider long-range objectives. Of course, that meant the Domestic Council was utterly without any worthwhile function. This once-promising instrument of the Executive was reduced to irrelevance. Previous major efforts of the national government at dealing with long-range objectives have not been much more promising. President Hoover's attempt produced a very competent, but ineffective report on ''Recent Social Trends.'' President Eisenhower's ''Goals for Americans'' report sank like a stone. When President Nixon attempted a similar operation, his political advisors quickly made him aware that the attempt would have been suicidal, so that the final report attempted very carefully to say as little as possible, as Daniel Patrick Moynihan, its principal sponsor, dolefully acknowledged.[2]

Seemingly, a more successful outcome could be realized by limiting the economic planning agency to merely planning the activities of the national government. To the rational mind, it does appear absurd that different government departments and agencies should be working at cross-purposes. But here, too, the rationalist is bound to be disappointed. It is no accident that government departments are doing different things, because they have been established individually by the Congress to serve the real or perceived needs of important elements in their constituency. The Small Business Administration is supposed to be stimulating economic activity which almost necessarily must pollute and therefore be regulated by the Environmental Protection Administration. Amtrak is supposed to be supporting railroads at the same time as the Interstate Commerce Commission is hobbling their activities. Even the classic example of working-at-cross-purposes so often cited—support for tobacco farmers while attempting to discourage smoking—is perfectly rational; the subsidies are to farmers through the Department of Agriculture while the discouragement of smoking is presumably a Public Health measure *via* HEW.

Moreover, any coordination or rationalization of government policies and programs cannot include the activities of the largest and most generously-funded function of the federal government—national defense. The military have their own plans, and claim that their "service" is of a different and higher order than the rest of government. And to a large degree defense plans are necessarily secret.

But let us imagine that the above difficulties can be dealt with one way or another, and that the economic planning authority can indeed plan the entire apparatus of the national government, and that it can identify options, assign priorities and make trade-offs. It has then appropriated to itself the functions of Congress. It would take a most imaginative forecaster to write a scenario for Congress surrendering the bulk of its power and rights.

So, I think the most likely scenario is that the economic planning authority as established will shortly become viewed like the other major planning apparatus in the United States— city planning. Practically every city in the United States has a plan for its future physical development. These plans are often beautifully detailed and illustrated. Considerable thought and money go into them (usually federal money). But, for the most part, these plans are a dead letter. The mayors, councils, and city managers of these cities almost completely ignore them. The city planners are frustrated and cynical people, who spend most of their time merely collecting data and publishing them. It seems likely that this function will be the major output of the national planning board. But even this relatively modest function will almost certainly create problems, because major competitors in the data and information business are already in the Federal Government. The U.S. Bureau of the Census is a well-established bureaucracy and is not about to let these *parvenu* economic planning board people cut in on its constitutionally-established prerequisites. The same is true of the Bureau of Labor Statistics and the Treasury. The Economic Planning Board will probably be reduced to producing ingenious input-output models and other harmless fancies.

But even the seemingly innocuous exercise of data collection will not be without effect. The information will always be inadequate and the "data dogs" will demand more and more (needless to say, utterly indifferent to the cost to the data provider). As they get deeper into their work, they will recognize how difficult it is to obtain systematic and consistent information in our complex economy and will become more and more sympathetic to schemes for simplifying and "rationalizing" it.[3]

But let us assume that a plan is actually written and put into effect. "Put into effect," however, does not mean that anything will actually be done about the plan. After all, in 1946 the Congress indicated its intention that there be full employment in the United States. In 1949 it was established that every American should have "a decent home in a suitable living environment." Over the years there have been definitive and unambiguous mandates for "peace," "justice," "equal opportunity," "clean air," "pure waters." As time goes by, it will be noticed that the world has not quite worked out the way the planners anticipated it would. There will be some annoyances, perhaps even a disaster. The Congress will become rightfully and righteously indignant. The planners will be dragged before committees and put through "dog-and-pony shows" to be blamed for the nation's woes. The planners will respond that they did the best they could with the limited resources the plan made available to them. They will be asked why they did not anticipate event "x" and when they deny that anyone could have foreseen it, will be presented with a paper or even an internal memo by some individual who vociferously claimed that such an event was highly likely and should have been anticipated and planned for. Such shows are important to Congressmen—they will have somebody to blame—and this in itself is the strongest argument for the passage of a national economic planning bill.

The same process will occur over and over again. Most of the failures will be trivial or minor. To some stalwarts these shortcomings will demonstrate what they knew all along—that the "free market" is the most efficient allocator of economic resources and capabilities. Others, who may have been sympathetic to a mild amount of planning, will become skeptical and disillusioned, seeing just so much more proof of the inadequacies of American institutions and/or human nature. Hardier spirits will draw from the lessons of failed planning the moral that more planning is needed, perhaps even government ownership, in order to reduce the real world to the parameters of the plan.

III

It seems reasonable to conclude that a centrally-planned America presupposes economic and political conditions which are not now foreseeable, or at least are so ugly that even the most fervent advocate of national economic planning could not wish them to occur. So we must abandon any futures methodology, however frail and inadequate, and resort to the purest speculation. Ignoring how it might be accomplished, therefore, let us imagine that a real, centrally-planned economic planning capacity was installed in the United States in this, the two-hundredth year of the Republic. What would it look like, assuming that the entire existing society, economy, and policy remain intact?

To begin with, only the most naive junior high school civics teacher would doubt that the political institutions of the country are highly sensitive to economic and ideological interests. At the present time, and in the immediate future, the Executive of the national government must be under the control of one of two important leadership groups in our society and its plans and implementation of plans will reflect the desires and interests of those groups. Let us start with the group currently (1975) in control of the Administration:

Central economic planning operated by business interest through its political instrument, the national Republican Party, will forward those goals and desires presently advocated by its constituencies. It would commit the nation to more rapid economic growth through subsidies and tax breaks for business profits, for investments, and for relatively prosperous individuals. Priority goals would be set for national security, GNP growth, and capital formation. Secondary goals would be set for disposable income and unemployment. The existing federal budget would be brought much closer to balance, principally through the trimming of "social programs," but not their entire elimination. The government "take" of GNP would stabilize, but not significantly decline, because of higher government spending for national defense.

By placing emphasis on economic growth, there would be a "tilt" against environmental protection. To be sure, there would not be major retrograde steps, but rather a lack of initiative in adding regulations, a reassessment of many existing regulations, and selected modifications of some of the more obviously arbitrary and/or counter-productive of environmental regulations. A similar process would occur in other areas of government regulation, but these would not be substantial because interests in economic regulation are much too strong to be overcome.

Energy policy would depend upon the relative power of the players in the game. A "conservative" national economic plan would most likely overcome the objections of the international oil companies and move rapidly toward energy independence by effectively guaranteeing a high domestic price for energy in order to assure the safety of investments in high-cost energy projects. Although strict controls would be required, environmentalist objections to off-shore oil drilling, strip mining, nuclear electric plants, and development of oil substitutes would be thrust aside.

While giving lip service to business in general, the national economic planning authority would of course be primarily the servant of big business, although the interests of small business (particularly if well-organized into pressure groups) and those peculiar corporations that sell labor that we call "trade unions" could not be ignored entirely. Special provisions would almost certainly be made to protect American jobs and markets from foreign competitors who would have the advantage of lower cost fuel. Higher tariffs are a possibility, but would more likely be quotas erected in product sectors most strongly threatened by foreign competition. Nevertheless, the national economic board would have a commitment to international free trade. A strong possibility would be some sort of instrument to coordinate and promote American business interests abroad—very much like that of all other industrial countries, even those which are nominally socialist.

The economic plans would rest on the assumption of "trickle down"—that all of the economy and society would benefit from the benefits to business. To some degree this cannot be denied, although critics would and will call attention to the great costs. Surely, in the short run, many of the less economically-powerful elements of the society will pay the most. In trade-offs between inflation and employment, the planning authorities will tolerate substantial unemployment rates. The gains to the consumer from less stringent regulation would be more than cancelled out by higher fuel costs. The recipients of social welfare benefits will see their doles and services eroded. The middlemen in the social welfare business—the bureaucrats—will be extremely unhappy, to say the least, and their colleagues in academia and the media will be bitterly critical of the system calling it "the corporation state" or even "genteel fascism." The laissez-faire Right will be extremely unhappy and mutter about Third Party movements.

IV

The alternative picture of a planned America puts it under the command of the leadership group currently out of power—"the new class" of nonprofit bureaucrats, academics, and intellectuals who identify themselves as "liberals" and whose political instrument is the national Democratic Party. National economic planning conducted under its auspices would have a quite different set of priorities. Lip service would be given to the importance of some economic growth, but it would be repeatedly sacrificed for "higher goals." Social welfare programs would be expanded and funded from incremental gains in GNP as well as increasingly rigorous tax levies on big business and high-income earners. However, because members of the new class make up a substantial block of the top 10% of the income-distribution spectrum, "soak-the-rich" schemes will only be able to tap the relatively trivial amounts transferred through inheritance, capital gains, and very high incomes. Income surtaxes, therefore, should only begin to take effect at levels immediately above the salaries of "upper grade" civil servants, full professors, and Senior Fellows of the Brookings Institution.

The "military-industrial complex" will not be a very rewarding source of diverting funds because it will be staunchly defended by organized labor. Probably the defense budget would remain fixed in current dollars and be somewhat eroded away by inflation. The bulk of the taxing must therefore fall upon the great middle class, including the unionized and white collar working people of the country. Needless to say, the government's share of GNP will increase sharply, mostly through the "fiscal dividend" created by inflation pushing individual tax-payers into higher brackets and through higher business taxes which will cut into private capital formation.

The regulation of all forms of economic activity will continue apace. In the name of environmentalism, safety, and consumerism, the difficulty in introducing new products into the market and the cost of those products will increase. Entry to markets will become more and more difficult, and small business will be slowly throttled. Nevertheless, free enterprise will flourish in the black market. More and more transactions will be for cash (and even barter). The increasingly complex compilations of the planners will be founded on increasingly fictional data.

An important thrust of national economic planning will be controls over land development. Conscious government effort would be directed toward maintaining the older urban areas in the Northeast and Midwest and thwarting shifts toward suburbs and the South and Southwest. "Urban sprawl" will be restricted and land values pushed up in existing urban areas. The American people will be advised that the day of the single family house is over, and they must perforce expect to live at best in a "town house" in a cluster development.

The energy problem will be primarily handled through enforced conservation of energy sources partially through higher taxes but more by means of allocations and rationing. Little would be invested in highways and much in collective transit facilities. Large cars will be discouraged through European-type escalating taxes on weight, engine displacement, or gasoline consumption. Natural gas prices will be controlled and natural gas will be allocated. As shortages mount, the same will be done for petroleum and coal. The failure of the private sector to deliver resources under such conditions will be taken as evidence of its incompetence and/or voraciousness, and it will rapidly become a completely regulated industry in the public utility model. Nationalization, particularly of the international oil companies, is a distinct possibility.

Throughout the entire economy, decisions will be made less and less by individual entrepreneurs and corporation managers, and more and more by bureaucrats and politicians. The taxing policies of the national government will leave relatively little capital available for major products and general expansion. The principal source of capital will be the Treasury and it will go to those sectors that the polity determines to be deserving. One obvious priority area is education. The current recession in academia would shortly be ended by influxes of new funds. Research money will again flow freely. There will be growing subsidies to upper middle-class arts and humanities.

Another prime target will be the reconstruction of the older American cities. Massive subventions to existing municipal governments can be expected, but will show little effect because most of this will be income transfers to members of municipal trade unions. Of course, teachers and professors will pick up most of the support for education. The rebuilding of older cities will be a major source of support for the construction industry.

From a material point of view, the real standard of living of the average American will probably fall. But this would not greatly trouble those in command of the economy, it being their view that the masses are entirely too coarse and materialistic in their desires. The new dispensation will be said to provide a better "quality of life" and there will certainly be many gains for the average American. He will have the opportunity for extended education which, judging from the present quality of the product, will to a large extent be a form of entertainment as more and more people take advantage of subsidized courses in subjects that they find "interesting" or "relevant" or "self-actualizing." Health care will be another priority item on the national agenda. Some sort of national health scheme will be installed and an increasing amount of GNP and Federal revenues devoted to it, but escalating costs will require tighter controls, particularly of individual behavior which might lead to injury or sickness. The air and water will be unquestionably cleaner than it would be under ''conservative'' control. Unemployment will be lower, although many of the ''make-work'' jobs will perform, at best, marginal economic functions.

American productivity, both of individual firms as a result of tightened factory safety, ''equal opportunity,'' and other regulations, and national productivity, as a result of increasing amounts of energy, capital, and labor being devoted to unproductive or even counter-productive purposes, will stagnate. The U.S. competitive position in the world will suffer. Other industrialized and industrializing nations will seize U.S. markets abroad and begin to increase their penetration of American markets, only to be thwarted by increasing restrictions on imports, and upon the export of capital. The U.S. will gradually withdraw from world trade and its decaying economic condition will be reflected in the perception of its military and moral strength abroad. Much of the world will be in the grip of various gangster cliques calling themselves ''socialists.'' This, however, will be reported by the national media as an indicative of ''the wave of the future'' and America's position relative to the world will be interpreted as a sign of the ''maturity'' of our society and economy; the prosperity and vigor of countries abroad will be smiled upon as illustrative of their adolescence.

Many readers will doubtless consider either or both of these pictures overdrawn. Perhaps some will find one agreeable. Nevertheless, I strongly suspect that the bulk of the American people are quite satisfied that America has no consistent, rational, comprehensive economic planning capability. And it seems almost certain that whoever puts such a process into effect will erode what little economic, social, and political power that now remains to the mass of Americans.

NOTES ON THE IDEOLOGY AND PSYCHOLOGY OF PLANNING

ERNEST VAN DEN HAAG
Lecturer in Sociology & Psychology, New School for Social Research

I

People and organizations, such as business firms, select means so as to achieve ends, i.e., desired effects. When suitable means are deliberately used to attain ends, we act rationally. The process of mentally working out the adaptation of means to ends is called planning. Thus, in its most general sense, the word "planning" refers to the design that precedes *rational deliberate action*. A further connotation of planning, at least as an ideal, is to be systematic, to take into account all the probable and possible effects of alternative courses of action, and all the likely costs, rather than just the most immediate ones.

The ends of planning justify the means when (a) the ends themselves are justified; (b) the means are suitable (effective and efficient); (c) the means are not too costly in using up other means or defeating other ends. Means can be justified only as, or by, ends. Ends can never justify all, yet must always justify some, means; ends that are not attainable by some means, or cannot justify any, are literally fantasies rather than goals.

Traditional actions that have proved effective in the past suffice to meet customary problems. There is no need for deliberation, for considering the selection of means, for conscious determination of priorities among ends, no planning. Conscious planning occurs only when problems are felt as problems, usually when they are new or disturbing. One drives to work in the usual way and engages in one's routine tasks. But if there is a road block, one deliberately plans how to go around it; one consciously decides to act appropriately, to make plans. The housewife prepares breakfast routinely without much planning; but she plans for a party. The difference between the appropriate but unplanned action and planning is that new thought is expended when we plan, either because the problem is new, or because dissatisfaction is felt with the customary way of meeting it.

II

Whether an action is a means to an end, or an end in itself, is often uncertain, particularly on the psychological level. It is tempting and logical to assign the status of means to all efforts made for a declared (conscious) purpose. However, often the expenditure of effort is an end in itself; its actual as distinguished from its alleged usefulness lies in the expenditure of effort. This is admitted only with regard to sports; yet even in sports effort is usually called forth most easily when it is presented or felt not as an end in itself but as a means, e.g., to win the game. This suggests that people feel uncomfortable with ends in themselves and more comfortable when they see their efforts and activities as means to an end. One of the appeals of planning may well be that it allows us to order our activities into a means-ends framework, and to extend that framework to all our activities and the activities of all social bodies, each seen as striving to achieve visible, rationally-intelligible goals, intermediate and ultimate. We may have missed that sort of planning since the religious world view lost its hold; and, psychologically, central planning may appeal as a secularization of or substitute for what was thought of as God's plan.

Confronted with activities that are not easily seen as anything but ends in themselves, a means-ends analysis is sometimes persisted in by defining a psychological state (e.g., happiness) as an end. But this largely avoids the problem to be met: that activities may not have tangible *external* goals, yet be felt to be worthwhile.

While ends are irrelevant to many activities, which therefore cannot be analyzed as rational in a means-ends framework, other activities may only appear irrational to an observer: the means seem unsuitable to the ends he assumes, or to the actor's stated ends. However, the means may be quite suitable to actual (unstated) ends: the action may be rational in the light of ends which differ from those assumed or declared. (Sometimes even the actors may become aware of their actual ends only *post factum* by analyzing their own actions.)

One difficulty of deliberate planning in any form, and particularly of planning for others, then, is that it tends to disregard unstated, or to accept mistated ends. Emerging ends, that appear only as activity goes on or succeeds—or vague, as yet unspecifiable ends—also tend to be neglected.* Finally, the weight given to ends changes as they are fulfilled, often in unpredictable ways. Usually to plan ahead is to pay little attention to the unforeseen.

III

Because it means to act rationally, to use suitable means to achieve one's ends, or to find more effective ways of doing so, planning used to have an approving connotation. However, lately the psychological costs of planning, of rationality, in individual life have become prominent. It is often thought now that spontaneity, open-ended nonplanning, leads to a more ready detection of one's actual desires, of the structure of one's priorities, than the deliberate approach which, by presuming such a structure on the basis of imitation, prescription, or habit, may actually rigidify or limit one's desires or replace true ones with pseudo-desires. Planning also is felt to close the door to unforeseen opportunities, changes, or to newly-felt desires. For

---

*Ends as here used may be positive (what one wishes to achieve) or negative (what one wishes to avoid or get rid of).

these reasons, less approval is attached to individual planning
and to rationality in general than used to be the case.

Much of the approval that used to surround individual planning is now attached to central planning. It is as though people
were saying: "We do not care to be rational any longer; the
government should be rational for us and spare us the trouble."
But is central planning rational? Specifically, is it rational to
centrally allocate resources by postulating a structure of social,
and ultimately individual, ends for which they are to serve as
means? And is central planning an efficient way to achieve such
ends?

IV

Man is not easily reconciled to the niggardliness of Nature,
which condemns him to work and to economize—to be rational;
or to the conventions of his own society, which endows with
prestige mainly those who rise above the average, thus causing
most people to feel deprived. This is bearable in an immobile
society, but hard in a mobile society (such as ours) that asks
everybody to rise above everybody else. Perhaps an age in
which communication, and therewith competition (and, as a
reaction, egalitarian sentiment) have become literally boundless, in which the world ceases to be divided into noncompeting
segments—an age which pushes us all into the same race—was
destined to turn to a new redemptionism.

When, with the Industrial Revolution, mankind bent its gaze
from the heavens to the earth, it did not give up its millenarian
aspirations. Chiliastic hopes were merely shortened and sec-
ularized: promises of material improvement were found acceptable as a way of redemption. "Planning" is among them, the
more so because it promises the benefits of competition without
the competitive race so many people are tired of.

Planning seems both "scientific" and 'commonsensical. It
appears to make intelligible an economy which had become
even more complex and mysterious as markets widened and
technology progressed. It promises remedies for every ill. It

places someone in charge of the economy, where no one seemed to be in charge.

Although types of central planning differ in the degree to which they attempt to do so and in the ways of attempting it, all types of planning, by definition, shift the making of plans and the effective allocation of resources from individuals and firms to a central authority. Individuals and firms become subordinated to the central authority; to carry out its plans they must subordinate their own; they become planned rather than remaining planners, sources of plans themselves. Central planning, by definition, takes the ability to make effective plans out of the hands of individuals; at least it greatly reduces their autonomy.

Before continuing, let me deal with a common objection to this depiction. It is generally conceded that central planning will reduce the ability of the present middle and upper classes to plan, to dispose of resources. The members of these classes may regain this ability in a different legal form if they become planners. Or a planning class that replaces the present upper classes may enjoy some of the advantages that the old upper classes enjoyed. In any case, however—and herein lies the force of the objection and its political weight—central planning hardly changes or reduces the effective autonomy of the non-rich, and may even increase it. (It will certainly increase it in relative terms.) While quite free to make their own plans in a non-planned economy, the poor are unable to carry them out for lack of means. Thus they may plan, or dream, to become educated, to travel, to locate and to work where they choose, and to purchase what they want. Yet they may be effectively so restricted in all this by lack of means or of opportunities that they cannot feel that they have much to say about their own fate. Although reducing their theoretical choices, central planning deprives them of little effective choice. Only the rich suffer a reduction of effective choices.

This argument may well be half true: central planning will not reduce the effective choices of the majority of the poor. But neither history nor theory suggest that central planning will actually increase their effective choices. Indeed, it is hard to see how central planning could. Since there are many poor and comparatively few rich, redistribution could not significantly increase the means at the disposal of the poor. And so far nothing indicates that central planning could enrich the poor faster or more than they are enriched without it. Nothing indicates that the major gains in the utilization of resources, in efficiency, that would be needed, can be achieved by central planning. On the other hand, central planning can and necessarily does reduce the options and opportunities of the rich, indeed of all but the poorest segments of the population.

Let me focus the argument more specifically. When the poor are extremely poor, very little can be taken from them by definition. *Ipso facto* central planning cannot greatly reduce their effective as distinguished from their theoretical autonomy. However, as soon as the poor reach the standard of, say, European—as distinguished from Asiatic—poverty, the theoretical reduction of their options does in many cases interfere with the practical planning ability of workers, farmers, etc. It follows that the effects of central planning are felt to be the least oppressive where poverty is most extreme and widespread; though it does not increase, central planning may not decrease the effective autonomy of most people in these countries. Central planning is felt to be most oppressive where most people are not in extreme poverty; there the effective as well as the theoretical autonomy of many individuals and organizations is curtailed by central planning. The political import of this distinction is obvious.

V

Consider now the appeals central planning has for poor and rich alike. Since most people still do regard planning as desirable in their own activities they readily think, or rather feel, that it is generally desirable, that what is good and desirable for them as individuals can hardly be bad for the community as a whole. Yet to think so is to commit the fallacy of composition: to believe that what is good for the parts is, therefore, good for the whole. Those who commit this fallacy often make a material mistake as well: they assume that the central planners do not originate the ends for which they plan, but merely allocate means for the achievement of ends that are determined by the tastes of the community or of the individuals in it. But historically—and theoretically as well—the ends of central planners always have differed from the ends of the individuals in the community for which the planning is done. Usually the variety of individual ends is reduced, and many are frustrated. One type of soap is produced instead of ten, serving fewer tastes or one standardized taste only. The allocation of resources between consumption and investment also differs from the allocation preferred by the community; so does the mix of goods produced and of employments offered. One can only speculate on the distribution of income, prestige, and power.

It is unlikely indeed that central planning can achieve more efficiently what individuals would have wanted to achieve by their own plans. The market is far more responsive to the wishes of individuals than even the best central planning bureaucracy can and, above all, will be.

Central planning, however, is more efficient than the market could be in carrying out the wishes of the central planners and in defeating those they disapprove of. Therein lies the appeal of central planning for those who expect to do it, and for those who disapprove of the wishes consumers fulfill in a market economy.* Unlike the market, central planning is not a neutral instrument registering consumer demands and allocating resources accordingly. Central planning registers the demands of the planners and not those of the planned.

The bureaucratic planning machine would be likely to be staffed by people who now hold little power, but feel they ought

---

*A great number do. John Kenneth Galbraith believes that these wishes are "contrived" by industry. Herbert Marcuse believes that they arise from "false consciousness." Both believe that they can discern the true desires and needs of consumers, which seem to coincide with their own preferences.

to hold more by virtue of their education. Planning would be done by college graduates who, through their education, have acquired the ambition to plan other peoples' lives more rationally than they can. The college-bred ambitions cannot be fulfilled without central planning; wherefore, educated groups clamor for it. Because college education has made them on the average more articulate than the noneducated, these groups can be very persuasive if they play on the equivocations listed before. They do. And it is to their advantage to do so.

Although the logic of central planning does not permit other interpretations, the purpose of central planning usually remains hidden. Consumers often disapprove of the wishes of other consumers. They are led to believe that central planning will fulfill theirs and not those of others. The delusion here does not differ much from the delusion that has often attracted people to dictatorships: they tacitly see themselves among those who will do the dictating and not among those dictated to.

Planning also holds out the promise of security for all. Regardless of the extent to which the promise is kept, it is very largely believed. Many people prefer security, even if it limits their horizons, to a less secure existence, even when it opens wider possibilities. Whether this is an actual preference manifested in actual specific choice situations or an imagined preference relevant only to abstract general policies, such as planning vs. the free market, is a question on which one may speculate because conclusive answers are not available (people do engage in gambling; but they also vote for social security). Perhaps, too, wider possibilities do mean greater responsibilities, more decisions to be made and, above all, less possibility of blaming one's failure to achieve a goal on external circumstances. To put it positively, in a free economy one cannot escape blaming oneself for failure.* In a planned economy it is, after all, beyond one's control.

---

*Perhaps one can by means of elaborate ideologies. But these ideologies themselves function as defenses against blame either for one's failure, or in some cases for one's feeling that success is undeserved. These last guilt feelings play a major role in attracting the upper classes to various forms of egalitarianism.

VI

Central planning concentrates economic power, since by defini-tion it concentrates the planning function by shifting all eco-nomic planning power to a central bureaucratic machine. Often it is believed that the bureaucratic planners will find it easier to coordinate their plans than the many individuals and firms which now plan independently from each other. It is assumed that individuals and firms have no coordinating mechanism, while government authorities do. Neither proposition seems correct.

In a market economy there is' a coordinating and directing mechanism—the market. It differs from the mechanism of planning by being automatic; it does not require human direc-tion or coordination, yet, through prices, it directs and coordi-nates the allocation of resources, whereas the controls of plan-ning are, as it were, manual. Since the market is visible mainly in its effects, people find it hard to realize the presence of design without a designer, of coordination without a coordinator, of direction without a director.

The idea of automatic, invisible adjustments is hard to accept; and without analysis—or worse, with insufficient analysis—the market seems "anarchic," even though the milk is on the doorstep every morning, whereas in a planned economy charac-teristically it is not. The free market allows anybody to reconcile his plans with those of everybody else. Individuals plan for themselves; they choose their own ends and means. Prices indi-cate to all the value placed on whatever can be bought or sold. By paying heed to prices, individuals economize. So does soci-ety as a whole: *Ceteris paribus,* more of the less-valued and less of the more-valued resources are consumed directly or used for production. And the goods most in demand are produced most often. Thus, in a free market, individuals, rationally striving to attain their own ends, provide one another with the goods and services most in demand at the least expense. The issue is usu-ally presented as if the central planners favored individual plan-ning, and the individual planners favored chaos, inefficiency, and anarchy. But the issue is not whether to plan, but who is to plan what, for whom, and with what powers.

In a bureaucratic machine—by definition not automatic—there are coordinators. However, the presence of coordinators does not assure coordination. On the contrary, the planning bureaucracy and those who are subordinated to it become aggregates of divergent interests often pursued through power clashes and without coordination. Although coordinators are more visible than the "invisible hand" of automatic coordination, in effect the navy and army and air force often are not coordinated, even though they share a common purpose, defense.

Planning is particularly bad at three functions which market competition excels in: (1) the introduction of innovation; (2) the phasing out of obsolete products, techniques, and services; (3) the avoidance of uneconomic investments. The record of government activities and agencies in the United States (and anywhere else) in housing, drugs, transportation, or postal service suggests no less.

VII

Let me briefly consider now some of the allegedly broader advantages of planning on which so much of its appeal rests.

Planning is said to reduce the harsh competition which injures many people. Indeed, planning abolishes the competition of the market. But it merely changes the terms and conditions in which psychological competition—vying for income, power, and prestige—takes place.

Competition among independent organizations is replaced by competition among organizations subordinated to the central planning board and by competition within them. This competition is likely to be more ferocious, and without escape for the defeated. Even if planning were to produce economic equality—a promise nowhere kept—competition merely would continue for power and prestige. It might well be socially more dangerous, psychologically more troublesome, and economically less fruitful than vying for wealth. But central planning cannot do without monetary rewards. Good performance would have to be rewarded by promotion—more money, power, and prestige. Central planning differs from a market economy not because the rewards differ, but because fewer would be awarded by an impersonal market mechanism: instead promotion would depend altogether on the subjective judgment of one's superiors. In a market system this is now the case only within a firm; and the subjective judgment is restrained and corrected because discontented employees have alternative opportunities, other firms, or independence. These, to say the least, would be narrowed with central planning. However the "profit motive"—the incentive to perform for the sake of monetary reward—would still have to be used in "planning." Only in a technical sense—as a return to the owners of capital—would profit disappear. Unequal monetary reward would remain. But the reward would depend more on the favor of superiors and on bureaucratic intrigue. It would be likely to be more capricious and less economically rational than it is in a market economy: without becoming morally just, it would be economically less so, and the striving for it would be intensified.

Thus the two factors which contribute to the pejorative connotation that dogs "profit"—(a) that it is a monetary reward, and (b) that the monetary reward is unequally and "unjustly" (from a moral viewpoint) distributed among the population— are not changed by central planning. The distribution remains monetary, except where power and prestige directly take the place of money. It remains unequal even though it benefits or deprives different people. Finally, it is likely to be more capricious than it is now.

The market system is often alleged to be not only anarchic, but also to produce for profit rather than use, thereby somehow producing the wrong things for the wrong reasons.

Production is carried out "for profit" in a market system, but it does not follow that it is not carried out "for use." On the contrary, in the price system, profit (or loss) is the difference between the value of the input of resources and the value added (or lost) by using them to produce the output. If consumers regard the output as more useful to them than the resources that went into producing it, there is a profit; if the resources are regarded as more useful, a loss. Producers shift production accordingly: they are led, *nolens volens,* by their profits or losses, to produce what consumers regard as most useful. Thus, "production for profit" is a means to "production for use," not an alternative.

On the other hand, in "production for use," when usefulness is not indicated by profit, planners determine for themselves what goods are most useful, and their judgment is not informed by consumer demand.

Since profit and loss are powerful automatic coordinators of individual plans and lead to the most economic utilization of resources, the market system is not "anarchy," but an automatic mechanism which coordinates the plans made by individuals. Central planning, in contrast, is nonautomatic: adjustments do not take place impersonally by means of automatic price changes, but must be made "by hand" by the planners. They are more visible yet less responsible to consumer wishes and less efficient.

Originally, those who felt that the market produces the "wrong" things argued that unequal income led to the production of mink coats or liquor, when babies starved for lack of milk. This is at best an argument for correcting the income distribution (by giving the mothers of babies more money, which would permit more milk production and consumption), and not against the market mechanism that responds to it. For the market will simply produce what consumers are inclined and able to buy—milk or mink. It obeys votes cast in dollar ballots, and far more accurately so than politicians respond to constituents. Even if reapportionment (i.e., more votes to those who earn too little because of circumstances beyond their control) were needed it is not accomplished by abolishing voting and substituting dictatorship—by giving all the votes to the planners.

ON ADVERSARY GOVERNMENT AND THE LIBERAL AUDIENCE

PAUL H. WEAVER
Associate Editor, Fortune *Magazine*

The Balanced Growth and Economic Planning Act of 1975 would be a promising piece of legislation if it really mapped out a way to bring some semblance of order to the inchoate jumble that is federal economic policy today. Alas, it doesn't do that. Disorder prevails in Washington, not because the bureaucracies lack the services of a coordinating agency, but because the policies they carry out are in too much conflict with one another to be coordinated at all. The procedures spelled out in this act will not harmonize public policy because they do not force policymakers to be consistent. To the extent that they have any effect at all, they will merely foment conflict within the government and cause delay.

Similarly, the act would be an ominous one if it really provided for the establishment of a comprehensive central economic planning agency with power to take basic economic decisions and to make them stick. That sort of planning has been tried in countries all over the world for the better part of this century, and for all its authentic social and political benefits, economically it has been more or less a disaster. But this legislation doesn't set up such a planning agency; what it envisions is merely the creation of yet another economic-policy staff organization, one that will take its place alongside the CEA, the OMB, the Fed, the Treasury, the Commerce Department, the Council on Wage and Price Stability, the Congressional Budget Office, and many other agencies, not least among them the White House Staff and Committee of Congress themselves.

The Balanced Growth and Economic Planning Act of 1975, then, is a silly piece of legislation. Despite the implications of its title, the agency and activities it will actually bring into being are redundant and unnecessary. There is nothing this agency will do that isn't already being done by half a dozen other government organizations. There is nothing it will know that isn't already known or knowable. There is no technical contribution it can make to the clarification of means and ends in U.S. public policy that isn't already being made, and beyond making such a clarification there is nothing it can do to induce Congress and the President to engage in the kind of long-range analysis of ends and means that the act posits as desirable. In the terms of its own announced intentions, then, this legislation is certain to contribute nothing positive. It is strictly another case of political posturing, buck-passing, and job-creation for the upper middle class—which is to say it is hardly noteworthy at all, being but one more instance of a familiar pattern of policymaking, and in view of the modest scale of the enterprise lacking interest even as an act of wastefulness.

And yet the matter does bear discussion. It is, after all, the joint proposal of two of our most distinguished and intelligent Senators. It has won itself a vigorous body of supporters and is about to be given full consideration by the committees of Congress. It may even pass, though one may doubt that it will be signed; but whatever eventually becomes of it, having come this far is no mean achievement. Since the bill is so obviously silly, and since the planning idea has been so thoroughly discredited in our time (for example, by the spectacle of the "planned" Soviet Union making regular and massive purchases of "unplanned" U.S. grain), why is it being taken so seriously by so many able and responsible persons? What is it commends this legislation to the elected representatives of the American people?

The answer, of course, is that it serves a variety of useful purposes in the circumstances. To some, undoubtedly, it is desirable on its merits. There are, after all, Congressmen who want to establish economic planning, primarily for social rather than strictly economic reasons; there are others who would like to infuse more coherence in American public policy. For both groups, this bill is obviously no more than half a loaf, but clearly it can be justified as being better than nothing—and no doubt, for them, it is. To others, it is precisely because this bill is half a loaf that it is so attractive. It offers a plausible way of responding to widespread complaints about public policy and the U.S. government without really doing anything concrete and therefore potentially dangerous. And for all, one suspects, this bill has a further advantage, the nature and appeal of which is my subject in these pages: namely, the fact that it embodies a mood and style that have become touchstones of what passes for good politics among our elected representatives.

ADVERSARY GOVERNMENT

For the Balanced Growth and Economic Planning Act of 1975 is no isolated aberration; to the contrary, it conforms in almost every particular to a pattern of politics and legislation that has developed over the past many years to the point where it has become very nearly typical of the way the national government deals with all the needs and desires of the polity. This pattern reflects and intensifies pathology in American politics and culture, and it derives both from fundamental changes in the structure of American institutions and beliefs and from the vicissitudes of our national politics since the late 1960s. I call it a pattern of adversary government, and it provides the key to any understanding of the character of American public life over the last decade.

What is adversary government, and where is it found? The answer to that last question, at least, is easy enough. It is found at all levels of government, but most especially in the U.S. Congress, particularly the Senate. Its spirit shines forth clearly in a long series of bills passed during the last decade. It is powerfully and distinctively present in the Clean Air Act of 1967 and its various amendments; it is no less visible in the Auto Safety Act of 1966, in the various water pollution measures enacted in recent years, and in the War Powers Act of 1973. It is embodied in the Occupational Safety and Health Act of 1970; in the Consumer Product Safety Act and Noise Control Act of 1972; and in the legislation that authorizes the activities of the Equal Employment Opportunity Commission. Whiffs of it can be got from the campaign finance reforms of 1974, the killing of the U.S. SST project, the Congressional pursuit of the Watergate scandals, the Watergate scandals themselves, the Church committee investigations of the CIA, and so on through nearly the entire catalogue of major governmental events in recent memory. And the effects of this pattern of governing can be seen in the growing public disillusionment with American institutions that has become the single most definitive and dangerous political phenomenon of our time.

Adversary government arises out of the politics of complaint rather than the politics of deliberate action; what its legislative acts have in common is a distinctive kind of incompleteness. Each of them, to be sure, spells out a clear objective. In some cases—the various environmental laws come to mind—the objective is made extraordinarily specific; in others—the Balanced Growth and Economic Planning Act is an example—it is general almost to the point of meaninglessness. Each provides a set of powers to accomplish the stated tasks; in some cases the powers are enormous, in others woefully inadequate. Each also provides for active participation by any interested citizen or group, including participation that assumes the form of a suit for failure to comply faithfully with the letter and spirit of the law. And each is strongly backed by the committee or subcommittee that gave birth to it, though it may not be so strongly supported in Congress or the government as a whole.

What adversary legislation lacks is a sense of limits, of context, of discipline, and so of responsibility. The goals are not only clear, they are also ''pure''—uncontaminated by such mundane and unedifying concerns as cost, feasibility, and the whole swarming host of competing values that, at one point or another, collide with any one goal when it is taken to an extreme. A classic example of this phenomenon is to be found in water pollution policy, which, in mandating a campaign to clean up our rivers and lakes, specifies that by 1985 literally zero waste is to be discharged into American waterways. Cost, feasibility, fairness, even commonsense are not to be allowed to qualify the pursuit of this single objective. This, the legislation implies, is an anti-pollution law, not a money-saving law, or a public welfare-enhancement law, or a fairness law; only the reduction of pollution—no: the *elimination* of pollution—is to concern those who administer the program. Comparable, if often less absolute, prohibitions against attending to legitimate competing and contextual goals are written into many of the works of adversary governance.

Lacking a sense of limits, this legislation inevitably lacks a sense of context as well. It proceeds as if water pollution, or the influence that supposedly accrues to wealthy donors to political campaigns, or the incoherence that characterizes U.S. economic policy were *sui generis*—there for no good reason; continuing to exist only because it never occurred to anybody to do something about them; and capable of being done away with the minute it's decided that they should be done away with. But of course, this is virtually never the case. The presence of water pollution signifies the coexisting presence of a large and complex industrial order; money can have influence because this is a free and wealthy society; overall economic policy is incoherent because there are so many different objectives that the government has decided to seek. And simply deciding to "do something" about any of these problems in isolation is likely to lead to an unhappy result. Either nothing will happen, as is almost certain to be the case with the proposed economic Planning Board, lacking as it does any powers to impose its decisions on government. Or something happens, but at an unanticipated often unacceptable cost to the society as a whole—as is likely to be the case when superhighways are drilled through densely-populated areas without regard to the social and political costs of doing so.

Lacking a sense of limits and context, adversary legislation also lacks any sense of intellectual honesty and discipline. It refuses to see things whole, as in the case of pollution and industrialism; or, alternatively, it blithely aggregates entirely different things together even when they are contradictory. The latter is clearly visible in the Balanced Growth and Economic Planning Act of 1975, as may be seen in the nature of the problem it addresses itself to. Obviously it is not a single, coherent difficulty, but rather a mishmash of very different sorts of problems: recession, inflation, erratic short-term policies, imbalanced growth, the absence of an agency whose main function is to perform long-range planning, and so on. In other words, this bill addresses itself simultaneously to the predominant economic concerns of the right (inflation, short-term policies), of the left (recession, structural economic problems like the business cycle, and income distribution), and of various other groups such as the environmentalist movement ("balanced growth"). Inasmuch as what is a problem to one of these groups is likely to be an economic virtue to another, it's hard to see what the entire bill amounts to. It's a mixture of the immiscible; it adds up to zero, or at least to nothing intelligible.

A QUESTION OF RESPONSIBILITY

And lacking a sense of limits, context, and discipline, adversary governance also lacks any sense of responsibility. It is perfectly capable of moving from the identification of a nonproblem (as with the Balanced Growth and Economic Planning Bill) to the elaborate prescription of non-solution, which it nevertheless foists off upon the public as an authentic solution. And when, eventually, the Congressional practitioners of this style of legislation are then forced to concede that nothing good has come of all their efforts, they can usually lay the blame at the feet of someone else—the "bureaucracy," which failed to do its job;

or the "interests," which have foiled the bureaucracy's efforts to get its plans and projects carried out; or the Administration, whose indifference "allowed" the plans to be eviscerated or completely rejected by Congress. Who, having read the Balanced Growth and Economic Planning Act of 1975, can doubt that it maps out precisely such a nonsolution and that all these evasions will be employed when the entire scheme comes to naught, as eventually it is certain to?

But adversary legislation entails forms of irresponsibility that go deeper than the mere promulgation of schemes that are known in advance to be unlikely to work. The first duty of the public servant, after all, like that of the physician, is expressed in the ancient Latin injunction: *primum non nocera*—"first do no harm." In practical terms, this means that people who make and administer the laws must take care that what they do is needed, and that what they do will not make matters clearly worse overall. This requires first, that lawmakers assess the costs and other "unintended consequences" that are likely to flow from a projected course of action. Then they must settle on that limited definition of the goal and the goal-pursuing activity that takes into account, and stops short of, those costs and other side-effects which are clearly not worth it. To govern responsibly, in short, is to seek not the maximum, but the optimum; it is to act with at least a faint intimation of the tragic quality of political life.

Adversary governance rejects this first principle. It denies the ideal of the optimum in favor of an infantile aspiration to the maximum; it imagines that political action belongs to the genre of comedy rather than tragedy. Instead of fashioning an anti-pollution, or auto-safety, or campaign finance program by deliberating in advance the limits as well as the goals of the proposed enterprise and then explicitly striking a balance among all the competing desiderata at stake, the apostles of adversary government articulate a pure and unqualified political goal, establish an agency to pursue it, and enjoin upon that agency a role in which it must act as a zealous advocate rather than a judicious optimizer. The general idea behind this strategy is that if one sets extreme enough and pure enough goals, if one establishes a zealous enough agency, and if one then sets that agency loose on American government and society, it may well eventually be stopped short of the extreme, pure objective by a gathering array of political forces that have been alienated by the ever more expensive and disruptive consequences of the pursuit—but it will get farther in the end, and get there faster, than a more judicious agency would working with a more moderate and considered mandate.

The practitioners of adversary government, then, do not merely set up agencies to pursue immoderate social goals; they also, by their very way of defining goals and the manner of their pursuit, set up agencies whose mandate is nothing less than that of making war—in principle, *total* war, with no quarter asked or given—on those sectors of American government or society affected by the achievement of these goals. The Environmental Protection Agency, for instance, may be working to clean up the water and air; but it is also engaging major sectors of the American economy in the political, if not the administrative, equivalent of war. It is thereby engaging those ordinary citizens whose lives depend on the companies, products, or services affected in a comparable conflict. Will reducing the level of sulfur dioxide in the air by 1976 add 10 or 20 or 50 percent to the cost of electricity? It doesn't matter, says the law to the EPA: add it—you're not in the business of making electricity cheap or life agreeable, you're in the business of cleaning up the environment, and companies or persons who are thereby harmed have, as far as you're concerned, no legitimate grievance or claim on you. That is in effect what the law says. But of course, as citizens, they *do* have a legitimate claim; it is, alas, one that the adversary mode of governance refuses to recognize.

IMPLICATIONS FOR DEMOCRACY

And this brings us to a further form of irresponsibility— enshrined in the practice of adversary government—namely, the irresponsibility of those whose duty is to govern, but who chose instead to act in a way that constitutes an evasion of that duty. The job of democratic government, after all, is to represent public opinion and to make policy. At first glance, perhaps, The Balanced Growth and Economic Planning Act, like other measures taken in the adversary spirit, seems to stand up on both these counts. Actually, it represents a default on those obligations. To govern is to identify choices and then to find some authoritative resolution of the issue so identified. What is involved, at bottom, is a process of exclusion: first of false, or irrelevant, or unappealing definitions of the question; and then of solutions that are unacceptable or ineffective. In making these exclusions, persons are taking actions—exercising power, fulfilling duties, and accepting responsibility for the result. And eventually, through elections, they are held to account; in light of the alternatives, the voters affirm or deny the correctness of the representative's decision.

In the case of this bill, we observe just the opposite sort of process taking place: a process, not of exclusion, but of indiscriminate inclusion of everyone's definition of the problem; a process, not of decision in any meaningful sense, but of indecision; a process, not of taking responsibility for the course of events, but of evading it; a process, not of enhancing the electorate's ability to hold the legislators involved accountable, but of dissipating that ability. It is a pattern of legislative behavior that is wholly inconsistent with the basic premise of democratic government.

Consider, for a moment, what it would mean if the Balanced Growth and Economic Planning Act were to be passed. What would the U.S. government thereby be saying about the substance of U.S. economic policy? That it is officially committed to a program of central comprehensive economic planning? In a sense, yes; but then again, considering the puny powers and advisory character of the agency it sets up, clearly the answer is no. Does this act mean that it is the policy of the U.S. government to bring unemployment and inflation down to low levels and to keep them there as well as it knows how? Well, yes, sort of; but then again, considering the vagueness of the charter and the incredible multiplicity of the goals that are spelled out, clearly Congress is saying no such thing. Then does this act say that Congress has decided that the overall pattern of economic policy is so bad that it needs drastic revision? That certainly would seem to be implied; yet it's equally clear, in light of the fact that Congress gave the Board only advisory powers, that Congress is expressing no such intention and would in fact be horrified if the Board came up with a plan that would really bring some coherence and efficacy to economic policy. In other words, the bill means all of these things, and none of them. As policy it is ambiguous and self-contradictory; and as an act of democratic legislation, it reflects an abdication of responsibility.

Thus adversary government does not make policy in any meaningful sense of the term. It attempts to "govern" by creating official adversaries of existing policies, institutions, and practices and then by pitting them against one another in an indeterminate struggle under ground rules established by Congress. This way of exercising the legislative power exacts a stiff price, the most important part of which is that it induces a disintegration of democratic society. It creates expectations that certain goals—zero water pollution, comprehensive economic planning, perfect safety for children who use toys, and so on—will be met, and yet it does this in the foreknowledge that they cannot and will not be met. It effectively declares that certain kinds of activities and attitudes—supporting the concept of a free market, or running a paper mill, or selling bicycles, or wanting cheaper products even if they are less safe—are illegitimate, the province and pleasure of out-and-out enemies of the public welfare; and yet, of course, this is not at all the case. It guarantees that when people find themselves beset by problems of one kind or another, they won't have to look very far or for very long before they find one or another of the agencies of government busily at work creating or perpetuating or worsening the problem. Above all, adversary governance shatters the links of communication, deliberation, persuasion, and trust which ought to join the people of a democratic society with its elected representatives.

WIRE PULLERS AND HASTY GENERALIZERS

To be sure, some degree of official game-playing and symbolic politicking are inevitable in a representative democracy, and any bicameral legislature of 535 members is bound to enact laws that aren't models of purposive coherence and instrumental rationality. But perfection, and the failure to attain it, are not the issue here; what is at issue is a deep-seated and pervasive change in American life which has transformed a political system that generally approximated a kind of responsibility into one in which adversary government, and the evasions on which it rests, have become the rule rather than the exception. To understand how this has come about, it is useful to recall a distinction made almost a hundred years ago by Sir Henry Sumner Maine.

Maine's interest—and it wasn't an altogether friendly one—was in the nature of democracies and the quality of life they permit. He argued that the basic determinant of that quality of life is the way power is organized. When everyone has the vote, he argued, there is great power but it is so dispersed that it's a waste of time for any individual to spend much effort in exercising it. So the crucial determinant of life in such a society is the basis on which votes are amassed into a majority and the character of the people who do this sort of work. There are, Maine argued, two sorts of people who can dominate in such circumstances: "wire-pullers" and those adept at "hasty generalization." In modern times, one would say that the political boss and the demagogue are the characteristic leadership types in a democracy, and that appealing to people's narrow self-interest or to their sentiments are the two basic sources of power in a democratic system.

The emergence of adversary government has taken place against the background of—and in part as a result of—a broad tidal shift in American politics. From having been built upon a foundation of wire-pulling, the political system has moved slowly but massively toward the pole of hasty generalizing. The political party—and the party *style* of doing politics—has given way increasingly to the spoken and written word as the medium of assembling consent, a shift that has quietly but profoundly altered nearly every aspect of the American political system. For whereas the disciplined, narrow, wire-pulling mode of politics is characteristically alive and responsive to the complexities of governance, to the demands of specific interests, the necessity of settling questions, and the centrality of keeping promises (lest the entire cooperative "machine" break down), the hasty generalizer's way of politicking and governing is just the opposite. Like the actor and the con-man, he lives in a world of appearances, and his first imperative is to get the audience's attention and to make a favorable impression. What actually happens is, to him, less important than what is *seen* to happen; and oddly enough, settling questions and resolving disputes is less desirable than keeping them alive—inasmuch as a settled question is no longer capable of attracting interest, and so no longer a suitable vehicle for advancing the politician's career. So the hasty generalizer not only lives in a world of appearances, he thrives in a world of melodramatic conflict, crises, heroes, and villains.

A second crucial characteristic of the politics of hasty generalizing is to be found in the fact that a different social element tends to succeed in it. Wire-pulling politics is the politics of ordinary folks—of the great mass of citizens and those gifted entrepreneurs who are both from the people and of them, who excel only in respect of their ability to translate their skill in personal relationships into deliverable blocs of votes. But in the politics of hasty generalization, the persons who rise to the top are the ones who excel in the arts of rhetoric. In the badly misused word that prevails today, it is "intellectuals"—i.e., people with education and a knack for verbalization—who dominate the politics of hasty generalization. These people, of course, are always a small minority in any society, and they quickly come to have an influence out of all proportion to their numbers.

THE NEW CLASS

It is against this background that two developments—one broad and general, the other quite particular—have prompted American institutions to conform themselves increasingly to the adversary mode of governance. The first of these is the emergence, in the U.S. and other advanced Western nations, of what Daniel Bell has termed the "post-industrial society"—a social order characterized by, among other things, a prevalence of "knowledge work" as against blue-collar work (manufacturing, etc.). With the post-industrial society has come a new social and political class, committed to a new political ethos—ostensibly egalitarian, liberationist, statist, but above all skeptical of, if not downright disbelieving in, the moral adequacy and political legitimacy of the advanced liberal, capitalist, democratic order to whose continuity and prosperity this new class owes its very existence.

In recent years, this new class has become a matter of growing interest to a wide variety of Western intellectuals, and the term has come to possess two very different meanings. To a number of writers on the Left, such as C. Wright Mills or Charles Reich, the New Class is a providential and revolutionary idea, the logical successor, in function, to the proletariat as it was understood by Marx: as the bearer of revolution and a utopian future, as the nemesis of modern capitalism, and as the cause in whose name enlightened people will fight. This New Class, however, has not yet found its Marx; it remains an unrealized idea, and the future order it is destined to usher into being is an imperfectly-known quantity. But what is clear about it is that it carries within it the seeds—and the hope—of the destruction of capitalism; it is an idea of opposition.

To others, however—Daniel P. Moynihan and Irving Kristol come to mind—the term has a much more concrete referent. It denotes, not any theoretical successor to the proletarian revolution, but a very specific class with specific interests and a specific ethos. It consists of large fractions of the traditional upper-middle class: college-educated with advanced degrees, practicing a profession, and engaged seriously in the business of constructing and practicing a chosen "life-style." This class is committed, in Brigitte Berger's telling phrase, to "people-work"—to a "meaningful" occupation which will make life better, by some standard, for other people, and which is located in the public sector. Politically, this class espouses a "humanism" and "egalitarianism" which opposes themselves to what are seen as the salient characteristics and vices of liberal, capitalist democracy. In foreign policy it favors movements of "national liberation" and opposes any variety of traditional "great power" diplomacy; domestically, it advocates a redistribution of power from the private sector, which is tainted by selfish motives, to the public sector, and a redistribution of wealth. Culturally, this new class is full of self-confidence and sees itself as the wave of the future. It does not confine itself to the traditional commitments and disciplines of the Old Left, though it obviously has much in common with it. But its principal *de facto* urge is to establish for itself social space within the existing society commensurate with its own sense of self-importance; and though it does redistribute power from other elites to itself, the effect of many of its programs—from increasing educational opportunity to cleaning up the environment—is to redistribute income and other benefits from the poorer to the richer!

In truth, there is no necessary contradiction between these two senses of the phrase "new class," and indeed they are complementary. Those who understand it to be a revolutionary idea nevertheless believe that the public-sector upper-middle class is the nearest embodiment around, and to those who see it as a specific group in modern society, a large part of its significance and energetic elan derives from its (and the critics') sense that it is indeed the harbinger of something radically new in the modern world.

The emergence of this new social force has had a powerful impact on the character of the ideas which thrive in American public discussion. The leading national audiences, from having been diverse and generally resistant to radical ideas, have become ever more unified around the cultural and political positions of the new class. Thus has been born what James Q. Wilson terms "the liberal audience" which has increasingly set the tone and the terms of national politics—and even of the politics of many of our cities, suburbs, and states. And in an astonishingly short-time—certainly over the course of the 1960s—this liberal audience has come increasingly to sanction—indeed, to demand—a mode of government that is as adversary in its style as the liberal audience is in its sentiments towards bourgeois culture and capitalist democracy.

THE IMPORTANCE OF RICHARD NIXON

It is easy to overspecify the makeup and beliefs of the new class and the liberal audience it formed and led. It would be at least premature—and in truth it would be dishonest—to insist on anything more about this class than its existence, its commitment to public-sector enterprise, its aspiration to "meaningful" occupations, and its generalized sense of distance from the American society. Its more particular attributes and positions have been heavily influenced by events, persons, and circumstances; and of all these, none has been more influential, in an odd and widely-ignored way, than the person and presidency of Richard M. Nixon.

For it was Nixon's approach to most domestic policy issues that had more influence than any other single factor in driving liberal Democrats in Congress into embracing adversary modes of governance, and it was these Congressmen's commitment to such modes that made the general approach appealing and plausible to the liberal audience. The heart of the matter is that on domestic issues Nixon was damn liberal. Was there a problem with the welfare system? Far from taking a stance of resolute hostility to welfare, Nixon proposed a responsible reform that would have vastly increased its size and cost. Were liberals talking about instituting a system of comprehensive national health insurance? Nixon developed his own initiative on the subject, one that called for the direct federal expenditure of many billions and for an elaborate system of mandated private insurance coverage. Were Americans worried about environmental degradation and occupational safety and the dangers of toys and other consumer products? Nixon didn't choose to resist any of these liberal initiatives. Rather he tried to make them his own, and in the case of each he proposed a careful and moderate program of his own.

In this situation, what could liberal Democrats in Congress do? They could let the Administration dominate the development of legislation in the traditional fashion and confine themselves to dealing with matters of degree and detail—but in that case they would be letting the President get the credit and denying themselves an opportunity to dramatize the proposition that they were liberal and Nixon conservative. The other alternative, of course, was for them to fashion a much more drastic and intransigent program and to insist that *it* properly represented the spirit of liberal reform, whereas the Nixon Administration's version was a weak and insincere counterfeit of a proper legislative resolution of the problem at hand. And if, in doing so, they wrote legislation that denied the bureaucracy charged with administering the program the right to let legitimate contextual goals (cost, feasibility, etc.) affect the content and timetable of their regulations, so much the better: how better to suggest that the Nixon Administration was so much in the thrall of special business interests, and so indifferent to the public welfare, that it literally could not be entrusted with the most elementary forms of administrative discretion?

The Congressional liberals chose the second alternative. If the administration proposed a 90 percent reduction in auto emissions to be accomplished by 1980, thereby giving manufacturers time to thoroughly explore all alternative means of achieving that goal, Edmund Muskie changed it to 1975, which meant that only the catalytic converter would be a realistic option. If the Administration favored only catastrophic health insurance, liberal Democrats decided it was necessary to enact a 75 billion-dollar program for universal, comprehensive health care. Thus did liberal Democrats distinguish themselves from the Administration and appropriate the mantle of progressiveness while castigating the Administration as callous and indifferent. Such is the perverse logic of the politics of the hasty generalization in the post-industrial age that a moderate, responsible course of action by a conservative Republican President created, in the liberal majority, an intensifying commitment to an irresponsible and destructive adversary style of governance.

TOWARD A RESTORATION OF POLITY

But whatever its origins, we today are left with a heritage of adversary government to which the liberal audience and its new-class political leaders seem strongly committed, and with which Americans must begin to cope seriously. It may be that this condition will prove to be reversible, and that as soon as the division of the government between Republicans and Democrats comes to an end, the adversary approach to governing will be abandoned, and the liberal audience's appetite for it will wither for want of nourishment by the only people with standing to sustain it. In which case, American citizens are advised to vote a straight party ticket.

Yet one may doubt that unified government will suffice. There is, after all, something about the politics of hasty generalization that encourages public officials to make political melodrama. Given the weakness of political parties in the nation, there will be a continuing incentive for Senators and Representatives to make good media politics. In these circumstances, a remedy is going to be harder to come by. Americans are going to have to learn how to make arguments for what once upon a time they were able to take largely for granted—namely, the idea that responsible government is prudent government, and that the pursuit of one policy objective does not relieve government of the duty to consider the many contextual and competing goals which are affected by the pursuit.

It may also be necessary to undertake a major political public works project as well: the rehabilitation and refurbishment of the political party. For without a large and continuing supply of political wire-pulling and politicians who are adept at it, the nation will remain prey to the hasty generalizer. He is, in the nature of things, an unreliable character, especially in an age when the audience to which he plays has the unformed, mercurial, but potentially-radical qualities that one observes in the new class liberal community. Until the hasty generalizer is put in his place, that is to say, we are probably going to have to look forward to more adversary government, more disorder and de-legitimation in our political system, and more legislation like the Balanced Growth and Economic Planning Act of 1975.

Confronted with that dismal prospect, perhaps Americans will be persuaded that bringing back the DeSapios and the Daleys and the Baileys is by far the more attractive and respon-sible course of action.

PART V
SUMMARY AND CONCLUSION

THE GOD THAT CANNOT FAIL*

A. LAWRENCE CHICKERING
Executive Director, Institute for Contemporary Studies

In his endorsement of the Balanced Growth and Economic Planning Act of 1975, which introduces this volume, Myron Sharpe concludes by saying that we must bring to national economic affairs the same commonsense that we use in driving from Boston to Washington. Planning makes sense; everybody does it. So why all the fuss?

Individuals do plan. And yet their relative success in ordering their own affairs stands in almost total contrast to the failures of virtually every attempt we know about to plan collectively and centralize decision-making. There seem to be two broad reasons: first, as Vincent Ostrom argues, because a planner cannot begin to know enough in a complex society to plan successfully; and second, because even if the information were available to him, the chances are overwhelming that the planner either would not or could not use that information in making his plans.

The availability of information is a fairly straight-forward problem. As society becomes more complex, information describing it becomes more complex, and the result is the increasing problem, as Ostrom puts it, of the "learned ignoramus." The more complex society becomes, the more hopeless it be-

*The author would like to thank Eugene Bardach for his valuable comments on previous drafts of this paper.

comes to centralize decision-making—and this is true not only in nation-states, but in all institutions: corporations, universities, hospitals, labor unions, whatever. Advocates of national economic planning invoke the analogy of business planning. Murray Weidenbaum lays to rest the value of any such analogy: centralized decision-making has apparently worked no better for business than it has for governments.

Individuals can plan for themselves because they have fairly ready access to information affecting them. But no planner, regardless of the sophistication of his techniques and hardware, can begin to know what they all know individually.

But there seems to be a more fundamental reason for the failures of planning. It runs throughout this book, and it concerns the context within which planners make their decisions. Even if the information for successful planning were available, it will only be useful and relevant if it is used in the formulation and implementation of plans. If not—if the economic and social information bearing on the subjects of planning plays no significant role in planners' decisions—then it is hardly surprising that their decisions consistently fail.

There are two parts of the problem. The first concerns the self-interest of planners. When individuals plan, they act for themselves. Planners, on the other hand, are expected to act not for themselves, but for something called "the public interest." Apart from the problem of knowing what the public interest is—a problem which is itself practically insurmountable—successful planning depends on the planner's ignoring his own personal interests and ambitions and acting like a philosopher king. Put another way, the planner is expected to act on information bearing on the problem he confronts, and not on such "extraneous factors" as his own prospects for career advancement. But it isn't even necessary to put the problem so narrowly. Even if a planner *wanted* to make decisions based only on the information available to him—apart from his own personal ambitions—how long would competing interests, constituencies and pressure groups permit him to do so? If planning is all that important, no one will let planners do it.

Planners operate within a general incentive structure made up of all the constituencies and interest groups who have any kind of stake in planning decisions. A major task in understanding the planning process involves relating different incentive structures to different decisions. This issue is treated in different ways and with great skill particularly by Sheahan, Hilton, Buchanan and Tullock, and Bruce-Briggs.

Beyond the narrow problem of self-interest is the broad social and cultural context that influences both planners' decisions and the general enthusiasm for planning. Planners, after all, do not act in a social and cultural vacuum. In some ways the social and cultural context is the most serious and important problem, but it also is the least discussed and least understood. It is touched on by Bruce-Briggs and van den Haag in general terms, and more specifically by Sheahan and Weaver. The broad problem concerns such issues as how and under what circumstances will support for planning increase (decrease)—within individual societies, and between them. What factors, to pick an extreme example, were involved in promoting stringent economic planning in Germany in 1934, and then relaxing it into the relatively free social market economy in 1948? Why is the planning impulse so much stronger in Great Britain than it is in France or the United States? And—most important of all—why has the Planning Idea grown as it has over the decades, defying the overwhelming indications of its failure?

THE PATTERNS OF PLANNING

Central economic planning, as Ernest van den Haag notes, is visible and manual, unlike the invisible and automatic planning routinely performed by the market. The visible, conspicuous nature of central planning is perhaps the dominant factor in the incentive structure influencing planners. Moreover, changing degrees of visibility will change the constituencies planners must serve.

Following are certain themes, some of them overlapping, that run through much of the history of economic planning:

1. Political demands tend to arise for economic planning
when something goes seriously wrong. Planning will thus respond both to specific economic problems and to more fundamental social and cultural changes in a society. The economic
problems may be caused externally (such as energy, by the oil
boycott and cartel), or internally (the Great Depression or problems resulting from mismanaged monetary and fiscal policies).

More fundamental than specific economic problems are the
social and cultural conditions which, if they are sufficiently
aggravated, will eventually bring on a totalitarian state. These
include the collapse of authority and social trust which brought
on both Stalin and Hitler. As Hayek has reminded us, political
totalitarianism in both Nazi Germany and Soviet Russia were
accompanied by total economic planning, enforced by all the
means at the disposal of a police state. It is interesting, as
Willgerodt notes in his chapter on West Germany, that the first
systematic economic planning in that country was introduced in
1934—the year after Hitler and the National Socialists came to
power.

Among lesser underlying social and cultural conditions, one
may note possible relationships between the class tensions in
Britain and Ralph Harris's depressing narrative of British planning, and between the collapse of social authority and trust in
the United States and the emergence of demands for new forms
of economic planning since that time. If social and cultural
influences often work very strongly in favor of planning, in
some cases they also work against it. John Sheahan, for instance, in his chapter on France complains that the basic conservatism of French culture has prevented effective planning in
France.

In a dictatorship paths of resistance must be more subtle.
Thus in the Soviet Union—perhaps the most planned society in
the world—consumer satisfaction with that system is perhaps
best indicated by the fact that Soviet citizens routinely risk
imprisonment in order to pay from $85 to $100 on the black
market for a pair of Levis. That amounts to about a full month's

wages for the average Russian worker, who will often go as high as $145 if he can get the jacket along with the pants.

2. Though general factors and influences provide the dominant pressures for the visible, conspicuous forms of planning, its precise configurations are governed by politics. All decisions to plan as well as all planning decisions are ultimately political decisions, influenced only incidentally by the economic and social facts that form the substance of planning issues.

a. Politics influences planning in several different ways. Direct political influence is simple and obvious. In many instances decisions are made not because of economic and social realities but because of the fortuitous location of political strength. Explicit bribes need not necessarily be involved, often only the desire to avoid penalties. Thus Amtrak schedules are fitted out to serve the location of ICC members and of Congressmen on key transportation committees without substantial regard for population densities or service needs: as George Hilton indicates, Montana and West Virginia are lavishly served by Amtrak despite limited service needs, whereas without interested politicians representing it, the city of Cleveland got no service at all under the original Amtrak plan. For similar reasons the federal highway program builds thousands of miles of superhighways across vast empty spaces of the country. The same is also generally true of planning programs that subsidize obsolete technologies (passenger trains and rail transit), as initial mistakes produce constituencies that push for perpetuating the mistakes.

James Buchanan and Gordon Tullock analyze the general political constraints operating on planners, applying their analysis to the problem of minimum wage laws. Could a central planning agency succeed where others have failed in having the minimum wage law repealed or modified to reduce its disastrous effects in producing (especially minority) teenage unemployment? Buchanan and Tullock conclude they would fail for precisely the same reasons that policy-makers are unable at the present time to do anything about the minimum wage. Because the interests and constituencies influencing minimum wage policy would be no different, there is no reason to believe that the content of policy would change.

Recent energy policy, such as it is, has been fashioned by political pressures of a more general nature. The policy on price controls on old oil was made with November 1976 rather explicitly in mind, while the general problem of price controls (currently on oil and in the four Nixon phases on most everything else) responded to the more general political problem of pricing policy.

b. Besides direct political influence on planning, political pressures are often responsible for inefficient government intervention in the economy. Perhaps the most pervasive problem caused by this class of pressures is the almost universal government avoidance of marginal pricing of public goods and services. Rather than using marginal prices to allocate resources to their most valuable uses, government pricing policies give us such things as airport congestion and queuing, rush-hour freeway congestion, queues for public housing, gasoline, and health care (where, as in Britain, prices are controlled). And everything else at times (as recently) of general price controls. The pricing problem appears almost everywhere as politicians come under constant political pressure to use individual sector planning (energy, housing, medical care, transportation) for economic redistribution.[1] In every case the result is enormous waste, for keeping prices artificially low only encourages consumption for less valuable uses.

In addition, keeping prices artificially low does not eliminate the problem of price. It tends only to change the rationing system and to force people to pay the price in other forms—by queuing, increased search costs, etc. The effects of the policy are particularly noticeable in a place like the Soviet Union which, Pejovich notes, pretends it can do without prices altogether. The result is that Soviet consumers measure the inflation rate in part by the increasing time it takes to find what they want to buy.

Price controls (or refusing to apply marginal pricing) favors people who do well in non-price competition: pretty girls, non-minority group members, relatives, friends, and people of low time valuation who don't mind waiting.

c. The final political influence on planners' decisions relates to the visibility of the planner's manual system. It is the tendency in all areas of "social policy" to distribute "merit goods" or services to recipients rather than giving them cash and permitting them to use it in the most valuable ways to them. This tendency is particularly noticeable in housing with urban renewal and the public housing program, but it is also evident in education, legal services, and other areas. It is not clear that this tendency is entirely due to the planning process itself. Part of the tendency may simply be that for any number of reasons the public prefers to give its subsidies in this manner—to the providers of social services rather than its recipients.

There are reasons, however, to believe that the visibility of central planning provides some bias toward merit good subsidies. One important consideration is the planners' need to have something to plan. After all if social policy were limited to giving cash to the poor, what would be left for planners to do? This is part of the new class problem described by Paul Weaver—to maintaining "meaningful" "people work." On the other hand the implications for low income recipients are mildly disturbing when one considers the results of preliminary studies indicating that when given an opportunity to relate to a computer as opposed to a professional mental health worker, clients with emotional problems prefer by an overwhelming margin to problem solve with the computer.

From the standpoint of the poor, Richard Muth analyzes the severe waste and inefficiency in providing direct housing (as in the public housing program) or mortgage subsidies. As he points out, at least from the standpoint of the poor, the problem is poverty, not poor housing or poor diets. The cure for poverty is to give the poor money or its equivalent.

Politicians and planners give social services in kind rather than cash so that they can say they are *doing* something about social problems. To give merely cash would be to risk accusation that they are "ignoring" problems. But giving visibly, so that the public and the media will think you are doing something, means concentrating large assistance on few low income recipients—which as Muth argues with respect to housing subsidy programs, wastes large amounts of resources while ignoring most needy recipients.

3. Political influence on planning is by no means limited to the influence of politicians. Planners operate within broad incentive structures, which include the private special interests and constituencies that are governed by various regulations and plans.

Political scientists and economists have several theories about the politics of regulation, but all of the major theories indicate that most regulations yield substantial long run benefits to the regulated interests. Many regulations and plans seem to be born in impassioned rhetoric, ideology, in populist appeals to "the people" and denunciations of capitalism and the unregulated market, and then gradually yield to the influence and incentive structure that the regulated interests construct for them. In this scenario political liberals and progressives actively press for "reform" against the equally active opposition of business and labor. But over time general acceptance of the program deprives it of its progressiveness, and industry and labor representatives gradually replace the reformers on the boards and commissions. As this happens, the two partisan groups find themselves changing positions: the progressives now begin to denounce the regulatory agency, while lobbying fiercely for a new and highly exciting regulatory and planning scheme; and business and labor interests now begin to support the regulatory system, citing "complexities that others don't understand," and "special circumstances," while opposing the new proposal.

An alternative scenario is offered by other observers, such as George Hilton, who argue that regulatory agencies such as the Interstate Commerce Commission were established with business support and that they served and perpetuated cartels from the outset. These contrasting scenarios do not conflict in their observations of the influence of the regulated over the regulators. John Sheahan offers some interesting comments on the same point in his narrative on French planning.

4. One final thread in the patterns of planning concerns the pressures that arise for economic planning from failures in monetary and fiscal policy. The most common problem in this family is evident in Germany in the latter half of the 1930s, in Great Britain throughout much of the post-war period, and at present in the United States and most other Western countries. Some critics regard this as the problem of inflation resulting from pushing too hard with monetary and fiscal expansion for reduced unemployment.

Governments have long regarded it as their objective to provide price stability. But since the Depression, they have been increasingly influenced to use macroeconomic policies to reduce unemployment and trade reduced unemployment for increased inflation. The difficulty, these critics argue, is that the Phillips Curve trade-off between unemployment and inflation only seems to work in the short run, and if government ignores price stability and pushes too hard to reduce unemployment, it will buy both escalating inflation *and* high unemployment. Milton Friedman has argued that the long term trade-off is between unemployment and escalating inflation and that in the long run excessively expansionist policies will produce a *positive relationship* between unemployment and inflation—the worst of both worlds. This is exactly what we seem to have had in the United States and other countries in the past few years.

The pattern seems particularly clear in Britain over a much longer period. The "stop-go" policies described by Ralph Harris reveal the severe problem that may result from excessively ambitious efforts to "fine-tune" macroeconomic policy. Initial efforts to reduce unemployment by fiscal and monetary expansion bring inflation. In response, fiscal and monetary restraint is applied, and when unemployment rises, often before inflationary pressures have fully receded, political pressures mount again for renewed expansion. And so the cycle repeats. Whether inflation and unemployment escalate, of course, depends on the point where restraint is applied. In recent years both inflation and unemployment have risen sharply in most Western countries.

The recent history of economic planning is filled with examples of political pressures for planning to deal with the results of inflationary monetary and fiscal policies. As inflation accelerates, demands arise for wages and price controls; and when they don't work (as they never do), pressures mount for still more extensive controls. As shortages and other problems develop, including unemployment, demands increase for planning to solve problems the market no longer seems able to solve.

The point is important because although many prominent economists now oppose central planning, they nevertheless advocate (expansionist) fiscal and monetary policies, which if followed will almost certainly increase the pressures for planning. This existential impatience underlies the fragility of our economic and social system.

PLANNING FOR NO-GROWTH

For roughly a century and a half up to the mid-1960s, economic planning has been a major vehicle of the rationalist belief in Progress. Throughout that period progress meant material progress, economic growth, and (following the decline of traditional religion and its replacement by science's promises of secular redemption) the triumph of man over nature. Until recently planners were overflowing with optimism. In the 1940s, when the idea was at its apogee, there was hardly a problem or vexation of modern society that people thought was beyond the ability of planning to solve. Unemployment, slums, housing shortages, unequal distribution of wealth—they all existed because of the inefficiency, haphazardness, or selfishness of the market place and all could be solved by transferring the powers exercised by markets to government and by vesting those powers in organizations of experts, who would rationally survey society's needs and allocate resources accordingly.

In its optimistic pursuit of material progress planners of the Old Left set out to correct the institutional failings of capitalism. In pursuing this course, they were following a well-traveled path that went back to Marx: that the Inevitability of the Planning Idea was rooted in the institutional weaknesses and failures of capitalism.

In the mid-1960s a major change of emphasis appeared. Largely with the rise of the New Left the traditional optimistic planning commitment to material progress and economic growth gave way, and a new impulse emerged to take its place. Instead of economic growth, the new planning sought no-growth. In place of the old optimism, a new pessimism spoke about a world of ''scarcity'' and warned that we must conserve our ''limited resources'' and stop ''wasting'' them. Even the rhetorical case in support of planning changed abruptly: instead of attacking capitalism's failures, the new planning idea assaulted capitalism for its successes—for producing abundances of ''useless'' consumer goods, ''imposing'' them on the public through advertising, and so desecrating ''the quality of life.''

The new planning emphasis on limitations brought with it both a new vocabulary and a new agenda for planners. The limits to growth became a dominant theme in planning efforts on behalf of population control, safety, and product quality legislation, and especially in legislation involving land use and the environment, including controls on pollution. While certain former objectives of planning remain—the Balanced Growth and Economic Planning Act of 1975 recites growth as well as no-growth objectives—in the past ten years the emphasis on limitation has provided the dominant emphasis of every major consideration of economic planning. Because of its current importance and because it indicates certain interesting things about planning in general, I shall concentrate on this recent planning emphasis.

In California Jerry Brown has come to symbolize the new strain of planning for limits. Brown's commitment to limits touches everything, including government itself; and like many no-growth planners he expresses an attitude toward government and politics whose ambivalence is often expressed by outright hostility. (But while Brown expresses opposition to central planning, his opposition remains an ambivalent one—which cannot finally be separated from the Planning Idea.)

In certain areas, particularly involving the environment, no-growth planning has powerful intellectual arguments to support it. Most important among these involve the problem of external effects—what the economists call "externalities"—which are unpriced activities, in which the social cost of the external effect is not reflected in the private cost of the activity. Air and water pollution are common examples: the costs of pollution are not fully borne by polluters because of the absence of legally-enforceable property rights in air and water.

Despite the validity of these arguments, it is puzzling that planners only discovered them at the end of the sixties. The reasons for the discovery may become clearer if we consider certain other events that occurred at about the same time.

ENTER THE NEW CLASS AND ADVERSARY GOVERNMENT

It is particularly interesting to consider the rise of no-growth planning in relation to Paul Weaver's arresting thesis about the new class and adversary government. Weaver's concept of adversary government is adversary in two separate respects. First, he describes current legislation as adversary in the sense that its purpose is to attack traditional American society. Here he describes it precisely:

> The practitioners of adversary government . . . do not merely set up agencies to pursue immoderate social goals; they also, by their very way of defining goals and the manner of their pursuit, set up agencies whose mandate is nothing less than that of making war—in principle, *total* war . . . on those sectors of American government or society affected by the achievement of these goals.

But there is another, more profound and more disturbing sense in which his analysis describes current practices of government as adversary. It occurs in his treatment of Nixon—his blaming Nixon, in effect, for sponsoring what Weaver himself describes as responsible, moderate approaches to national problems. What, he asks, were the liberal Democrats to do? Let Nixon steal their fire? The Democrats were not about to let that happen; and so Nixon forced them to behave irresponsibly and even irrationally. But if Weaver's thesis is true, there is no escaping the conclusion that the horrors of adversary government are directly and completely attributable to the responsibility and moderation of Nixon's leadership.*

Mr. Weaver has described not an intellectual but a theatrical process. To borrow his word, the political arena in America today is like a good melodrama, with heroes and villains, conflict and confrontation, and much gnashing of teeth—all of the ingredients of a good afternoon soap opera. As an adversary process, it is thereby empty of intellectual or philosophical content: to maintain the mythology of Republican irresponsibility and reaction, the Democratic Left are driven to hasty generalization and adversary government.

The advent of adversary government occurred at precisely the same time as the emergence of planning for limits and no-growth. The rhetoric and program of both are the same, and so are their practitioners. In fact, for the most part adversary government and no-growth planning are simply different ways of describing the same phenomenon.

Both no-growth planning and adversary government look with great suspicion on the objectives of planning for growth. If you think true progress resides in turning back material progress, then you will likely regard any effort to plan for material progress as perverse. Thus, planning for limits often embraces

---

*One logical extension of this proposition creates an extraordinary responsibility for the minority party in the contemporary American political system. From Weaver's conclusion it logically follows that the minority party—the party that does not control the political and social idiom—has a responsibility to be irresponsible. Or put the other way around, it is irresponsible for the minority party to be responsible.

and seeks to perpetuate the material failures of planning for growth. For this reason no-growth planners will receive as successes many of the arguments recited throughout this book on planning failures. If defenders of the market list its innovative power and its ability to phase out obsolete technologies among its prime virtues, to its new class critics the market's ability to innovate is one of its primary vices. The private automobile may be "efficient," but it disrupts the nostalgia of no-growth planning—which seeks ongoing subsidies of obsolete technologies such as passenger trains, not despite their antique quality, but because of it. In an odd sort of way, in rejecting modernism, modern progressives have rediscovered the past, and they resent the market's disrespect for it.

The planning of "scarcity" may become clearer if we consider briefly the new planner's theory of value. Berkeley political scientist Eugene Bardach has recently described present concerns for energy conservation in terms of what he calls their "BTU theory of value."[2] In greatly simplified form his theory measures the social cost of any good or service in terms of the energy consumed in producing it. Energy conservationists therefore press for legislation opting for processes that minimize consumption of BTUs—"an integral part," as the $4 million Ford Foundation Energy Policy Project put it, "of the nation's life support system." Bardach sums up the position nicely: "Use BTU's and you sap the nation's vital bodily fluids."

Let's borrow the analysis and apply it elsewhere. The point will become quickly obvious if the reader places the phrase "theory of value" after each of the following ideas: prime agricultural land, coastline, open spaces, quality goods, product safety, clean water, clean air—the list could go on and on, but these examples are enough to make the point. In each case the concept of value is an absolute, pre-empting any possibility of trade-off or optimizing or balancing values—pre-empting, that is, the very basis of the economist's effort to deal with the problem of scarcity.

Perhaps the best symbol of this theory of value is contained in widely-publicized statements by environmentalists who argued in opposition to off-shore oil drilling in the Santa Barbara Channel that no amount of oil was worth the life of a single bird killed by an oil spill. In reporting Santa Barbara economist Walter Mead's efforts to place a dollar value on each bird, the *Wall Street Journal* quoted one environmentalist who marked that "economists know the price of everything and the value of nothing."

When no-growth planners say we live in a world of scarce resources, they do not mean that statement in the sense that economists regard scarcity as the basic economic problem. They mean scarcity in the sense that people should value a few specific values—each of which, following the "theories of value," is very nearly absolute and has close to infinite value. In simpler terms, the no-growth planners mean that people should consume fewer things, while concentrating their resources on *quality goods*. In its extreme (though logically extended) form this means consuming what the upper-middle class "consumer" wants: an Audi or BMW, maybe a black-bodied Nikon camera, a full-sized Mont Blanc pen and the best French wines. Consumerist legislation has not yet been permitted to enjoin these items on the American consumer but it certainly tends in that direction.*

Scarcity under this scheme is not a natural constraint imposed on public policy; it *is* a public policy. It is the modern planner's penance for the older planner's *hubris* in attempting to dominate nature. The modern planner is here to serve nature, not to dominate it. The commitment is particularly evident in the rather open and explicit environmentalist determination to protect the land from people.

---

*Unfortunately even if the upper-middle new class were willing to underwrite a program and subsidize the poor to buy these items—say, by special vouchers for black-bodied Nikons—the problem would remain. Such programs would only shift the standards of quality. In place of the $700 Nikon would be a $2,000 Hasselblad, or we would see a marked increased in inverted snobbery ("You bought *what*? . . . a *new* black Nikon?") If everyone had a BMW the new standard would require a higher priced Mercedes or an antique Rolls. It is a view of the world best satirized in the writings of Tom Wolfe and the cartoons of Wm. Hamilton.

PLANNING AS SOCIAL MYTH

If the new planners are pessimistic, hope nevertheless remains at the heart of the Planning Idea. Aaron Wildavsky, Dean of the Graduate School of Public Policy at Berkeley, put the issue quite directly:

> Planners are men of secular faith. The word "faith" is used advisedly because it is hardly possible to say that planning has been justified by works. Once the word is in them it leaps over the realm of experience. They are confirmed in their beliefs no matter what happens. Planning is good if it succeeds and society is bad if it fails. That is why planners so often fail to learn from experience. To learn one must make mistakes and planning cannot be one of them.[3]

Wildavsky concluded that "Planning is not so much a subject for the social scientist as for the theologian."

Economic planning is a social myth. It does not yield to evidence of repeated failures, because arguments for it do not recite its successes. No one *claims* it works. Sharpe's endorsement of the Planning Bill is particularly instructive. Nowhere does he suggest or even hint that planning works. On the contrary, he goes out of his way to concede almost every argument against planning. It has not worked in France, he says, citing John Sheahan's article (which is reprinted in this volume). Nor in Japan, citing another *Challenge* article. And after reciting a whole list of things he does not have in mind, he concludes by saying that planning advocates support "effective planning."

Sharpe has no problem with Vincent Ostrom's information problem. He concedes it: It is true, he says, "it is impossible to see a year ahead, much less six." So, as circumstances change, plans must change. There is no problem with bringing out six-year plans every two years, or even presumably every six months. The six-year plan is a "rolling plan, subject to change as unforeseen difficulties or opportunities arise." Nevertheless, the plan provides a "sense of direction." It provides a "framework" within which to consider goals. It will be "rational," and "systematic," "comprehensive." All of the magic words that Ostrom argues are at the heart of the planner's rite. It will be "coherent," serving "vital needs," "coordinated," "consistent," "efficient"—"effective planning" will be all these things and more while seeking to improve "the quality of life."

The importance of hope in Planning, following Weaver's analysis of adversary government, suggests why the objectives of planning shifted abruptly toward the end of the sixties from planning for economic growth to planning for "scarcity." Weaver notes that at the end of the sixties the Republican Party and its leader Richard Nixon celebrated the decade's unremitting news of planning failures by moving rapidly into every social and planning area. This development would have caused problem enough for the Democrats and the liberals, but the problem was aggravated because Nixon was not content merely to adopt as his own the substance of liberal social policy—he also—especially in the trip to China—often went out of his way to seize the symbols of political Leftism and even to flaunt them. The problem was especially aggravated because all of this was done by Nixon, the old Red-baiter and symbol of all that the Left detested. Under these circumstances the symbols of moral struggle were difficult to maintain. Gone were the symbols of the old Republican reaction: John Foster Dulles and cold-war politics, George Humphrey and balanced budgets. During the fifties under Eisenhower, the Republican Secretary of Defense and former President of General Motors (Charles E. Wilson) could actually say that "What is good for General Motors is good for the United States!" For liberals those were the good old days, when Republicans were Republicans and there was no doubt where the angels were.

If Nixon was determined to become a planner as he said he had become a Keynesian then how could the Planning Idea remain as a symbol of hope? If Nixon was to be an optimist—promising peace in Vietnam and abundance at home—how could the Idea remain optimistic and rational? It could not and did not. Thus adversary government and planning for limits and scarcity were born together.

Considering planning as a social myth, the inadequacy

of information discussed by Ostrom and others is more an advantage than a disadvantage to Planning. If centralized decision-making makes it impossible for planners to know enough to plan successfully, on the other hand the more centralized a system is, the more removed the decision-maker is from pressure by individual citizen "bourgeois" preferences. Furthermore, the more complex the situation and the more impossible information is to get, the more difficult it is to know and evaluate what a planner is doing. For those who see planning as concerned with real economic and social problems, these considerations will seem uniformly negative, but to those committed to the Planning Idea—especially to planning for limits—they are all decided advantages.

As decision-making is centralized, it not only becomes increasingly removed from individual citizens, it also becomes increasingly visible. Centralization thus changes the incentive structure for planners, substituting (the more it is centralized) James Q. Wilson's new-class liberal audience of foundation executives and media types for the individual citizen. Centralization and visibility thus increase the importance of Planning myths and symbols. Far from inconveniences to the Planning Idea, these features of centralization are all indispensable to it.

WHY PLANNING CANNOT FAIL

As van den Haag, Wildavsky and others have argued, the Planning Idea draws its ultimate strength from the decline of the traditional sources of personal structure and identity in Western culture. As the agent of rationalist individualism and utilitarianism, liberal capitalism has been a major force in undermining traditional authorities and communities such as the family, church and local community—all of which provided important places of belonging in generations past. While the rationalist emphasis on efficiency and utility has produced most of what man has traditionally regarded as progress, the emphasis on usefulness has been hard on the pre-rational underpinnings of family and church, as well as other institutions of the social bond. Robert Nisbet has argued that the decline of the traditional communities and authorities and their gradual replacement by the central state is the most important theme in the history of the West. The decline of traditional communities has of course been celebrated by libertarians such as Hayek, whose exclusive emphasis on individualism often ignores the importance of personal structure to individual freedom. Such an emphasis also often obscures the possibility of understanding how the decline of traditional community and the rise of the central state are causally related.

People cannot function without some kind of structure and identity. Those who are cut off from the traditional source of structure are often left, like adolescents, in the painful position of defining themselves by opposition to the larger society. Many of those cut off from traditional values often find that for them opposition is the only legitimate value.

The Planning Idea emerges from the decline of social authority. It is no accident that the advocates of planning—the upper-middle new class—come from the group in modern society most estranged from the belonging and identity once provided by the traditional communities of family and church. Nowhere is the search for personal structure and identity more obsessively pursued than it is by the new class. A major instrument of that search is the opposition to traditional society offered by the symbols and myths identified with Planning.

As Dostoyevski warned us through the words of his Grand Inquisitor, the problem of structure and identity is absolutely critical to the problem of freedom. For without personal structure, people cannot tolerate political freedom either for themselves or for others. The problem of identity has been aggravated by the steady decline of the traditional communities and authorities—family, church and local community. The loss of the smaller, intermediate associative communities has gradually given way to larger and larger organizations and institutional structures, which do not satisfy as the older communities once satisfied the need for a sense of belonging.

The religious underpinnings of planning for limits are rather explicit. Planning for limits trades on constant rhetorical appeals to man's lowly condition, to his imminent extinction, and to the sinfulness of his profligate nature. It is unlikely that the advocates of planning will be impressed by demonstrations of planning failures because such demonstrations will not tell them anything they don't already know and even embrace. If anything, even as the evidence of its failure grows, the continued decline of social authority will increase the demands for planning. Turning the point around, only by discovering new sources of personal structure to replace those we have lost can we have any hope of halting the advance of the Planning Idea.

All of this explains why planners do not learn from their mistakes. Planning is a god that cannot fail because planners' eternal hope won't let it.

APPENDIX A

THE CASE FOR PLANNING*

The Initiative Committee for National Economic Planning
Co-Chairmen
    WASSILY LEONTIEF, *Harvard University*
    LEONARD WOODCOCK, *President, UAW*

Few Americans are satisfied with the way in which the economy is now operating. Unemployment and rising prices are endemic. Inflation in the United States has become a source of instability in the world at large. No reliable mechanism in the modern economy relates needs to available manpower, plant, and materials. In consequence we have shortages of housing, medical care, municipal services, transportation, energy, and numerous other requirements of pressing importance.

We have not made it our business to foresee these critical problems and to take steps to forestall them. We do not plan. But in a modern economy planning is not a matter of preference or ideology. It is one of immediate need. In its absence we will all suffer. This suffering is avoidable.

We therefore urge that provision be made for planning at the highest level of the United States government and through regional, state, and local units of administration of the methods and objectives of planning, and by full public participation in the planning process.

---

*Reprinted with permission of The Initiative Committee for National Economic Planning.

NATIONAL ECONOMIC PLANNING

We believe that economic leadership must be exercised in a new way through an Office of National Economic Planning. This office must be in a position to perceive our country's economic and social needs now and for many years to come and to provide the public, Congress, and the executive branch with alternative plans of action, not only to enable us to avert hardship and disaster, but to guide the economy in a direction consistent with our national values and goals.

Planning is neither strange nor unfamiliar. Every individual and business plans for the years ahead. Without passing judgment on its merits, our space program is a good example of planning in its most sophisticated and successful form. It also illustrates the magnitude of the effort that must go into national economic planning. Nevertheless, the principles are simple. First, from a set of feasible alternatives, a definite and realizable goal was decided upon: to carry a man to the moon and bring him back to earth. All the necessary information had to be gathered together in a consistent and useful form. Then, step by step, the program had to be carried out in the required sequence, the results monitored, and corrections made whenever necessary.

Just as it would have been impossible for a man to go to the moon and back by accident, it is impossible for us to achieve our economic objectives by accident.

But the most striking fact about the way we organize our economic life is that we leave so much to chance. We give little thought to the direction in which we would like to go. We do not attempt to ensure that resources are allocated to meet our most urgent national needs. In fact, we know that they are not so allocated.

Instead of systematically trying to foresee the needs of the nation in years ahead, we have dozens of separate, uncoordinated agencies making policy in this area, and that without any thought of how it all fits together. We have over fifty federal offices collecting economic data, in most instances insufficiently detailed, frequently obsolete, often contradictory and incompatible. No single office is responsible for setting appropriate standards and for bringing these data together so that they can be used to pursue coherent national objectives. We make economic policy from quarter to quarter or year to year without any perspective on where the economy is going or where we want it to go.

HOW PLANNING COULD WORK

The mere cataloguing of these problems reveals the inadequacy of our present economic techniques. We therefore recommend that an Office of National Economic Planning, described below, be established with

—authority to accumulate, collate, and analyze detailed economic information from all sources;

—a mandate to examine major economic trends and work out realistic alternative long-term economic programs for periods of fifteen to twenty-five years, to be submitted to the President and Congress;

—a mandate to work out alternative plans of intermediate length, such as five or six years, to be submitted to the President and Congress, designed to carry us toward our long-range objectives;

—responsibility to specify the labor, resources, financing, and other economic measures needed to realize these programs and plans.

Needless to say, all programs and plans must be periodically reviewed and revised as changing circumstances required.

Let us examine how the planning office would go about its work. Its function would be to develop programs in specific areas where there are discernible national needs. Energy, transportation, and housing are obvious examples. But it is clear that a planning office cannot look at energy alone, transportation alone, housing alone, or at any other sector of the economy in isolation. All these sectors interact, draw on scarce resources, require definite numbers of workers with specific training, and require financing. Above all, planning is a way of looking at economic problems as a whole, providing the information needed to set explicit priorities in the use of resources, and guiding all sectors of the economy toward the attainment of our chosen goals. A planning system must balance resources with needs, set goals that can be realized, and inform the public what the choices really are.

PLAN AND MARKET

The heart of planning is to go from information to action. Most of the action in the U.S. economy takes place in the private sector. Democratic planning is not a substitute for a decentralized economy nor does it replace the millions of private decisions that are made in the market every day. Rather, to reach democratically-chosen objectives, it influences those decisions with a consistent set of economic techniques. The means of influencing those decisions are already familiar to us. Some, such as tax incentives and disincentives, and traditional monetary and fiscal policies, influence individual actions indirectly. Others, such as selective credit controls, guidance of basic capital flows, limits to the use of air, water, and land, and mandatory resource allocation, affect individual actions directly. All these measures have been used at one time or another by the federal government, but—save in World War II—in a haphazard fashion, with no view to their overall effect. The purpose of planning is to provide that view.

It should be clear, however, that the planning office would not set specific goals for any individual firm. But it would indicate quantitatively the input and output of various sectors of the economy necessary to achieve balanced growth.

One of the best persuaders available to the planning office is information. The flow of goods, services, and money from one industry to another can be grasped in great detail through the use of input-output and other programming techniques. The planning office can provide a continuous stream of detailed information about how various sectors of the economy mesh—and are expected to mesh in the future—enabling individual firms, as well as federal, state, and local governments, to make enlightened and coherent decisions about production and consumption.

ORGANIZATION

In order to be effective and useful, an Office of National Economic Planning must be set up at the center of our economic and political life as one of our most influential institutions. To provide leadership at the highest level, we propose the establishment of such an office within the Executive Office of the President, provided with sufficient funding and supported by a professional staff large enough to carry out the many functions discussed here. The Director of the Office of National Economic Planning should be designated as the chief adviser to the President for economic affairs. The office should oversee the implementation of the national economic plan within the executive branch of government. Accordingly, the membership of the board of this office should be composed of high administration officials and be supported by an advisory group representing the best talent of business, labor, farmers, consumers, minorities, and other sections of society.

We also propose that the Council of Economic Advisers continue to concentrate on short-run problems of full employment and stabilization, usefully supplementing the long-run concerns of the office.

PLANNING AND DEMOCRACY

It goes without saying that the final choice among all feasible alternative planning objectives and programs belongs to Congress; and the execution of all laws embodying planning policy is the responsibility of the Administration. Congress and the executive branch must be equal partners in planning. We therefore recommend that a Joint Congressional Planning Committee, supported by a Congressional Office of Planning, with the necessary funding and technical assistance, be established to oversee all planning activities of the executive branch, and to initiate and review legislation related to planning.

But, to be successful, planning has to be undertaken with the full understanding, acceptance, and support of the public. The participation of representatives of all important economic and social interests in every phase of planning is essential. Regional, state, and local units of government must fully share in the planning process. Every national forum—the press, Congress, and the executive branch—should be used for a continuous airing of opinion on planning goals and methods. A network of committees representing every area of economic life should be available for mutual consultation with members of the planning office.

No one can possibly argue that planning will solve all our problems. Nor will it reconcile conflicting interests between different sections of our society. These will continue to be contested in the political arena as before. But planning can spare all of us the sense of helplessness we feel as the economy drifts from crisis to crisis and can replace frustration with a sense of hope, with the conviction that we can, in fact, exert some control over our affairs.

Nor is planning an easy task. It is one of the most difficult enterprises that any society can undertake. But the technical capability and know-how exist to do the job. We believe that the hard thinking, work, and experimentation required by a planning effort will be repaid many times over. We are convinced that the American people will respond to the challenge.

NOTES

PART I. INTRODUCTION

Myron Sharpe: "The Planning Bill"

[1]This editorial was printed a few days before Senators Humphrey and Javits announced their sponsorship of "The Balanced Growth and Economic Planning Act of 1975." Several changes were made in the bill in that interval, and they are noted herein:

—Instead of an Office of Balanced Growth and Economic Planning with a director and a staff, there is now a three-member Economic Planning Board with a chairman and a staff.

—The length of long-term plans is to be decided by the President and Congress. The specifications of six-year periods has been deleted.

—The Administrator of the Federal Energy Administration is added to the Economic Planning Council.

—The President rather than the director appoints four of the twelve members of the Advisory Committee.

Herbert Stein: "Economic Planning and the Improvement of Economic Policy"

[1]Jacob Javits, "The Need for National Planning," *Wall Street Journal*, July 8, 1975, p. 14.

The Balanced Growth and Economic Planning Act of 1975 (S. 1795) was introduced into the Senate on May 21, 1975; an identical bill (H.R. 7678) was introduced into the House of Representatives on June 5, 1975. For the text of the bill and statements by its supporters, see *Congressional Record*, May 21, 1975, pp. S8831–8833.

[2]MES (Myron E. Sharpe), "The Planning Bill," *Challenge*, May/June 1975, p. 7.

[3]*Notes from the Joint Economic Committee*, vol. 1, no. 19, July 1, 1975, p. 2.

[4]Vera Lutz, *Central Planning for the Market Economy* (London: Longmans, 1969), p. 17.

[5]"The Need for National Planning," p. 14.

[6]Quotations are from *Notes from the Joint Economic Committee*, p. 18.

[7]"The Planning Bill," p. 7.

[8]Gustavo Velasco, "Planning and Reason," *Modern Age*, (Fall 1974), pp. 394–95.

[9]One should not infer from the foregoing analysis of recent proposals for economic planning that I consider either Federal economic policy or the process by which that policy is made to be beyond improvement. On the contrary, I think improvement is both possible and urgent. I do not believe that the proposals which go under the name "planning" would make a positive contribution. I have made some suggestions for improving the process of policy formation in the American Enterprise Institute pamphlet from which the foregoing was excerpted.

PART II. NATIONAL EXPERIENCES WITH ECONOMIC PLANNING

Ralph Harris: "Great Britain: The Lessons of Socialist Planning"

[1]Published in 1965.

[2]*Planning in Practice* (Cambridge University Press, 1950). Professor Devons was concerned with the single issue of aircraft planning which presented baffling choices between a wide variety of (changing) alternative possibilities, each implying differing requirements for raw materials, manpower, equipment, servicing, spare parts, etc. The perfect coordination which planners take for granted would require what Devons described as "superhuman capacity [to] comprehend fully and realistically . . . the whole range of choices open to the Ministry of Aircraft Production in deciding what to produce."

[3]*Ordeal by Planning* (Macmillan, 1948); second edition published as *New Ordeal by Planning*, 1968.

[4]But what Hutt has described as the "strike-threat system" in view of the coercive monopolistic powers exerted by labor unions. *The Theory of Collective Bargaining, 1930–1975* (London: Institute of Economic Affairs, 1975).

[5]In *Management of the British Economy 1945–1960* (CUP, 1964), J. C. R. Dow showed that economic management in the name of "stabilisation policy" had a de-stabilizing effect. By ignoring the time lags, the alternation between tardy "disinflation" and premature "reflation" caused oscillations in output and employment without preventing the almost continuous rise in prices.

[6]Doubts about the claims made for "indicative planning" were brilliantly exposed by Dr. Vera Lutz in *Central Planning for the Market Economy* (IEA/Longmans, 1969).

[7]Of course, market economists understand that all elements in an economy are inter-related, often in ways that no planner—or anyone else—can fully know.

[8]Such forecasts are bound to lean heavily on extrapolating past trends; they are in large part backward-looking and have been compared to steering a ship by its wake.

[9]An exposé of the fundamental contradictions of French "indicative planning"—with its evasive shifts between "targets," "forecasts," "flexible estimates"—will be found in Lutz, op. cit.

[10]Reprinted with other essays in *Full Employment at Any Price?* (Institute of Economic Affairs, 1975). See also Hayek's classic "Scientism and the Study of Society" in *The Counter-Revolution of Science* (Glencoe: Free Press, 1952).

[11]Published in 1968 by the University of Strathclyde where Frank McFadzean (now Chairman of the Royal Dutch/Shell Group) was a Visiting Professor.

[12]Many of its 250 studies analyze the reforms in the legal and institutional framework that would impel competitive enterprise to serve more harmoniously the interests of consumer, investor, employee and environmental desiderata.

Hans Willgerodt: "Planning in West Germany: The Social Market Economy"

[1]For instance: K. Mandelbaum, "An Experiment in Full Employment. Controls in the German Economy, 1933–1938," in *The Economics of Full Employment* (Oxford: The Oxford Institute of Statistics, 1946), p. 183f; F. C. Child, *The Theory and Practice of Exchange Control in Germany* (The Hague, 1958).

[2]J. K. Galbraith, "The Germany Economy," in *Foreign Economic Policy for the United States,* ed. by S. E. Harris (Cambridge, Mass., 1948), p. 94f.

[3]Cf. Werner Obst, *DDR—Wirtschaft. Modell und Wirklichkeit* (Hamburg, 1973).

[4]The founded the yearbook *Ordo,* which is a periodical dealing with problems of economic order and economic policy in general.

[5]Cf. Alfred Müller-Armack, *Wirtschaftsordnung und Wirtschaftspolitik* (Freiburg, 1966); *Genealogie der Sozialen Marktwirtschaft* (Bern and Stuttgart, 1974).

[6]Later Müller-Armack himself became Undersecretary of State in the Federal Ministry for Economic Affairs.

[7]See Lucius D. Clay, "Gratulation," in *Ludwig Erhard. Beiträge zu seiner politischen Biographie. Festschrift zum 75. Geburtstag,* ed. by G. Schröder, A. Müller-Armack, K. Hohmann, J. Gross, R. Altmann (1972), p. 40.

[8]Walter W. Heller, "The Role of Fiscal-Monetary Policy in German Economic Recovery," *The American Economic Review, Papers and Proceedings,* vol. 40 (1950), p. 535. Heller mentioned also the structural difficulties to increase employment.

[9]H. Besters, "Economic Policy in Western Germany 1949 to 1961," in *Economic Policy in Our Time,* vol. 3 (Amsterdam, 1964), p. 407.

[10]Cf. Wilhelm Röpke, "Deutschland—Massengrab falscher Voraussagen," in Wilhelm Röpke, *Gegan die Brandung* (Erlenback–Zurich–Stuttgart, 1959), pp. 206–18.

[11]For instance, by H. Mendershausen, "Fitting Germany into a Network of World Trade," *The American Economic Review, Papers and Proceedings,* vol. 40 (1950), pp. 548–67.

[12]Wilhelm Röpke, *Ist die deutsche Wirtschaftspolitik richtig?,* with preface by Chancellor Konrad Adenauer (Stuttgart-Köln, 1950), p. 88.

[13]Cf. Norbert Sandner, "Die Grenzen der mittel- und langfristigen Prognosen des Energieverbrauchs," in *Glückauf,* vol. 23, no. 11 (1972), p. 1147–60.

[14]For many details, see Ludwig Erhard, *Wohlstand für Alle* (Düsseldorf, 1957).

[15]For further details see the excellent article of Egon Sohmen, "Competition and Growth: The Lesson of West Germany," *The American Economic Review,* vol. 49 (1959), pp. 986–1003; and ibid., the debate, vol. 50 (1960), pp. 1015–31.

[16]R. G. Opie, *The American Economic Review,* vol. 50 (1960), p. 1024.

[17]Cf. Hannelore Hamel, "Die Marktwirtschaft der Bundesrepublic als 'staatsmonopolistischer Kapitalismus'," in *25 Jahre Martwirtschaft in der Bundesrepublic Deutschland,* ed. by D. Cassel, G. Gutmann, H. J. Thieme (Stuttgart, 1972), pp. 65–74.

[18]Galbraith, "The German Economy," p. 101, recommended alignment of the United States with the SPD, because in his opinion the Christian Democrats and the Liberal Democrats were "defensive rather than programmatic." The economic and political reform after 1948 was accomplished under the leadership of the Christian Democrats.

[19]Automatic stabilizers were preferred to discretionary actions, but the latter were not excluded, at least by Müller-Armack, who had proposed systematic anticyclical policies in the twenties; cf. his article, "Konjunkturforschung und Konjunkturpolitik," in *Handwörterbuch der Staatswissenschaften,* 4th ed., supplement (Jena, 1929), pp. 645–77.

[20]Cf. Hans Herbert Götz, *Weil alle besser leben wollen . . .* (Düsseldorf, Wien, 1963), pp. 199–202; *Monatsberichte der Deutschen Bundesbank,* November, 1957, pp. 16–18.

[21]Cf. Günter Schmölders, *Die Politiker und die Währung* (Frankfurt am Main, 1959); idem, *Finanz- und Steuerpsychologie* (Hamburg, 1970), p. 145ff.

[22]Cf. R. Plate, "Das 'Professorengutachten' von 1962 aus heutiger Sicht," in *Agrarwirtschaft,* Jahrgang 17 (1968), pp. 193–201.

[23]For further details see Hans Willgerodt, "Warum Staatsplanung in der Marktwirtschaft?" (Why State Planning in the Market Economy?), *Ordo,* vol. 17 (1966), pp. 153–228.

[24]For details, see R. Hasse, H. Werner, H. Willgerodt, *Aussenwirtschaftliche Absicherung zwischen Markt und Interventionismus* (Frankfurt, 1975).

[25]Cf. Christian Watrin, "Globale Wirtschaftssteuerung und Einkommenspolitik," *Ordo-Jahrbuch,* vol. 25 (1973), p. 125ff.

[26]Cf. Kurt Schmidt, Eberhard Wille, *Die Mehrjahrige Finanzplanung. Wunsch und Wirklichkeit* (Tübingen, 1970).

[27]For further details, see "Sachverständigenrat zur Begutachtung der gesamtwirtschaftlichen Entwicklung," in *Vor dem Aufschwung* (Stuttgart, Mainz, 1975), pp. 94ff, 137ff.

[28]Cf. Hartmut Bebermeyer, *Regieren ohne Management?* (Stuttgart, 1974).

[29]*The Wealth of Nations,* book 4, chapter 2.

Svetozar Pejovich: "The End of Planning: The Soviet Union and East European Experiences"

[1]G. Warren Nutter, *The Strange World of Ivan Ivanov* (New York: The World Publishing Co., 1969), p. 39.

[2]James Blackman, "The Kosygin Reforms: New Wine in Old Bottles," in B. Treml (ed.), *The Development of the Soviet Economy* (New York, 1968).

[3]G. Warren Nutter, "How Soviet Planning Works," *New Individualist Review,* 4 (Summer 1965), pp. 20–25.

[4]Evsei Liberman, "The Plan, Profits and Bonuses," *Pravda,* September 9, 1962.

[5]The extent of environmental disruption in the Soviet Union is suggested by economists Philip Gramm and Robert Ekelund:

> The Black Sea coast in the Soviet Republic of Georgia is disappearing and sea encroachment has moved to 40 meters inland at some places. Hospitals, resort hotels, and even the beach sanitarium of the Ministry of Defense have collapsed. Excessive construction loosened the soil but the major source of land erosion is simply attributable to the fact that contractors have hauled away much of the Black Sea area in their quest for a cheap source of sand and gravel. In a resort area of the Caucasus, a protective semicircle of mountains is being eroded by lime facilities constructed by the Ministry of Railroads (to increase freight density in that region). The erosion has had disastrous effects upon the climate and ecology of Kislonodsk. . . . [T]he examples are but two of a large number reflecting massive environmental disruption in the Soviet Union.

Quoted from "Land Use Planning: The Market Alternative," in *No Land Is an Island* (Institute for Contemporary Studies, 1975), p. 165. The author has also traveled extensively in the Soviet Union and has observed the same phenomena. See also Marshall I. Goldman, "The Convergence of Environmental Disruption," *Science,* 170 (October 2, 1970), pp. 37–42, for additional discussion of air, water, and land pollution in the U.S.S.R.; and Lucille Sheppard Keyes, "Planning Gap and the Role of Regulation," *Land Economics,* 41 (May 1965), pp. 111–19—both cited in Gramm and Ekelund, op. cit.

[6]Armen Alchian and William Allen, *University Economics* (Belmont: Wadsworth Publishing Co., 1972), p. 8.

[7]Lowell Gallaway, "The Folklore of Unemployment and Poverty," presented at the Conference on Individual Liberty and Governmental Policies in the 1970s, Ohio University, 1975.

[8]Zev Katz, "Insights from Emigrés and Sociological Studies on the Soviet Union," in *Soviet Economic Prospects for the Seventies* (U.S. Congress, Joint Economic Committee, 1973), p. 110.

[9]David Bonson and Barbara Severin, "Soviet Consumer Welfare: The Brezhnev Era," in *Soviet Economic Prospects for the Seventies,* p. 379.

[10]Keith Bush, "The Implementation of the Soviet Economic Reform," manuscript, pp. 29–30.

[11]Gertrude E. Schroeder, "Recent Developments in Soviet Planning and Incentives," in *Soviet Economic Prospects for the Seventies,* pp. 35–36.

[12]Svetozar Pejovich, "Liberman's Reforms and Property Rights in the Soviet Union," *Journal of Law and Economics,* 12 (April 1969), pp. 155–62.

PART III. ECONOMIC PLANNING IN AMERICA
Peter P. Witonski: "The Historical Roots of American Planning"

[1]Seymore E. Harris, "The New Economics," in *Paths of American Thought,* Arthur M. Schlesinger, Jr., and Morton White (eds.) (Boston: Houghton Mifflin Company, 1970), pp. 345–71.

[2]John Jewkes, *The New Ordeal by Planning* (London: Macmillan, 1968), p. 45.

[3]Max Lerner, "The Triumph of Laissez-Faire," in *Paths of American Thought,* pp. 147–66.

[4]Ibid., p. 147.

[5]Oscar Lange, "Marxian Economics and Modern Theory," in *The Review of Economic Studies,* 2 (1935), pp. 189–201.

[6]It has been argued by some critics of the free economy that the availability of cheap land and the egalitarianism of the frontier slowed the advance of social democracy in America. See V. L. Parrington, *Main Currents in American Thought* (New York, 1930), 3 vols.

[7]E. Durkheim, *Le Socialisme: sa définition, ses débuts, la doctrine Saint-Simonienne* (Paris, 1928).

[8]In an introduction to the 1928 edition of *Le Socialisme,* Durkheim's student, M. Mauss, tried to explain his mentor's anti-socialist attitude. "All his life he shrank from adhering to socialism . . . on account of . . . its violent nature, its class character . . . and its political character. . . . Even the social and moral crisis of the Dreyfus case, in which he [as a Jew] played an important part, did not change his opinion. . . . He never gave himself to [the socialists]." Durkheim shared his student's passion for the suffering of the poor, but, unlike Mauss, he could not bring himself to chuck his positivism and embrace what he considered to be a half-baked religion of economics.

[9]H. Stuart Hughes, *Consciousness and Society* (New York: Vintage Books, 1958), p. 78.

[10]Robert Heilbroner, *The Worldly Philosophers* (New York: Simon and Schuster, 1953), chapter 6.

[11]Walter Lippmann, *Drift and Mastery* (Englewood Cliffs, N.J.: Prentice-Hall, 1961), pp. 23–25.

[12]Robert Hessen, *Steel Titan: The Life of Charles M. Schwab* (New York: Oxford University Press, 1975), pp. 111–44.

[13]Quoted in Richard Hofstadter, *Social Darwinism in American Thought* (Boston: The Beacon Press, 1959), p. 51.

[14]William Graham Sumner, *The Challenge of Facts* (New Haven, 1914), p. 5.

[15]G. B. Shaw et al., *Socialism: The Fabian Essays*, with introduction by E. Bellamy (Boston, 1895), p. xi.

[16]Louis Hartz, *The Liberal Tradition in America: An Interpretation of American Thought since the Revolution* (New York: Harcourt, Brace, 1955), p. 187.

[17]Martin Diamond, "The Problems of the Socialist Party after World War One," in *Failure of a Dream? Essays in the History of American Socialism*, John H. M. Laslett and Seymour Martin Lipset (eds.) (New York: Doubleday, 1974), p. 376.

[18]Adam Smith, *The Wealth of Nations*, Book 4.

[19]Werner Sombart, *Warum gibt es in den Vereinigten Staaten keinen Sozialismus?* (Tübingen, 1906), pp. 112–42.

[20]Hessen, op. cit., p. 242.

[21]John Dewey, *Liberalism and Social Action* (New York, 1935).

[22]Arthur Schlesinger, Jr., "Sources of the New Deal," in *Paths of American Thought*, p. 387.

[23]See John P. Diggins, *Mussolini and Fascism: The View from America* (Princeton, N.J.: Princeton University Press, 1972), p. 162.

[24]Ibid., p. 164.

[25]Quoted in Schlesinger, op. cit., p. 390.

[26]Harry G. Johnson, "Revolution and Counter-Revolution in Economics: From Lord Keynes to Milton Friedman," *Encounter*, 36, 4 (April 1971), pp. 23–33.

[27]Axel Leijonhufvud, *On Keynesian Economics and the Economics of Keynes* (New York: Oxford University Press, 1968).

[28]Alvin H. Hansen, *The American Economy* (New York: McGraw-Hill, 1957), pp. 158–59.

[29]J. M. Keynes, *The End of Laissez-Faire* (London, 1926), pp. 34–35; idem, *Essays in Persuasion* (London, 1931), p. 300.

[30]Johnson, op. cit., p. 25.

[31]J. M. Keynes, *The General Theory of Employment, Interest, and Money* (London, 1936), pp. 383–84.

[32]Raymond Aron, "The Diffusion of Ideologies," *Confluence*, 2, 1 (March, 1953), pp. 3–12.

[33]It has been argued by the socialist economist, Thomas Balogh (Lord Balogh), that Keynes moved away from the classicism of Alfred Marshall under the influence of his younger Cambridge colleagues, Joan Robinson and Richard Kahn. In his essay, "Keynes and the IMP," *The Times Literary Supplement*, 10 October 1975, pp. 1211–14, Balogh argued that the Keynes who wrote *The End of Laissez-Faire* was an entirely different man from the Keynes who became an advocate of convertibility and non-discrimination of free trade at Bretton Woods. In endeavoring to explain Keynes's change, Balogh suggests that it was partly due to the fact that Keynes was no longer under the influence of Robinson and Kahn, and partly due to the fact that Keynes had always been pro-capitalist. On p. 1214, he writes:

> The Keynesian Revolution gained acceptance because ultimately it was . . . deeply conservative in character. Its adherents believed that our economic problems could be solved by painless new gadgets, by the right number of policy weapons, mainly in the fiscal and monetary field. There was first of all the perfection of fiscal and monetary intervention which would regulate and "fine-tune" demand to achieve full-employment.

Ultimately, however, under the influence of a renascent monetary school, Keynes, like many of his disciples, came to the conclusion that "Keynesian" economics would not work in the modern world. Balogh, who styles himself a Keynesian socialist, concludes that the Keynesian revolution was only an *intermezzo* rather than a new departure "towards a socially valid analysis and solution." For a further elaboration of Keynesians against Keynes, see Joan Robinson and John Eatland, *An Introduction to Modern Economics* (London: McGraw Hill, 1974).

[34]Joseph Schumpeter, *Capitalism, Socialism, and Democracy* (New York: Harper & Brothers, 1942), pp. 121ff.

[35]Ibid., p. 121.

[36]Paul H. Weaver, "Liberal and the Presidency," *Commentary,* 60, 4 (October, 1975), pp. 48–53.

[37]See Roger Freeman, *The Growth of American Government: A Morphology of the Welfare State* (Stanford: Hoover Institution Press, 1975).

[38]Albert Jay Nock, *The Memoirs of a Superfluous Man* (Chicago: Henry Regnery Company, 1964), pp. 112–16.

[39]Jewkes, op. cit., p. 46.

[40]Ibid., p. 46.

[41]Ibid.

[42]Quoted in ibid., pp. 46, 47.

[43]See Vera Lutz, *French Planning* (Washington, D.C.: American Enterprise Institute for Public Policy Research, 1965).

[44]See E. H. Carr, *Socialism in One Country* (Baltimore: Penguin Books, 1970), 3 vols.

[45]F. A. Hayek, *The Road to Serfdom* (Chicago: University of Chicago Press, 1962), p. 35.

[46]See Leszek Kolakowski's introduction to *The Socialist Idea,* Leszek Kolakowski and Stuart Hampshire (eds.) (London: Weidenfeld and Nicholson, 1974). The Kolakowski-Hampshire anthology contains contributions from leading socialist scholars from both Western and Eastern Europe, as well as the United States. In most cases, the contributors have abandoned their classical socialism for mixed-economy planning.

[47]During the 1972 General Election, George McGovern, the most left-wing candidate ever to receive the Presidential nomination of a major American political party, constantly praised the free enterprise system, and insisted on describing himself as a defender of that system.

[48]*Time,* July 14, 1975, p. 63.

George Hilton: "American Transportation Planning"

[1]Ann F. Friedlaender, *The Interstate Highway System—A Study in Public Investment* (Amsterdam: North Holland Publishing Co., 1965).

[2]This point has been stressed by William Vickrey in several publications, e.g., "Pricing in Urban and Suburban Transport," *American Economic Review,* 52 (1963), pp. 452–65; "Pricing as a Tool in Coordination of Local Transportation," in *Transportation Economics* (New York: Columbia University Press, 1965), pp. 275–91.

[3]Michael E. Levine, "Landing Fees and the Airport Congestion Problem," *The Journal of Law and Economics,* 12 (1969), pp. 79–108.

[4]A. Carlin and R. E. Park, *The Efficient Use of Airport Runway Capacity in a Time of Scarcity* (Santa Monica: RAND Corporation, 1969), pp. 92–95.

[5]The argument of this section is derived from Ross D. Eckert, *Airports and Congestion* (Washington, D.C.: The American Enterprise Institute, 1972).

[6]Ross D. Eckert and George W. Hilton, "The Jitneys," *The Journal of Law and Economics,* 15 (1972), pp. 243–325.

[7]On the non-optimality of vehicles of urban transit, see J. Hayden Boyd, Norman Asher, and Elliot S. Wetzler, *Evaluation of Rail Rapid Transit and Express Bus Service in the Urban Commuter Market* (Arlington, Va.: Institute for Defense Analysis, 1973).

[8]William B. Tye, III, "The Capital Grant as a Subsidy Device: The Case Study of Urban Mass Transportation," in *The Economics of Federal Subsidy Programs* Part 6 (1971) (U.S. Congress, Joint Economic Committee), pp. 796–826.

[9]On the UMTA program more generally, see George W. Hilton, *Federal Transit Subsidies* (Washington, D.C.: American Enterprise Institute, 1974).

[10]With the inception of the federal program to restore an American merchant marine in 1936 by a mixture of construction subsidies, operating subsidies, flag discrimination, and similar devices, the United States Maritime Administration brought forth a series of standardized tankers and dry cargo vessels. Although these ships were largely conceived in the late 1930s, because of World War II they were built primarily in the immediate World War II period. The development of containerization in the mid-1950s by the White Pass & Yukon Railway and other operators caused American shipping lines to convert their technology away from the standard hold-type dry-cargo vessels of the sort brought forth in the Maritime Administration's plans. One of the standard designs, the C-2 cargo vessel, was widely adapted to containerization of cargoes. Subsequently, American operators have typically chosen newly-designed vessels as container carriers. The Maritime Administration did not anticipate containerization and had no standard design for a container vessel in advance of the technological improvement.

[11]See George W. Hilton, "The Hosmer Report: A Decennial Evaluation," *ICC Practitioners' Journal,* 35 (1969), 1470–86.

[12]Idem, *The Transportation Act of 1958* (Bloomington: Indiana University Press, 1969), chapter 4, passim.

[13]Ernest W. Williams, *The Regulation of Rail-Motor Rate Competition* (New York: Harpers, 1958), esp. pp. 213–14.

[14]This section summarizes George W. Hilton, *The Northeast Railroad Problem* (Washington, D.C.: American Enterprise Institute, 1975).

[15]Personal rapid transit is a technology of unmanned rubber-tired vehicles guided by wires imbedded in concrete structures capable of low speed movement between a variety of points of origination and destination. Such systems, if practical, will serve rather as horizontal elevators between a limited number of points as, for example, in an airport or a central business district. The UMTA has built such a system in Morgantown, West Virginia, between three stations in the central business district and the West Virginia University campus. The investment has proved to be over $60 million and the system has not, at the time of writing, become fully operational owing to mechanical difficulties. A system installed in the Dallas-Fort Worth Airport has recently been shut down and its future is currently in doubt. A linear installation of this character planned for Pittsburgh has tentatively been rejected in favor of conventional streetcar technology. Personal rapid transit, if practicable, appears to require about the same investment as conventional rapid transit with lower peak-load capacity, much lower speed, but greater flexibility in origins and destinations. The private sector of the economy has shown no indication of willingness to invest in it.

[16]Beginning in 1962, the federal government expended to date $1 billion in an effort to produce an aircraft capable of flying at approximately triple the speed of sound. Previous improvements in commercial airliner technology had in general increased speed, safety, and comfort, and at the same time had lowered the cost of operations. The supersonic transport (SST) was expected to increase speed, but probably to reduce the safety and comfort levels and to entail a very great increase in cost of operation. The private sector had not brought forth the aircraft for the usual reasons: the marginal cost of providing the additional speeds exceeded the expected marginal benefits.

In addition, the externalities of the plane were thought to be strongly negative. It would increase the noise level around airports, create a sonic boom while in flight, and possibly reduce the ozone layer of the atmosphere so as to increase the admission of ultraviolet rays and other potentially harmful rays from outside the atmosphere. The project was thought to be strongly inequalitarian on the grounds that only travellers of the highest time valuation would be willing to pay fares considerably in excess of subsonic first-class fares in order to make a small marginal saving in time. Mainly because of the anticipated adverse ecological effects, the program was terminated by Congress in 1971. Had the project been continued, the plane would apparently not have been economic for operation in rivalry with conventional subsonic jets, except under subsidy.

Richard F. Muth: "Government Planning of Housing and Land-Use"

[1]Richard F. Muth, *Cities and Housing* (Chicago: University of Chicago Press, 1969).

[2]Ibid.

[3]Ibid.

[4]Ibid., chapter 10.

[5]Ibid., pp. 254, 266.

[6]Otto A. Davis, Charles M. Eastman, and Chang-I. Hua, "The Shrinkage in the Stock of Low-Quality Housing in the Central City," *Urban Studies,* 11 (February, 1974).

[7]Beverly Duncan and Philip M. Hauser, *Housing a Metropolis-Chicago* (Glencoe, Ill.: The Free Press, 1960). The authors compared data contained in the 1950 Census of Housing and the 1956 National Housing Inventory which used identical definitions of dwelling unit conditions.

[8]Muth, op. cit. The 1960 Census of Housing contained a more detailed breakdown of structural conditions than the 1950 Census, but in making the comparison I was able to calculate measures from the 1960 Census corresponding to the 1950 ones.

[9]Davis, Eastman, and Hua, op. cit., p. 14.

[10]According to census income data, the median income of the lowest fifth of urban families by income rose from $1,000 to $3,302 per year between 1949 and 1969. Allowing for the rise in consumer prices over the period, the purchasing power of the lowest fifth of urban families more than doubled over the twenty-year span.

[11]National Commission on Urban Problems, *Building the American City* (Washington, D.C.: U.S. Government Printing Office, 1969), Table 6, p. 82.

[12]The effect of government housing on private market rentals depends on the elasticity of private market supply. If the supply is relatively elastic, as I believe it to be, the long-run effect will be small.

[13]"Capital and Current Expenditures in the Production of Housing," in C. Lowell

Harris (ed.), *Government Spending and Land Values* (Madison, Wis.: The University of Wisconsin Press, 1973), pp. 75–76.

[14]This is the so-called Section 8 program.

[15]For a good summary of this evidence, see Frank De Leeuw, "The Demand for Housing: A Review of Cross-Section Evidence," *Review of Economics and Statistics*, 53 (February, 1971), pp. 1–10.

[16]Indeed, it has been estimated that families living in public housing in the middle 1960s had almost exactly the same income and spent almost exactly the same amount on housing on the average as families whose incomes made them eligible for public housing but who were privately housed. See Edgar O. Olsen, "A Welfare Economic Evaluation of Public Housing," Ph.D. dissertation, Rice University, 1968, p. 84.

[17]I have estimated that the public housing program enables a family to consume almost four times as much housing as it would have in the absence of the program. See Richard F. Muth, *Public Housing, an Economic Evaluation* (Washington, D.C.: American Enterprise Institute, 1973), p. 25.

[18]Ibid., p. 28.

[19]I have appraised them in ibid., chapter 3.

[20]I have compared differences in urban decentralization with a variety of factors, including the quality of central-city housing and other aspects of its physical condition. I concluded that deterioration of physical conditions in the central city was not a cause of post-war decentralization. See Muth, *Cities and Housing*, chapter 7.

[21]Ibid., p. 181.

[22]"Numerical Solution of Urban Residential Land-Use Models," *Journal of Urban Economics*, 2 (October, 1975), pp. 328–29.

[23]Ibid.

[24]Ibid., pp. 323–24.

[25]Muth, *Cities and Housing*, pp. 101–14.

[26]"Numerical Solution of Urban Residential Land-Use Models," op. cit., section 6.

Richard Mancke: "Energy: The Record of the Federal Energy Administration 1974–75"

[1]Public Law 93–159 (27 November 1973)

[2]*Congressional Record*, 1 October 1973, p. S18142.

[3]For more elaboration, see Richard B. Mancke, *Squeaking By: U.S. Energy Policy Since the Embargo* (New York: Columbia University Press, forthcoming 1976), chapter 7.

[4]*Congressional Record*, 7 November 1973, p. S20034.

[5]Ibid.

[6]Ibid.

[7]Statement of John E. Swearingen before the U.S. Senate Commerce Committee (5 February 1974), p. 7.

[8]Two suggestions for encouraging greater competition within OPEC are M. A. Adelman's proposal to reimpose oil import quotas and auction off the quota rights to the highest bidder, and my suggestion that the U.S. impose higher tariffs on all oil imports from countries classified as insecure. See Mancke, *Squeaking By*, chapter 5, for elaboration. Rather than attacking the oil cartel directly, the administration has followed the fruitless approach of attempting to "talk down" oil prices.

Robert B. Hawkins, Jr.: "Regional Versus Local Government: The Lessons for National Planning"

[1]See *The Economic Planning Proposal* (Washington, D.C.: American Enterprise Institute, 1975) for an excellent summary of the pros and cons of this legislation.

[2]For an example of this literature, see *Modernizing Local Government* (New York: Committee for Economic Development, 1966), pp. 11–12.

[3]Ibid.

[4]Advisory Commission on Intergovernmental Relations, *Regional Decision Making: New Strategies for Substate Districts* (Washington, D.C.: U.S. Government Printing Office, 1973), p. 2.

[5]Idem, *Size Can Make a Difference,* Bulletin No. 70–8 (Washington, D.C.: U.S. Government Printing Office, 1970), p. 2.

[6]Gregory C. Krohm, *Findings on the Organizational Structure of Local Government and Cost Effectiveness* (Sacramento: Office of Planning and Research, 1974), pp. 33–36.

[7]Idem, *Survey of Cities and Counties* (Sacramento: Office of Planning and Research, 1974). The findings of this study are comparable with other studies that have been conducted on the subject of contracting with private producers.

[8]James H. Thomas and Henry M. Levin, "Financing Community Schools," in the Brookings Institute, *Community Control of Schools* (Washington, D.C., 1969), pp. 250–55.

[9]California Division of Forestry, *Alternative Fire Protection Systems for Privately Owned Woodlands* (Sacramento: State Printing Office, 1974).

[10]Krohm, *Findings,* pp. 33–36.

[11]James E. Delaney, *Satellite Vehicle Waste Collection Systems* (Washington, D.C.: Environmental Protection Agency, 1972), p. 11.

[12]Roger Ahlbrant, *Implications of Contracting for a Public Service: A Case Study of the Provision of Fire Services* (Los Angeles: Sage Publications, 1972).

[13]California Local Government Reform Task Force, *Public Benefits from Public Choice* (Sacramento: Office of Planning and Research, 1974), pp. 26–27.

[14]Subcommittee on Intergovernmental Relations of the Committee on Government Operations, United States Senate, *Confidence and Concern: Citizens View Americans and Government,* vols. 1 and 2 (Washington, D.C.: U.S. Government Printing Office, 1973).

[15]Jorgen Westerstahl, "Decision Making in 36 Swedish Communes," presented at the 1970 annual meeting of the American Political Science Association. Jorgen is a professor at the University of Gothenburg, Sweden.

[16]See Steven P. Erie, John J. Kirlin, and Francine F. Rabinovitz, *Reform of Metropolitan Governments* (Washington, D.C.: Resources for the Future, 1972).

[17]Advisory Commission on Intergovernmental Relations, *Regional Decision Making.*

[18]Committee for Economic Development, *Modernizing.*

[19]See Robert L. Bish, "A Comment on V. P. Duggal's 'Is There an Unseen Hand in Government?'," *Annals of Public and Co-operative Economy,* 39 (January-March, 1968), pp. 361–65. Also see John R. Commons, *Legal Foundations of Capitalism* (Wisconsin: University of Wisconsin Press, 1957).

[20]See Vincent Ostrom, *Institutional Arrangements for Water Resource Development,* PB 207314 (Springfield, Va.: National Technical Information Service, 1971).

[21]California Local Government Reform Task Force, *Public Benefits,* pp. 21–23.

[22]J. C. McDavid, *Interjurisdictional Cooperation Among Police Departments in the St. Louis Metropolitan Areas* (Bloomington, Ind.: Workshop for Political Theory and Policy Analysis, 1974).

[23]Robert B. Hawkins, Jr., *District Government in the American Political System: The California Experience,* draft manuscript.

[24]See the testimony of Donald Dillion, Victor Jones, and Ray Remy before the Advisory Commission on Intergovernmental Relations in San Francisco, California; printed in *Hearings on Substate Regionalism,* vol. 6, A–43a (Washington, D.C., 1974).

[25]Testimony of Walter A. Abernathy, Deputy Executive Director of the Port of Oakland, appearing before the California Assembly, Committee on Local Government, 1972. The committee was hearing testimony on Assembly Bill #2040 that would consolidate a number of regional planning districts into the first stage of a comprehensive regional planning agency.

[26]Testimony of Donald Dillion, *Hearings,* pp. 6–11.

[27]California Legislature, *Assembly Bill No. 2422* (Sacramento, California, June 25, 1975), p. 69.

[28]East Bay Municipal Utilities District, ''Time Table of Events to Obtain Permit to Construct, Operate and Maintain Extension of Sewage Outfall Line.'' Data presented to the California Local Government Reform Task Force, February 19, 1974.

[29]Abernathy, testimony.

Murray L. Weidenbaum: ''The Contrast Between Government and Business Planning: Market Orientation versus Centralized Control''

[1]*The Balanced Growth and Economic Planning Act of 1975* (The Humphrey-Javits National Planning Bill).

[2]Jacob K. Javits, ''The Need for National Planning,'' *Wall Street Journal,* July 8, 1975, p. 14.

[3]George A. Steiner, *Managerial Long-Range Planning* (New York: McGraw-Hill, 1963), pp. 2–3.

[4]''Corporate Planning—A Sometimes Thing,'' *The Commercial and Financial Chronicle,* August 25, 1975, p. 12.

[5]David W. Ewing, *The Human Side of Planning, Tool or Tyrant?* (New York: Macmillan, 1969), p. 16.

[6]''Corporate Planning—A Sometimes Thing,'' op. cit., p. 11.

[7]Patrick H. Irwin, ''Why Aren't Companies Doing a Better Job of Planning?'' *Management Review* (November 1971), p. 11.

[8]E. Kirby Warren, *Long-Range Planning, the Executive Viewpoint* (Englewood Cliffs, N.J.: Prentice-Hall, 1966), pp. 2–3.

[9]Robert J. Mockler, ''Theory and Practice of Planning,'' in Robert J. Mockler (ed.), *Readings in Business Planning and Policy Formulation* (New York: Appleton-Century-Crofts, 1972), p. 103.

[10]Murray L. Weidenbaum and A. Bruce Rozet, *Potential Industrial Adjustments to Shifts in Defense Spending* (Menlo Park, Cal.: Stanford Research Institute, 1963), p. 20.

[11]George A. Steiner, ''Long-Range Planning,'' in Mockler, op. cit., p. 3.

[12]Mockler, "Theory and Practice of Planning," op. cit., p. 507.

[13]Irwin, op. cit., p. 12.

[14]Ewing, op. cit., p. 9.

[15]"Corporate Planning—A Sometimes Thing," op. cit., p. 12.

[16]"For a National Economic Planning System," *Challenge* (March/April 1975), pp. 52–53.

[17]Daniel P. Moynihan, "The Future of Federalism," in U.S. Advisory Commission on Intergovernmental Relations, *American Federalism* (Washington, D.C.: U.S. Government Printing Office, 1975), p. 98.

[18]Malcolm H. Sherwood, Jr., "The Definition of Planning," in Mockler, op. cit., p. 41.

[19]Robert G. Murdick, "Nature of Planning and Plans," *Advanced Management Journal* (October 1965), p. 40.

[20]David Ewing, *Long-Range Planning for Management* (New York: Harper and Row, 1964), p. 3.

[21]"For a National Economic Planning System," op. cit., p. 52.

[22]Ibid., p. 53.

[23]"Planning Economic Policy: An Interview with Hubert J. Humphrey," *Challenge* (March/April 1975), p. 23.

[24]T. A. Murphy, "National Planning," *Wall Street Journal,* August 18, 1975, p. 7.

[25]"For a National Economic Planning System," op. cit., p. 53.

[26]"Planning Economic Policy," op. cit., p. 23.

[27]Herbert Stein, *Economic Planning and the Improvement of Economic Policy* (Washington, D.C.: American Enterprise Institute for Public Policy Research, 1975), p. 25.

[28]"Planning Economic Policy," op. cit., p. 24.

[29]Cited in David Novick (ed.), *Current Practice in Program Budgeting* (New York: Crane, Russak, 1973), p. 22.

[30]Ibid.

[31]Bertram Gross and Michael Spring, *Annals of the American Academy of Political and Social Science* (May 1967), p. 9.

[32]Harold Henry, "Formal Long-Range Planning and Corporation Performance," in Subhash Jain and Surendra Singhri (eds.), *Essentials of Corporate Planning* (Oxford, Ohio: Planning Executives Institute, 1973), p. 31.

[33]R. Hal Mason, "Developing and Planning Organization," in Mockler, op. cit., p. 103.

[34]Ewing, *The Human Side of Planning,* op. cit., p. 19.

[35]Jack W. Carlson, "Recent U.S. Federal Government Experience with Program Budgeting," in Novick, op. cit., pp. 210, 216.

[36]John Jewkes, *The New Ordeal by Planning* (London: Macmillan, 1968), p. xi.

[37]John Sheahan, "Planning in France," *Challenge* (January/February 1975), p. 18.

[38]Murray L. Weidenbaum, "Shortcomings of Business Planning," in Jain and Singrhi, op. cit., p. 319.

[39]Ibid., p. 320.

[40]Cited in "Corporate Planning: Piercing Fog in the Executive Suite," *Business Week* (April 28, 1975), p. 48.

[41]"Corporate Planning—A Sometimes Thing," op. cit., p. 25.

PART IV. THE DYNAMICS OF CENTRALIZED PLANNING

Vincent Ostrom: "Some Paradoxes for Planners: Human Knowledge and Its Limitations"

[1]This problem has been examined by F. A. Hayek, "The Use of Knowledge in Society," *American Economic Review*, 35 (September 1945), pp. 519–30. See also Robert L. Bish, "The Assumption of Knowledge in Policy Analysis," *Policy Studies Journal*, 3 (Spring 1975), pp. 256–61.

[2]Milovan Djilas, *The Unperfect Society* (New York: Harcourt, Brace and World, Inc., 1969), p. 150.

[3]José Ortega y Gassett, *The Revolt of the Masses* (New York: W. W. Norton and Company, 1932), p. 112.

[4]Ernst Cassirer, *The Myth of the State* (New Haven: Yale University Press, 1964), pp. 277–96.

[5]Gordon Tullock, *The Politics of Bureaucracy* (Washington, D.C.: Public Affairs Press, 1965).

[6]This relationship was recognized by Alexander Hamilton when he observed in "Federalist No. 73" that: "The oftener the measure is brought under examination, the greater the diversity in the situation of those who are to examine it, the less must be the danger of those errors which flow from the want of due deliberation." Alexander Hamilton, James Madison, and John Jay, *The Federalist,* Modern Library ed. (New York: Random House, n.d.), p. 477. See also Vincent Ostrom, *The Political Theory of a Compound Republic* (Blacksburg, Va.: Center for the Study of Public Choice, Virginia Polytechnic Institute and State University, 1971), chapter 7.

[7]Vincent Ostrom, *The Intellectual Crisis in American Public Administration,* rev. ed. (University, Alabama: University of Alabama Press, 1974).

James Buchanan and Gordon Tullock: "Politics and the Bureaucracy of Planning"

[1]John F. Chant and Keith Acheson, "The Choice of Monetary Instruments and the Theory of Bureaucracy," *Public Choice,* 12 (Spring 1972), pp. 13–33.

[2]Abba Lerner, *The Economics of Control* (New York: Macmillan, 1944).

[3]Note that this type of economic crime is "victimless." Like prostitution, sale of drugs, usury, and sale of unlicensed weapons, it does not carry with it someone who is a victim and who is more likely to report the matter to the police. Such crimes are particularly hard for the law to deal with.

B. Bruce-Briggs: "Prospect of a Planned America"

[1]On the methodology of future studies, see Herman Kahn and B. Bruce-Biggs, *Things to Come* (New York, 1972).

[2]President's Research Committee on Social Trends, *Recent Social Trends* (New York, 1933). President's Commission on National Goals, *Goals for Americans* (New York, 1960). National Goals Research Staff, *Toward Balanced Growth—Quantity with Quality* (Washington, D.C., 1970).

[3]I recently heard a Boston economist make the case that the problem of the lack of adequate, consistent, and reliable data is a justification for the radical reorganization of our economy. He is a consultant to the U.S. Department of Labor.

PART V. SUMMARY AND CONCLUSION

A. Lawrence Chickering: " The God that Cannot Fail"

[1]For a brief though excellent discussion of this problem in relation to national health insurance, see Thomas Schelling, ''Government and Health,'' Discussion Paper 35D (Kennedy School of Government, Harvard University, 1975).

[2]Eugene Bardach, ''Save Energy and Save a Soul,'' Working Paper #41 (Graduate School of Public Policy, University of California, Berkeley, 1975.)

[3]Aaron Wildavsky, ''If Planning Is Everything, Maybe It's Nothing,'' *Policy Sciences* (June 1973), p. 151.